T0296896

Human–Computer Interaction Series

HCI is a multidisciplinary field focused on human aspects of the development of computer technology. As computer-based technology becomes increasingly pervasive – not just in developed countries, but worldwide – the need to take a human-centered approach in the design and development of this technology becomes ever more important. For roughly 30 years now, researchers and practitioners in computational and behavioral sciences have worked to identify theory and practice that influences the direction of these technologies, and this diverse work makes up the field of human-computer interaction. Broadly speaking it includes the study of what technology might be able to do for people and how people might interact with the technology. The HCI series publishes books that advance the science and technology of developing systems which are both effective and satisfying for people in a wide variety of contexts. Titles focus on theoretical perspectives (such as formal approaches drawn from a variety of behavioral sciences), practical approaches (such as the techniques for effectively integrating user needs in system development), and social issues (such as the determinants of utility, usability and acceptability).

For further volumes:
http://www.springer.com/series/6033

Mark Childs • Anna Peachey

Editors

Understanding Learning
in Virtual Worlds

 Springer

Editors
Mark Childs
Faculty of Engineering and Computing
Coventry University
Coventry, UK

Anna Peachey
The Open University
Walton Hall
Milton Keynes, UK

ISSN 1571-5035
ISBN 978-1-4471-6205-6   ISBN 978-1-4471-5370-2 (eBook)
DOI 10.1007/978-1-4471-5370-2
Springer London Heidelberg New York Dordrecht

Printed on acid-free paper

Springer is part of Springer Science+Business Media (www.springer.com)

Editors' Introduction: Understanding Learning in Virtual Worlds

This is a companion volume to the publication *Researching Learning in Virtual Worlds* (Peachey et al. 2010). Like that book, this is a collection of papers selected from those presented at the Researching Learning in Immersive Virtual Environments (ReLIVE) conference hosted by The Open University in the UK. ReLIVE 2011 saw a step-change in the nature of the presentations compared to the previous conference in 2008, a change reflected in the research within virtual world's education as a whole, and indicated by the change in title between the two books. Whilst ReLIVE08 provided the opportunity for a small core of researchers in the emerging field to come together physically for the first time, ReLIVE11 was one of a number of virtual world conferences that year where new and established researchers from a much wider group met to present and discuss their activity. Whereas before the educational community were developing the role of research into education within virtual worlds, that investigation is developing the maturity to be able to state that, to a large extent, what differentiates learning in virtual worlds is now being *understood.*

Virtual worlds are characterised by their use of navigable 3D space, by the representation of their users within them through the use of movable 3D characters, known as avatars, and by their persistence, i.e. that they are not created as and when needed, but continue permanently (Bell 2008). When the previous book was published the majority of educational activity took place in the virtual world Second Life™ (SL) created by Linden Lab, and although many educators have re-located to other virtual worlds since then (many due to the ending of the educational subsidy offered by Linden Lab), the majority of the authors represented within this volume still use SL as the platform for their education.

The characteristics that therefore represent the different nature of the experience of learning and teaching using a virtual world are these two features: the sense of *space* that they convey, and the digital *self-presence* of the user within that space. Understanding the nature of learning in virtual worlds, and how they can be essentially different from other forms of online learning, entails bearing these twin aspects constantly in mind.

These features do make the learner experience more demanding, particularly within the early stages of adapting to the use of the platform. Rather than simply needing to learn which button to click, or in which menu an instruction is located, navigation within a virtual world requires learning how to move and interpret the space around the user. The skills required of learners involve wayfinding, moving the avatar, interacting with objects, communicating with others and in a larger social world such as SL, to adjust to the sense of being in a community space and therefore interacting with other people. It is also an unfortunate but universal truth that users must develop the ability to recover from a software crash and return to their task/location. The sense of virtual presence, i.e. the sense of being located *in* another place, which can occur when one becomes accustomed to interacting with the world, can be intimidating as well as enjoyable. The learner is exposed to these very different experiences, and the requirement to learn all of the skills listed above, simultaneously.

The plethora of skills that virtual worlds demand of the user may be more than other platforms require, but is still similar to what much online learning demands, a progression through Dubin's cycle of unconscious incompetence to unconscious competence (Childs 2011). Educators are familiar with the precursor activities of enabling learners to become familiarised with a technology before able to *use* that technology for learning. If the virtual world is to be used solely to convey information to the learner (e.g. the design of a particular theatre, the hazardous places around a building site, information about sexual health), a set of learning activities referred to as *associative* in the Mayes and de Freitas overview of learning theories (2004, p 7), then simply being able to navigate and communicate competently will probably be sufficient to observe and make sense of this information without the difficulties in using the technology intruding overmuch.

However, the competent use of virtual worlds as a space and a communication platform is, as mentioned above, only part of what they offer. When we introduce the role of the digital representation of the learner, the avatar, into the space, the available interactions within that space increases. Rather than simply experiencing the space, the learner has a sense of themselves having a reality in that space, known as self-presence. They have virtual bodies, and the presence of a body within that space opens up a whole new set of learning opportunities.

For example, many learning activities located in virtual worlds are based on providing learners with an opportunity to take part in experiential learning and other types of learning activities that take use of *cognitive* approaches (Mayes and de Freitas 2004, p 8). This experiential learning is made more authentic for the learner by placing them directly within the online environment, via their avatar; this direct placement is made possible through a phenomenon known as embodiment. To achieve this sense of embodiment, however, makes further demands on the learners than simply learning how to operate the software and navigate around the spaces. It takes time. For example, from the authors' own experience, in the study by Childs and Kuksa (2009), students with only 2 h experience of Second Life were taken on a field trip around various theatres there and asked questions on the spaces as potential locations for performance. Although able to comment on the suitability of

Second Life as a medium (a question which called on their experience of the technology), they were not able to respond to the question of how they felt a performer would have *felt* in the actual theatre in the physical world from their experience of the theatre in the virtual. Their responses indicated that they did not feel sufficiently embodied within the environment to form an emotional response to the space. A later study with students who had spent several months in Second Life (Childs 2013) indicated that by this stage they were able to form an emotional response to different environments. Their descriptions of their time inworld indicated that three things had led to this development of a sense of embodiment; these were:

Experience. This is both in terms of length of time inworld and exposure to a number of emotionally affecting activities; moving ones, such as the Holocaust museum, and fun ones, such as snowboarding.

Personalisation. The learners had, on the whole, experimented with appearance and settled on a form and outfit that they felt comfortable with. Shopping, experimenting (such as being a robot made out of cardboard boxes) and spending time finetuning their costumes all helped them feel connected to their avatar. A few reported that they did not feel the need to do this, as they felt connected with the generic avatar they adopted when they first entered the world, but they had reflected on their identity and deliberately chose to keep this form.

Intention. The learners all had discovered some aspect of the world that drove their continued interaction, beyond that of the designated learning activity. For some this was simple exploration, others enjoyed the randomness of simply teleporting. A desire to excel at the learning task also motivated learners to feel part of the world (Childs and Chen 2011).

Embodiment within a virtual world is possible because the "mental representation of the body" is not necessarily located in the physical body but can, in fact, be located elsewhere (Biocca 1997) due to the plasticity of most people's body schema. This can be seen in the physical world in phenomena like the rubber hand illusion (Botvinick and Cohen 1998), in which a participant's hand is hidden and a fake hand placed within their field of view. The two hands are then stroked simultaneously and even though it is obvious that the rubber hand is not real, about two-thirds of participants transpose a feeling of ownership to it. Where there is an external body onto which this sense of self can be transposed, and where there is some sort of illusion which can enable this transposition to occur, then this embodiment can take place.

In virtual worlds, the avatar on the screen becomes the user's extended body such that "users do not simply roam through the space as 'mind', but find themselves grounded in the practice of the body, and thus in the world" (Taylor 2002, p 42). However, as with the rubber hand illusion, embodiment within a virtual world only occurs in two-thirds to three-quarters of participants. Why a minority do not experience embodiment is not understood, but it may stem from some participants being "so strongly situated in the real world and their real body that they have a difficult time becoming involved in the virtual world" (Heeter 1995, p 200). Heeter's use of the word "situated" specifically describes the experience of being embodied within a space, rather than simply "located" within it, a distinction established by Merleau-Ponty (Smith 2007, p 16).

The distinction between being situated in a place and merely located within it is at the root of the concept of embodied cognition, this is that cognitive activity takes place in the context of a real-world environment, and it inherently involves perception and action. Furthermore, "We off-load cognitive work onto the environment. Because of limits on our information-processing abilities … we make the environment hold or even manipulate information for us." Thus the environment, our bodies, and the connection between them, are a fundamental part of the cognitive process (Wilson 2002, p 626).

That virtual worlds provide an authentic sense of embodiment has increasing support from techniques such as neuroimaging that reveal that for many longer-term players of online role-play games, the parts of the cortex that are associated with sense of self and agency (the left inferior parietal cortex) were also activated when the avatar was involved in action. As far as the brain itself is concerned, for many players, "self-location may transfer to the avatar body, alternate back and forth between the gamer's body and the avatar body, or may be present in both gamer and avatar" (Ganesh et al. 2012, p 1578). The same study also measured the participants' body plasticity, i.e. its ability to incorporate external objects into the body schema and found a similar correlation between this and reporting of self-identification with an avatar and activity of the left angular gyrus.

Thus, through the provision of avatars, virtual worlds provide a unique platform for enabling experiential learning. The embodiment experienced by learners enables embodied cognition to take place within an online environment, and so genuine experiential learning can take place. Furthermore, according to Biocca, the more that this sense of embodiment is enhanced, the greater the cognitive performance that occurs (1997).

As stated earlier, virtual worlds provide *space* and they provide a *self-presence* within an online environment. Self-presence not only includes embodiment through the potential for an extended body schema, but also the ability to develop and project identity, through the existence of body image (Biocca 1997). Avatars, in the words of Taylor (2002, p 40), "provide access points in the creation of identity and social life. The bodies people use in these spaces provide a means to live digitally – to fully inhabit the world".

Identity is not discussed in depth here, as it is the focus of a previous book edited by the editors of this volume, *Reinventing Ourselves: Contemporary Concepts of Identity in Virtual Worlds* (Peachey and Childs 2011). However, its role in learning, particularly in providing the mechanism by which activities that depend on social construction of knowledge, is paramount.

The avatars within most virtual worlds come with the capacity to be altered and personalised. The size, shape and colour of skin and hair can be manipulated, or new skins, hair and clothes can be added to the avatar to further change its appearance. In SL, as in many other worlds, a basic set of such items are available when first entering the virtual world in the user's inventory and further options can be acquired for free, with (usually more sophisticated) forms available for purchase with the inworld currency.

The importance that personalisation of one's avatar has in supporting learning is demonstrated by the work of Gonzalez et al. (2011). In their experiment a group of students were given the task of creating an avatar in Spore (a massively multiplayer online role-playing game, or MMORPG) that reflected their personality. Half of the students then had their personalised avatar swapped with a generic one before the students were set a series of tasks in that world. The researchers found that the students who used their personalised avatars were more involved and had better recall of the activities than those who used the generic avatar.

The alterations to their avatars that are adopted by users not only express their own individuality but also are important to make one's appearance distinctive, and distinguishable from other users. By creating a social presence within the environment, learners have already taken the first steps required in establishing a base on which *situative* learning can take place, situative learning being a collection of learning theories in which learning is acquired through social and cultural practice (Mayes and de Freitas 2004, p 9). Those who have a strong sense of their own self-projection within the medium are more likely to be sensitive to the communication cues of others (Caspi and Blau 2008, p 339) and conversely, those who feel the environment to be an impersonal one will limit their self-expression, which will create a barrier to communication (Barrett 2002, p 35). The social dynamics supported by identity, which given time can develop into cultural and community dynamics, all aid the ease of communication and openness of sharing, and moreover the sense of *others* within the environment, that are essential for effective social construction of knowledge.

Learning in virtual worlds, because they use navigable 3D space, and because they provide the potential for self-presence and a virtual body for learners, is therefore, in many ways, arguably more akin to learning in the physical world than other forms of online learning. Understanding learning in virtual worlds then demands an understanding of what learners need in order to make this connection between physical and virtual, so that they are situated, embodied and socially present within that world.

The authors of the chapters within this book all approach this task, but from a range of differing perspectives. The book is arranged into three parts. The first of the two chapters following this one are Chap.1, *An Alternative (to) Reality*, by Derek Jones, and Chap.2, *Guidelines for Conducting Text Based Interviews in Virtual Worlds*, by Carina Girvan and Tim Savage. These lay the groundwork for much of the rest of the book by presenting two essential aspects to work in virtual worlds. Derek Jones looks at the phenomenological *meaning* of virtual worlds by asking the deceptively simple question, "Why do we use gravity in virtual environments?" Derek draws on his background in architecture to address the question, and uses the philosophical ideas around the experience of place in the physical world to develop a deeper understanding of our relationship to place in the virtual world discovering that, in essence, they are not that dissimilar. Carina and Tim provide a practical guidance to a specific aspect of research in virtual worlds, that of interviews, conducted via text-based chat and taking place within the virtual world. Their analysis of the successful and unsuccessful strategies, employed by both the researcher and the research subject, when communicating in virtual worlds, also reveal both the barriers and affordances that virtual worlds present. In effect, understanding the communication, and social relationship, between interviewer and interviewee also informs an understanding of how learners learn together, and returns us to the question of how socially constructed knowledge can best be supported within virtual worlds.

The second part of the book builds on these fundamentals to establish many of the factors that support learning in virtual worlds. Chapters 3, 4, 5, and 6 touch on two of the three aspects referred to above, those of space and of identity. Chapter 3, *Designing for Hybrid Learning Environments in a Science Museum: Interprofessional Conceptualisations of Space*, by Alfredo Jornet and Cecilie Flo Jahreie examines how different professional perspectives view space in different ways. Drawing on activity theory, and in this context viewing space as a mediating artefact that is negotiated by the various participants, Alfredo and Cecilie reveal how although our experience of virtual space resembles that of physical space, as Derek contends, it also has a flexibility which enables that meaning to be negotiated and conceptualised, and re-negotiated and re-conceptualised, resulting in virtual worlds being design tool, learning tool and locus for cultural communication in one.

In Chap. 4, *An Examination of Student Engagement, Knowledge Creation and Expansive Learning in a Virtual World*, Brian Burton, Barbara Martin and Jenny Robins examine how students socially construct knowledge within a virtual world, by analysing interactions according to three separate theories of social construction of knowledge: the framework for student engagement, knowledge creation theory and the theory of expansive learning. Not only do they demonstrate the effectiveness of virtual worlds in supporting the social construction of knowledge, this approach also shows that all three theories of learning are applicable in understanding how learning in a virtual world environment can take place.

In Chap. 5, *The Strength of Cohesive Ties: Discursive Construction of an Online Learning Community*, Rebecca Ferguson, Julia Gillen, Anna Peachey and Peter Twining also look at the social construction of knowledge, but in the later stages of its development, when the expression of self and of identity have grown to a point where community ties and an emergent society have appeared. Through an analysis of discourse within Schome (a space that takes aspects of both school and home) Rebecca et al. analyse the learning, and also the affective relationships that bear on communications between learners. In this case, the results of bringing two different communities together, and the communications and miscommunications that occur, can also be understood by applying concepts of community founded on the physical world.

Chapter 6, *+SPACES: Serious Games for Role-Playing Government Policies*, merges the discussion on developing societies in virtual worlds with the role of space in virtual worlds. In their chapter, Bernard Horan and Michael Gardner explore the notion of virtual spaces as authentic simulations, which require both effective recreation of physical space with the recreation of specific roles for people to play in that space, and activities to carry out in those roles. These simulations do not only include a virtual world, but link this to a variety of social media such as Twitter and Facebook. Unlike many other simulations, +SPACES takes a "glass-box" approach – participants can see the model underlying the simulation – which learners felt was more effective, and they also responded well to the activities being more structured. As with many simulations, the authenticity of the experience needs to be balanced against the need for structure in learning design.

The final part of the book looks at applications of virtual worlds to three specific activities. The first of these, in Chap. 7 *Avatars, Art and Aspirations: The Creative Potential for Learning in the Virtual World*, by Simone Wesner, is using the environment of a virtual world to foster creative approaches. Simone's students used Second Life to create their own event spaces, as well as to meet, discuss and plan their projects. In her analysis, Simone finds that the models for creativity and learning established in the physical world, such as Weisberg's CHOICES model, still apply, but also discovers that the role of personalisation of the learner's avatar, as introduced above, applied to her students; the avatar became the first focus of their creative interest, and on occasion, where their appearance could not be modified, the participants reported a negative impact on their well-being. Rather than re-creating their physical world, as the students' experience developed they created exhibits that explored the discrepancy between the physical and virtual, in effect the virtual world itself was a springboard for reflection and creativity. Although the pedagogies of the physical world apply to the virtual, ontologically, Simone suggests, it "might encourage a discussion of virtual worlds from within, using a *new* terminology and accepting virtual worlds as a *reality of their own,* rather than trying to fit the limited understanding and interpretation of one reality to the virtual world."

In Chap. 8, *Second Language Acquisition by Immersive and Collaborative Task-Based Learning in a Virtual World*, Margaret de Jong Derrington looks at how theories of language acquisition apply across a range of platforms: the physical world, Skype and OpenSim. There are minor differences in functionality, and virtual worlds afford greater support for anonymity and authentic task-based learning than other environments, but yet again we see that an understanding developed in the physical world of how learners learn, in this case English as a Second Language, applies directly to understanding the acquisition of language in a virtual classroom. The techniques, of role-play, immersion and task-based learning translate exactly.

In Chap. 9, *Do Virtual Worlds Support Engaging Social Conferencing?*, as an appendix to this discussion on learning, Andreas Schmeil, Béatrice Hasler, Anna Peachey, Sara de Freitas and Claus Nehmzow look at the practical implications of conducting a conference within a virtual world. Many of the gains of such activity are self-evident – no travel costs, and the potential with three loci in different time-zones to run the conference over a 24 h period. However, replicating a physical world model alone meant that opportunities for networking and mingling, which happen spontaneously in a face-to-face conference, were less prevalent. In the move from physical to virtual, some aspects are easily translated, while others need more support and structure to occur.

As the range of these platforms expand, OpenSim, OpenWonderland, Minecraft and massive multiplayer online role-play games such as World of Warcraft will not only provide new pastures for those experienced in virtual worlds education, but will also draw in educators new to the nature and potential of virtual worlds. It is perhaps therefore even more valuable in periods like this, of transition and development, to take the opportunity to reflect and to review what we have learnt as practitioners and academics about the unique characteristics of these environments. Understanding how virtual worlds can support learners in their education through their special affordances and particular demands is important, but also within this volume the authors demonstrate how what we already know and understand about learning also applies, and that the physical and the virtual are not so different. It is hoped that this collection of reflections and experiences, capturing a snapshot of this ongoing development of understanding of learning in virtual worlds, will prove to be a resource for educators with both long-term familiarity with virtual worlds and those for whom using virtual worlds for education is a completely new endeavour.

Mark Childs
Anna Peachey

References

Barrett, S. (2002). Overcoming transactional distance as a barrier to effective communication over the internet. *International Educational Journal, 3*(4), Educational research conference 2002 special issue, 34–42.

Bell, M. (2008). Toward a definition of "virtual worlds". *Journal of Virtual Worlds Research, 1*(1), 1–5.

Biocca, F. (1997). The Cyborg's Dilemma: Progressive embodiment in virtual environments. *Journal of Computer-Mediated Communication, 3*(2), 113–144.

Botvinick, M., & Cohen, J. (1998). Rubber hands 'feel' touch that eyes see. *Nature, 391,* 756.

Caspi, A., & Blau, I. (2008). Social presence in online discussion groups: Testing three conceptions and their relations to perceived learning. *Social Psychology of Education, 11,* 323–346.

Childs, M. (2011, June 8–9). Enhancing learning, teaching and student success in virtual worlds: Why Rosa keeps dancing, opening keynote at SOLSTICE: Effective practices: Enhancing learning. In *Teaching and student success conference*, Edge Hill University.

Childs, M. (2013). The experience of virtual space. In I. Kuksa & M. Childs (Eds.), *Making sense of space*. London: Chandos.

Childs, M., & Chen, Y.-F. (2011, June 28–30). Roleplaying disaster management in second life. In *11th international DIVERSE conference*, Dublin City University.

Childs, M., & Kuksa, I. (2009, July 6–8). "Why are we in the floor?" Learning about theatre design in second life™. In *Proceedings of the Edulearn 09 international conference on education and new learning technologies* (pp. 1134–1145). Barcelona, Spain.

Ganesh, S., van Schie, H. T., de Lange, F. P., Thompson, E., & Wigboldus, D. H. J. (2012). How the human brain goes virtual: Distinct cortical regions of the person-processing network are involved in self-identification with virtual agents. *Cerebral Cortex, 22*(7), 1577–1585.

Gonzalez, G., Younger, J., & Lindgren, R. (2011). The payoff of Avatar creation: Investigating the effects on learning and engagement. In *Games + learning + society conference*, Madison, June 15–17 2011. http://www.glsconference.org/2011/program/event/147

Heeter, C. (1995). Communication research on consumer VR. In F. Biocca & M. R. Levy (Eds.), *Communication in the age of virtual reality* (pp. 191–218). Hillsdale: Lawrence Erlbaum Associates.

Mayes, T., & de Freitas, S. (2004). *Review of e-learning frameworks, models and theories: JISC e-learning models desk study.* London: JISC.

Peachey, A., & Childs, M. (2011). *Reinventing ourselves: Contemporary concepts of identity in virtual worlds.* London: Springer.

Peachey, A., Gillen, J., Livingstone, D., & Smith-Robbins, S. (2010). *Researching learning in virtual worlds.* London: Springer.

Smith, A. D. (2007). The flesh of perception: Merleau-Ponty and Husserl. In T. Baldwin (Ed.), *Reading Merleau-Ponty: On phenomenology of perception.* Oxon: Routledge.

Taylor, T. L. (2002). Living digitally: Embodiment in virtual worlds. In R. Schroeder (Ed.), *The social life of Avatars* (pp. 40–62). London: Springer.

Wilson, M. (2002). Six views of embodied cognition. *Psychonomic Bulletin & Review, 9*(4), 625–636.

Contents

Author Biographies

Brian G. Burton *Ed.D.* is an author, game developer, and professor of Digital Entertainment and Information Technology at Abilene Christian University. Besides writing multiple textbooks on mobile application and game development, and contributing to several academic books on serious games and learning in virtual worlds, Dr. Burton has created two university level game development degrees. He also enjoys researching and playing virtual environments. Dr. Burton presents and publishes internationally on his research and enjoys sharing what he has learned about game and mobile development. He has received teaching and research awards. When not travelling or teaching, he can be found at his home in the Ozark Mountains of Missouri with his beautiful wife of over 25 years, Rosemary. Brian can be reached through his website http://www.BurtonsMediaGroup.com

Mark Childs is a Senior Research Fellow for Elearning at Coventry University, in the UK, as well as working freelance within academia. Since 1997 he has worked on more than 30 projects involving technology-supported learning; as a researcher, consultant, evaluator, manager and principal investigator, at Coventry and in previous posts at the Universities of Wolverhampton and Warwick. Alongside his research he has also supported the delivery of a range of in-service professional development programmes, acting as an instructor, supervisor and evaluator. In 2010 he was awarded a Ph.D. from the University of Warwick for his thesis on Learners' Experiences in Virtual Worlds. Dr. Childs also works as an education consultant and evaluator for a range of private and public sector organisations, including Hewlett Packard, the Field Museum of National History in Chicago, Ravensbourne College and JISC. His main research interest is the user experience of synchronous communication platforms, with his most recent work including virtual teamworking and digital identity, but particularly learning and performance in virtual worlds and mixed reality.

Sara de Freitas is Director of Research and Professor of Virtual Environments at Coventry University with responsibility for applied research, teaching and learning and business development. She is currently an Adjunct Professor at the University of

Malta, a Fellow of the Royal Society of Arts and Visiting Fellow at the University of London. Her publications include 5 books and over 90 journal articles, conference papers and technical reports. She has been a leading academic developing the new field of Serious Games and has published widely in the fields of pedagogic modelling, game-based learning, e-learning and Higher Education policy development.

Margaret de Jong Derrington lectures at King's College London on various courses for teachers of computer science and information technology. Her research interests include the use of virtual worlds (Second Life, OpenSim and Open Wonderland) for education in collaborative and task-based learning, and for teaching and learning programming. She has been involved in teaching English Language since 2006 first in real life, then as Bracken Homewood in Second Life and subsequently on Skype and in her own OpenSim Grid called Homewood. Research in this area is the basis for her current Ph.D. studies.

Rebecca Ferguson is currently a full-time research fellow in the UK Open University's Institute of Educational Technology, focused on *Educational Futures*. She works as research lead on the *SocialLearn* team, developing and researching initiatives to improve pedagogical understanding of learning in online settings, to design analytics to support the assessment of learning in these settings, and to extend the university's ability to support learning in an open world. For the last 6 years she has been a core team member of The Open University's *Schome* project, working with UK and US teenagers online and in the virtual reality world of Second Life to develop 'an education system for the information age'.

Michael Gardner Ph.D. is a Research Fellow and Director of the Digital Lifestyles Centre at the University of Essex. This centre explores future lifestyles based around the technical vision of ambient and pervasive computing. He has over 25 years experience in knowledge media both within the industrial research environment and academia. During that time he has worked extensively in the areas of virtual reality, e-learning, collaborative working, social software and the semantic web. Over the years he has worked closely with many industrial partners on innovative research projects, such as BT, Sun Microsystems, and Apple Computer. Many of his projects have been involved in developing and deploying innovative technologies in a range of concrete user contexts, such as within the home/school boundary, call-centres, and higher education settings. His current research interests are focused on the use of virtual reality environments for work, research, learning and teaching.

Julia Gillen is Senior Lecturer in Digital Literacies in the Literacy Research Centre and Department of Linguistics and English Language, Lancaster University. Dr. Gillen is interested in researching relationships between language, learning and technologies especially concerning children and young people. Her books include *Digital Literacies* (Routledge, forthcoming); *Virtual Literacies: Interactive Spaces for Children and Young People* (co-edited with G. Merchant, J. Marsh & J. Davies, Routledge, 2012); *Researching Learning in Virtual Worlds* (co-edited with A. Peachey, D. Livingstone and S. Robbins, Springer, 2010) and *International*

Perspectives on Early Childhood Research: A Day in the Life (co-edited with C.A. Cameron, Palgrave, 2010).

Carina Girvan is a Ph.D. candidate at Trinity College Dublin where she is a member of the Centre for Research in IT in Education. Her research focuses on the perceived educational affordances of virtual worlds and aligning these to potentially appropriate pedagogies for use inworld. She is also involved in research into technology adoption by teachers. Carina's thesis focuses on constructionism in Second Life, explored through SLurtle based learning experiences in which learners programme SLurtles (Second Life turtles) using Scratch for Second Life to construct inworld objects. She has also been involved in developing data collection techniques and ethical considerations for conducting research in virtual worlds.

Béatrice Hasler holds a Doctorate in Psychology from the University of Zurich, Switzerland. She investigates the psychological and social factors in virtual team collaboration and technology-mediated conflict resolution. Her research is funded by the Swiss National Science Foundation and the European Union. She currently works as a Research Fellow at the Advanced Virtuality Lab of the Interdisciplinary Center Herzliya, Israel.

Bernard Horan is a senior researcher in the School of Computer Science and Electronic Engineering at the University of Essex. Prior to joining the University, Horan was a Senior Staff Engineer for Sun Microsystems Laboratories, where he was the Principal Investigator and technical lead of the successful collaborative project that used Project Wonderland to create a Mixed Reality Teaching and Learning Environment. Horan's earlier research has included work on the semantic web as part of Sun Labs' Advanced Search Technology project (he was a member of the W3C WebOnt WG) and wireless transducer networks.

Cecilie Flo Jahreie has a long research experience in different fields of educational research. She has in more than a decade been working with transcending boundaries between university and school in teacher education. She is also concerned with learning in multi-professional groups and learning between schools and museums. In her research Dr. Jahreie emphasizes the importance of creating coherent learning trajectories across institutional settings. She has several publications in a variety of international journals. Dr. Jahreie is affiliated with InterMedia, University of Oslo, Norway, and is a post doctor at the MIRACLE project.

Derek Jones is a Lecturer in Design with The Open University and course chair for U101: Design Thinking, the innovative and award winning Level 1 entry course for the university's Design and Innovation degree. His research interests include: the pedagogy and development of creativity in education, Building Information Modelling (BIM) design processes in practice and education, Virtual architecture and place, and Archetypes in architecture. Derek is also a qualified architect with over 13 years of experience in the construction design and procurement industries. He is currently an architect and BIM Manager for Keppie Design based in Glasgow,

Scotland. In his spare time, Derek is also an Associate Lecturer with The Open University, tutoring U101: Design Thinking and T307: Innovation.

Alfredo Jornet is licentiate in Psychology by the University of Valencia (Spain), and is currently a Ph.D. candidate at the Department of Educational Research and Intermedia, University of Oslo (Norway). Versed in cross-sectional and cross-cultural studies on technology use in adolescence, he is currently involved in design-based research across diverse educational contexts, including the school and the museum. His main interest is in developing analytical models for the study of learning that consider the intersection between cognition, culture and technology.

Barbara Martin is Professor, Educational Administration Department, at the University of Central Missouri and an Adjunct Professor, Department of Educational Leadership and Policy Analysis, at the University of Missouri-Columbia. Her current research and writing focus is on social justice issues in K-12 and higher education, and technology in education in K-12 and in higher education. She has addressed these topics in over 70 publications, including refereed journal articles and book chapters. Her articles are published in the *Journal of Woman in Educational Leadership, Women in Higher Education, Educational Leadership Review*, and the *Middle School Journal*, among others. Dushkin/McGraw-Hill and IGI Global publishers have published her book chapters. Dr. Martin is on the editorial board of *Urban Educator Journal, International Journal of Leadership in Education, Educational Management Administration & Leadership, Journal of College and Character*, and *Educational Renaissance*. She has received teaching, service and research awards from Missouri State University and teaching and research awards from the University of Central Missouri. Dr. Martin holds a B.S., M.S, and Educational Specialist, along with an Ed.D. in superintendency from the University of Missouri, Columbia, MO.

Claus Nehmzow CEO and founder of 3D Avatar School, is an entrepreneur and leader in developing strategic innovation for market success. He has over 25 years experience building businesses and consulting to premier clients worldwide. Prior to founding 3D Avatar School, Claus held a number of leadership roles including at brand and user experience agency Method (General Manager International), PA Consulting (Partner and Virtual World Practice Leader), Shazam Entertainment (Angel Investor, COO and Director International Business Development), Viant (General Manager Viant Germany), Booz Allen Hamilton (Partner), and Accenture (Senior Manager). Originally from Germany, Claus worked and lived in Zurich, New York, Munich, London and since 2008 resides in Hong Kong.

Anna Peachey spent 4 years (2006–2010) researching identity and community in virtual worlds as a Teaching Fellow with the Centre for Open Learning in Maths, Science, Computing and Technology at The Open University UK. She has published and presented widely on virtual worlds as sites of learning, and continues to teach and research with The Open University within a portfolio of other projects as an independent consultant.

Jenny Robins is a Professor of Library and Information Science in the College of Education at the University of Central Missouri. She teaches and researches in the field of school librarianship, at the primary and secondary education levels. Dr. Robins has a two-pronged interest in this field, promoting self-directed learning and structuring learning environments. Recent research includes examining the role of play in learning, including the impact of affective states on learning and the relationship between motivation, creativity, and information literacy. She has also done research on the processes involved in implementing 'response to intervention' programs in primary and secondary schools.

Tim Savage is an Assistant Professor in the School of Computer Science and Statistics in Trinity College, Dublin University. His research is into the use of virtual worlds for teaching and learning with a focus on the identification and evaluation of existing and novel pedagogical strategies for use in these emerging environments. He integrates virtual worlds into his teaching on the Masters in Technology and Learning and other courses within Trinity College. He has been the principal investigator on two funded research projects in the area. Project Murias was an investigation into the use of virtual worlds in the teaching and learning of Development Education (funded by Irish Aid, Irish Government). The V-Learning project involves the creation of a virtual world integrated into a range of learning management systems to support teaching and learning across a range of domains (with the National Digital Research Centre and V-Rising).

Andreas Schmeil is a postdoctoral research fellow with the BeCHANGE group at the University of Lugano (USI) in Switzerland. He holds a Ph.D. in Communication Sciences from USI and an M.Sc. in Informatics from Ulm University, Germany. Past roles include positions and fellowships at the Palo Alto Research Center (formerly Xerox PARC), Simon Fraser University, the Human Interface Technology Laboratory New Zealand (HIT Lab NZ), Fraunhofer FIT, and Fraunhofer IAO. His research focuses on visual communication, avatar-based collaboration, natural user interfaces, and innovative approaches to behavior change and support. He is further interested in experience design and a proponent of the design science paradigm.

Peter Twining is the Director of Vital, a £9.4 million UK Department for Education funded programme that is supporting teachers in enhancing their teaching of IT/Computing as specialist subjects and the use of ICT across the curriculum. Prior to leading the Vital Programme, Dr. Twining was the Head of Department of Education at The Open University and then the Co-Director of the Centre for Research in Education and Educational Technology. His career has been focused on issues to do with the management of educational change, linked with enhancing education, and informed by understandings of the potential of ICT. His passion is Schome (not school – not home – Schome – the education system for the information age).

Simone Wesner is a Senior Lecturer in Creative Industries Management based at the Centre for Research in Cultural Industries Management at London Metropolitan University Business School. Her academic career is built on her practical experience as curator, project manager and producer in the cultural sector. She studied cultural management, cultural studies and cultural policy at the Universities of Leipzig, Hamburg and Warwick. In her doctoral research she investigated cultural change among artist communities in Germany. This original interest developed into a longstanding research theme of cultural fingerprints, which combines cultural values with identity. Currently her research interests have expanded into the virtual world where she developed an experimental learning framework (ELF) that analyses participants' project management in relation to the learning process and skills transfer in the creative industries.

Chapter 1
An Alternative (to) Reality

Derek Jones

Abstract This chapter explores the idea that a generation of successful virtual environments relies on a better understanding of how we conceive virtual and physical realities in our minds, in particular, to recognise that our *conception* of these realities is at least as important as our *perception* of them. The failure and success of certain virtual environments are explained as the failure and success of the application of conceived phenomena.

Firstly, making use of philosophical phenomenology and recent scientific research, our understanding of physical reality is considered in terms of phenomenal conception and it is shown that 'objective' perception is only one part of our relationship to physical environments. Secondly, the other point of view is considered and virtual environments are argued to be just as valid phenomenal conceptions as their physical counterparts.

Finally, the translation of phenomenal conceptions between realities is considered, providing a different way of considering how we think about and design all types of reality. Several interesting potential avenues of investigation are identified and examples of the emergence of this approach are presented.

1.1 Introduction

Virtual Reality has become a recognisable phrase often referring to environments generated and hosted electronically, but the word virtual leads to natural conclusions about the nature of these 'places'. Virtual suggests simulated, copied, mimicked – that there is an *a priori* reality that is the thing of greater value and that the virtual version must therefore be nothing more than a simulacrum.

D. Jones (✉)
Faculty of Mathematics, Computing and Technology, The Open University, Milton Keynes, Buckinghamshire, UK
e-mail: derek.jones@open.ac.uk

M. Childs and A. Peachey (eds.), *Understanding Learning in Virtual Worlds*, Human–Computer Interaction Series, DOI 10.1007/978-1-4471-5370-2_1, © Springer-Verlag London 2013

Virtual worlds come in a variety of forms, from collections of information that generate a social body of knowledge (such as a virtual learning environments or social media environments) to multi-user virtual environments (such as Second Life or online gaming environments), where a computer generated 3D graphical representation of an environment is provided, within which a user can navigate and interact with the environment and other users.

The word *virtual* within all of these terms is the starting point for this paper and it is suggested that, by using it, we immediately frame the environment in terms of a duality – that there is a 'real' world and the 'virtual' world, and that the latter is in some way a copy or simulacrum of the other. Yet there is compelling evidence to suggest that such a simple distinction between the two may not be so easy to establish when we compare how we react and behave in both. Studies have demonstrated that some cognitive functions are observable in both physical and virtual worlds and there is growing observational evidence that other psychological and social behaviours are shared in both environments.

Our lack of deep understanding of these virtual worlds has not prevented their use – the popularity of virtual world gaming, for example, represents a significant part of the total entertainment market. Virtual worlds in education have seen a fashionable uptake followed by variable results with (arguably) only the most capable environments persisting. Similarly the use of virtual learning environments offering entirely online content seems to be increasing in response to economic and user demands. Some recent examples represent quite complex socially immersive 'places' to learn.

The tendency to use 3D virtual worlds to simply copy physical reality is well documented (Addison and O'Hare 2008; Gardner et al. 2008; Grove et al. 2008). There is also evidence to suggest that we do not use this new technology to its full potential (Hobbs et al. 2006; Hollins and Robbins 2008).

It will be argued that copying reality and unfulfilled potential are symptoms of the same thing – that the essential part of how we conceive of any environment is not properly recognised. It is proposed that this essence is the phenomenal conception we generate from an environment and not simply the perception or cognition that arises from it.

The first part of this chapter will consider how we conceive of physical reality and show that the *conceptions* we generate of the world around us are as important as the *perceptions* we have of it. The objective, physical world will be presented as only one aspect of our overall mental picture of reality.

Using this idea of conceptions of reality, it will then be argued that similar (if not identical) mechanisms of conceptualisation occur in virtual worlds. Direct examples and analogies of physical and virtual worlds will be presented and the link between these is suggested to be the conception we generate of both. The notion of conception in education is also introduced as an importance aspect of significant learning events.

Finally, the possible implications of making use of conception in the design of physical and virtual environments in education are considered in terms of the barriers and potential for transfer of practice between physical and virtual. Examples of physical and virtual places are presented to demonstrate that it is possible to design with the conception in mind and that the conception in education design is of significance and worth further consideration and research.

Let us begin by posing the question 'Why do we use gravity in virtual environments?' This apparently simple question may seem a strange starting point and, with a little thought, may also seem to be answered quite simply. But there is potentially another way of looking at this question, which also provides another way of looking at all realities, whether virtual or physical. Gravity is a physical element that affects almost everything we perceive and this in turn affects how we think about the world around us. It is this effect on our idea, or *conception*, of reality that is the subject of this chapter.

Gravity does more than appear to make things fall.

1.2 Physical Reality as Phenomenal Conceptions

1.2.1 A Brief Introduction to Phenomenology

Gaston Bachelard, in his book *The Poetics of Space* (Bachelard 1994), describes architecture in a phenomenological way, providing us with a vivid alternative view of how we conceive the physical world around us. Rather than simply viewing our environment as a series of (objective) elements, we are constantly interacting with it – interpreting, filtering, or applying value. The ultimate idea (or conception) we have of reality is very different to any objective measurement we may make of it. Bachelard presents a phenomenological view of architecture and of reality itself, where the ideas we conceive are every bit as important as the physical things we perceive.

Consider where you are just now and, in particular, how you feel about that place. What is suggested here is that your reaction to that place is not simply to do with the colour of the walls or how high the ceiling is – it is how you respond to these and thousands of other elements that matters. This is necessarily a subjective thing, generated by you from your memories, preferences, mood, activity, etc. It is this interaction with the world around us, these events or phenomena, which is the main consideration of phenomenology.

Philosophical phenomenology, as originally formalised by Edmund Husserl (Honderich 1995), considers the difference between the thing perceived in our environment and the thing in the mind. More importantly, we must realise that the perception of anything is necessarily subjective and relies on our cognitive interaction with it – that is, what we think about the thing.

Heidegger develops this in greater detail with respect to our interactions between perception and cognition (Heidegger 1995). We may see a thing, but once we have interacted with it, we have a different relationship with it. The interaction in itself has developed our idea of the perceived thing and this in turn affects our relationship to it. Both Husserl and Heidegger rely on a duality of (at least) perception and conception – i.e. that the perception of a thing occurs by a consciousness and becomes an idea in the mind.

But it was Merleau-Ponty who synthesised this duality to suggest that neither should be considered *a priori* (Merleau-Ponty 1962). For Merleau-Ponty, both must be considered as a single embodied entity – our perception of a thing and any conception of it are at once the same thing, separable only by definition (if at all). When we touch something, we actively conceive of it as we interact with it.

Once again, consider what you are doing right now. Your interactions with the physical aspects of these words are (hopefully) the least part of what is happening in your mind. Your relationship to the text is potentially far more fundamental than simply seeing light reflected (or projected) from whatever medium you are using. In fact, your basic relationship with the medium you are using to read has a considerable effect on what you think about it. Essentially, you are not just looking at words – you are considering them, playing with them in your mind, dismissing them, reacting to them.

It is this phenomenon that is of greatest interest in this paper. Even if you cannot subscribe to a phenomenological philosophy of reality, it is still perfectly possible to apply the arguments to the notion that the idea of the thing in our minds is necessarily different to the reality of the thing outside of our minds. The significant aspect of concern is the conception – the event we conceive in our minds.

This is a (very) brief description of the main points of philosophical phenomenology. Mingers (2001) is well worth reading for an expanded (and much better) summary.

1.2.2 Architecture as Phenomena

Returning to Bachelard, he provides the examples of cellar and attic as two very different conceptions of place in a house:

> Verticality is ensured by the polarity of cellar and attic, the marks of which are so deep that, in a way, they open up two very different perspectives for a phenomenology of the imagination. (Bachelard 1994)

Bachelard is suggesting that there is something very different in our conception of going up to an attic when compared to going down to the cellar. We do not only perceive the attic and cellar, we react to them as very different objects with different values attached. For Bachelard, the phenomena of attic and cellar are the 'real' events – not simply the physical objects themselves. Indeed, Bachelard uses the notion of dreaming to argue the fact that the ideas we generate about our physical existence are as important as our physiological interactions with it.

Moreover, he also suggests that these two examples, attic and cellar, are conceived so strongly that we actually generate a third conception – that of verticality. In doing so, Bachelard presents the importance of the mind in generating our notions of space, place and reality.

All architecture can potentially be considered in this way, from the feeling of entering a building to how we react to a particular shape of room. The conception we have of space generated by built form is where the architecture happens. As Clark and Maher (2001) suggest, Architects create space – people bring Place – and it is Place that is argued to be the most important element in terms of human interaction and understanding. In architecture, this is sometimes referred to as *genus loci* (Norberg-Schulz 1980) and the meaning that Place can embody in architecture has been discussed and used by many architects throughout history.

Aside from the philosophical argument, the fact that we respond cognitively to buildings is a well-documented phenomenon (see Anthes (2009) for some interesting examples), particularly when a physical and mental map do not align (Carlson et al. 2010). What is important in all these examples is the requirement for people to conceive of their environment – not simply perceive it. To generate the meaning or value we apply to (or take from) places, we must embody both the physical perception and the cognitive reaction. It is argued here that this embodiment, or conception, should be the object of interest.

It is worth noting that this is perhaps one of the reasons why superficial copying of physical reality does not always translate as expected to virtual worlds. It is possible to copy the elements but if the conception of these is not translated then a different phenomenology can occur – the triggers of the 'value' of a physical place must be translated as well, and these triggers are not always the simple physical elements.

1.2.3 Reality as Phenomena

It is also possible to extend this idea to events that may not seem to be traditional forms of architecture. In fact, it is argued that reality is, in some respects, 'virtual' when considered from the point of phenomenology. If we realise that the thing conceived is not the same as the thing perceived, then we must accept that a truly objective reality cannot exist (see Fingelkurts et al. (2009) for an interesting view on this).

This is not simply a philosophical construction – the difference between objectively measured reality and our conception of it is well documented. A good example is the finding that we do not conceive of colour the way it exits physically (by objective measurement) and that it can be influenced by cultural conditioning (Lotto 2004). Lotto demonstrates that two people may look at the same object and see different colours simply because of the way they been taught to see colour. This finding can be difficult to accept simply because we are so used to our own conceptions of reality – to each of us as individuals, 'red' is very well defined. But this is simply a projection of our own conception. A significant amount of the reality we experience seems to behave itself in quite a predictable way. For example, this sentence is extremely likely to make sense – or to at least be formed from recognisable shapes. So why should you not expect other people to share the same understanding of that simple observation?

It is this difficulty of discussing reality beyond our own conceptions that is precisely the problem and the subject here. The fact that an apparently objective object may be conceived in different ways only as a result of social conditioning seems counter-intuitive, but this is indeed the case.

This example from cognitive neuroscience is not isolated. The idea that the conceptions we form from perception are essential to understanding our world has support in Psychology (Velmans 1990), information systems theory (Mingers 2001) and, of course, philosophy (Merleau-Ponty 1962).

We must consider that, if we cannot even agree on seeing 'red', our notion of physical reality is, at least in part, as much an idea as it is an objective event. It may be difficult to accept the full phenomenology of Bachelard but the conception we create of the world around us is at least as important as the objective measurement of it.

Once again, what is important here is the difference between *perception* and *conception*. The idea we generate in our minds (conception) is more than perception of the physical world around us. Our conceptions are informed by our psychology, sociology, culture, memory, mood, attitudes, and many other complex elements.

In physical world design, when we ignore the conception people form in their minds, then we ignore a significant part of their experience of physical reality.

1.3 Virtual Worlds, Information and Education as Phenomenal Conceptions

1.3.1 Virtual Worlds as Phenomena

We now consider our relationship with virtual worlds and argue that similar conceptions of these 'places' are formed in our minds. This can be demonstrated directly from the arguments above. We copy physical reality in virtual worlds since we believe them to be a translation between physical and virtual and, generally, we observe that many of the perceptions formed in physical reality can also be formed in virtual worlds. For example, we generate physical 'rules' to maintain analogies; we make sure avatars cannot go through walls, we have gravity, we make use of spatial arrangements that make sense in terms of physical reality.

But in doing this, we are also providing conceptual environments – ones that make sense to us in terms of our interaction with and response to them. The simple physical elements of a virtual world can come together to form something that is greater than the sum of the parts and a sense of place can be achieved (Doyle 2008). Moreover, in an educational context, this sense of place seems to be an important aspect of the richness required in a virtual world (Clark and Maher 2001).

We often tend to assume that because the virtual world is simply 'virtual' that there is no physical interaction but as far as our minds are concerned this is simply not the case. Our mapping of physical and virtual worlds generate very similar cognitive responses (Dalton et al. 2002) and it is argued here that it is precisely these interactions that are vital to permitting the embodied phenomenology required for conceptions to form. As Hollins and Robbins (2008) state, "After all, all computer use is interactive."

There is also something about 'doing' that is important in this process; something that goes beyond being a passive observer. Doing is not just a physical act – it is also a mental one and this is especially true of generating conceptions. Merleau-Ponty requires his phenomenology to embody both object and person to generate a phenomenon but even if we consider dualist phenomenology the same argument can be applied. When we interact with the world, something happens. This simple act of interaction is one of the essential requirements for conception – without it we are simply engaging in perception and, as we have already seen, it is not possible to 'simply' do this without more complex conceptions being formed.

In addition to our physical interaction, virtual worlds can clearly allow social conceptions to exist, with communities forming and social interaction taking place (Twining and Footring (2008) describe one of many examples of this). Even negative aspects of any socially organised system can be found (Carr et al. 2008; Derrington and Homewood 2008; Minocha and Tungle 2008).

None of this would be possible without a conception of the virtual world. An event that is more than simple perception of the 'objective' reality being presented is *only* possible when it is conceived.

1.3.2   Information as Phenomena

The conceptions we generate in our mind are not limited to conceptions of physical elements. For example, it is suggested that *any* information can generate a conception. To be more precise, our interaction with information generates and relies on our conception of it.

On the simple level we could argue this from the fact that perception is information and this will automatically lead to conceptions of that information being formed. It is extremely difficult to conceive of data in isolation, without giving it meaning. To say that a thing is 'two' makes very little sense unless we apply that datum – i.e. that we have two things, or that two things relate. In each case we generate a relationship to construct a conception of the information and its meaning. Tim Berners-Lee refers to 'the information space' (Berners-Lee 1999), clearly indicating what we know intuitively – data have value only when a conception of them are created to give meaning and sense (in this case, a spatial/relational meaning).

For example, we naturally represent a value's magnitude in geometry by a line 'rising' or a data point becoming 'larger'. This might seem a truism, and in many ways it is – our 'natural' understanding of lower and higher will automatically be applied in an analogous way to anything we conceive of as having magnitude. But we need to recognise how many other things we apply the conception of lower and higher to and recognise this as a direct analogy to Bachelard's going 'up' to the attic and 'down' to the cellar. The information itself is given meaning by our conception of it.

In fact there is a growing tradition of interpreting abstract data in a visual or phenomenal way. Rosling successfully demonstrates how we can re-conceptualise data when we look at it interactively (2006). We Feel Fine (Harris and Kamvar

2011), takes blog postings starting with 'I/we feel…' and visualises them, providing the user with an interactive space to experiment with this data. In doing so, a user develops their own conception of the data and ultimately the meaning of it from this conception.

Mingers (2001) argues that Artificial Intelligence and Information Systems need to merge to break the duality they create, similar to the assumed duality created by a Platonic world view (or by early philosophical phenomenology). In other words, just as we must recognise that an objective reality and the perception of it can no longer be treated as separate entities, so too must information and the perception of information be reconciled.

This conception of information is important and should not be underestimated. Stories are nothing more than information, yet they create very vivid conceptions in our minds (in fact storytelling actively relies on this happening). Some of the earliest human communication was representative and descriptive. A cave painting of an animal is clearly not the animal itself; rather, it relies on the viewer conceiving the representation being made. All storytelling relies on a conception of the information being presented and we are asked by authors to imagine, project or immerse ourselves in this conception. Modern storytelling continues this tradition but it relies on the same principle. *Dreams of Black* (Milk 2010) presents an online example of modern storytelling where an interactive virtual world and traditional storytelling combine. And what of Shakespeare in Second Life (Chafer and Childs 2008) – is the story or the medium the conception being created?

As an example, Sweeney (2008) suggests that immersion and eye tracking are related in the virtual world game *Runescape*, created by Jagex Games Studios. It is argued here that the user's attention on the 3D element is simply one aspect of the conception of the environment. Having seen the deeply immersive effects of Runescape firsthand, it is clear that an immersion is occurring but it is suggested that this is one of conception and does not rely only on the physical representation of the environment alone.

When a Runescape player is immersed, they are considering all of the information being presented and generating an overall conception. The player statistics are as important a part of that environment as the virtual space – in fact, it is the information that gives Runescape its value and meaning for players. Without it, the player would simply be moving in a 3D representation of reality and this has very little immersive value indeed. It is suggested here that the eye tracking evidence in Sweeney's study is actually indicative of greater immersion in a phenomenological sense – more information is communicated and interacted with, hence a richer conceptual environment is formed.

In other words, users are immersed in the story being presented to them: the information, 3D environment and, therefore, the conception of the Runescape virtual world. To simply take one aspect and assume that it is the analogy without understanding the conception runs the risk that many virtual world designers face – that without all the parts that make up the conception, you are simply left with a simulacrum or representation.

It is also possible to imagine other information repositories as 'places' of information. Peachey (2010) refers to Oldenburg's 'third places' in virtual worlds, and cites Glogowski (2006) as suggesting that an online blogging community can also be viewed as such a 'place'. Here, information is suggested to generate some conception that is beyond the mere perception or interpretation of the information itself and many educators will be aware of the need to generate an 'atmosphere' or 'momentum' in an educational forum.

If information in this context is not a conception, then how is it that we can even conceive of an 'atmosphere' when we refer to a series of letters and colours in a forum?

1.3.3 Education as Phenomena

Education can be argued to rely entirely on the generation of conceptions – not the transfer of facts. In fact, information transfer is arguably the least part of education. Problem Based Learning, Constructivist Learning or Personal Learning Environments are all examples of approaches to education that focus on the generation of conceptions in the mind of the student. The transfer of information is of a lower priority to how that information may be used or how meaning may be derived from it – and there is some evidence that virtual worlds are suitable environments for this (see Sect. 1.4.1 below).

It is worth noting that this is not limited to virtual worlds and is certainly not new, despite the latest names or acronyms. We can all reflect on physical learning events that have stayed with us throughout our lives and might recall a specific teacher at school, a particular subject (or even concept) and certainly the sense of place. In each of these memorable cases, it is argued that the phenomenon is the thing remembered.

Ramondt (2008) discusses the 'gift of drama' in education and how a teacher can generate conceptions in learning rather than simply presenting information. So it is perhaps worth pausing for a moment to recall your own significant moments in learning. For me, a particularly memorable one would be Mr. ('Buff') Bailey explaining resonant frequency, making use of the full length of the classroom and the vivid image of him pushing his Aunt Maggie on a swing. Out of phase resonance was explained as the unfortunate collision due to bad timing (all appropriately acted out by a biology teacher, storyteller and stuntman).

Trivial as this may seem, I can honestly say that my understanding of this concept is directly linked to this moment of education. Through storytelling, physical demonstration and perfectly timed words, I conceived of the mechanism by which light of certain wavelengths were absorbed in plants. The conception was strong enough that it could be applied to any and all such analogous events.

Another example of this might be the teaching of multiplication. It is certainly possible to learn the information (i.e. that $1 \times 1 = 1$ $1 \times 2 = 2$, etc.) but it is surely of more value that students understand the concept of multiplication (i.e. that '×'

means 'of'). With the concept of multiplication in your mind, you realise the meaning of it – the value of it. It belongs to you as an idea of the mind and this is both a personal and rather fundamental conception to hold

In education, if we seek to develop more than the simple transfer of information, then we need to provide more than data. The creation of conception requires richer elements of learning – it requires a storyteller, dramatist, entertainer, psychologist, anthropologist, …

Tolstoy (quoted in Schon 1991) describes this well:

> …Each teacher must … by regarding every imperfection in the pupil's comprehension, not as a defect of the pupil, but as a defect of his own instruction, endeavour to develop in himself the ability of discovering new methods…

1.4   Synthesis of Physical and Virtual

If we accept that we can consider physical reality, virtual worlds, information and education in a phenomenological way, then it may be that we can translate conceptions between these environments. Moreover it allows us to start with, and focus on, the phenomena or conceptions themselves and these ideas are considered next. But before this we do need to understand the difficulties in doing so. Finally, we must also consider the implications for the design of such artefacts.

1.4.1   The Barriers to Phenomenal Design

There are good reasons why we do not just jump straight into an abstract reality made from conceptions. Design for virtual worlds requires just as much attention as design for their physical counterparts and in many cases these considerations are more important to ensure a reasonable translation of the design intent.

We know that students require induction to understand how to relate to virtual worlds (Addison and O'Hare 2008; Trinder 2008; Truelove and Hibbert 2008). Similarly, the challenges facing MUVE socialisation design are known (Minocha and Tungle 2008), and simply translating 'rules' from physical reality to virtual worlds can be difficult (Barker et al. 2008). But in each of these cited examples, evidence is also presented of how these problems can be managed or overcome. Once a conceptual framework is embedded there are genuine benefits to be gained and people can adapt to these new environments.

In fact, as Carr et al. (2008) note:

> A degree of disorientation or ambiguity might be productive in one learning context yet completely counter-productive in another.
>   and
>   The 'anything goes' nature of SL [Second Life] meant that our students took little for granted. For example, they questioned the various pedagogic decisions that had been made.

Moreover, it is often the challenge of the new environment that is the reason for it being created. In computer gaming, there are several examples of entire games generated around radical shifts in conceptions of physical reality. *Portal* (Valve Corporation), *The Company of Myself* (Piilonin) and *Shift* (Armor Games) are all examples that not only require the player to adapt to a different conception of the reality they are presented with, but require the player to actively engage with that conception in order to progress in the game. In effect, the method and mode are synthesised into a phenomenon – an embodied event of conception through interaction.

So making use of conceptions in design offers us an alternative goal for the design process or an alternative method of considering the designed object. At the very least, understanding the simple fact that our design intent may translate to a very different conception in the minds of the users is necessary.

This are, in addition to the opportunities, several other reasons that it might be worth considering these challenges:

- The formation of these places can be emergent (Minocha and Tungle 2008) and this emergence is already occurring. We naturally design phenomena but often at an instinctual level without understanding or recognising it explicitly. Being able to consciously design for the emergence of phenomena, or at least being aware of this mechanism, is required. The failure of physical copies of campuses in virtual worlds is an example of the failure to translate the phenomena or conception of those campuses.
- Designers are working beyond their 'expertise' and this, rather than being a negative outcome, is leading to some genuinely excellent inter-disciplinary solutions. This knowledge needs to be recognised and shared with further lines of design investigation followed. In fact the potential this may offer may be only now truly emerging.
- If we aim for student-centred and adaptive pedagogies, then we must consider the affordances of conception-based virtual worlds. Problem Based Learning has been demonstrated to be possible (Brown et al. 2008; Burden et al. 2008; Burton and Martin 2008). Constructivist Learning may operate more effectively in a virtual world (Grove et al. 2008). Atwell's Personal Learning Environments (Attwell 2007) are effectively conceptions of learning places.

There is also a self-referencing argument to be made with respect to educational virtual worlds. It is all very well starting with pedagogy but if we do not know what is possible with a new mode then we have no way of realising how a pedagogy can be applied (or even affected) by its use. A very good point is made by one of the educators interviewed in Minocha and Reeves (2010):

> I find the political correctness of 'pedagogy must lead technology' to be rather sterile. We need to be more interactionist about this. The teachers don't know what is possible [in Second Life], and the technologists don't know what the teachers might want to achieve if they could…

Perhaps our design of these places needs to learn from the duality of early phenomenology – that both should collapse to a single conception of mode and pedagogy. After all, if we acknowledge that the creation of conception requires embodied interaction (e.g. application of theory and practice), then we require an embodied pedagogy that does not assume a simple cause and effect model of education – we require an emergent pedagogy where the method is the teaching and vice versa.

1.4.2 Knowledge and Concept Transfer

It is now argued that phenomena or conceptions can translate directly between environments, allowing exciting opportunities for designers. For example, architectural design in education can be used in virtual worlds and knowledge from educational virtual worlds can be used in physical architecture. The ceiling height in physical schools has been previously reported to have a measurable effect on creation task type performance (Anthes 2009). Now consider the finding in Sweeney (2008), where the removal of the ceiling/roof led to claustrophobia. Here, it was considered that the space still led to a feeling of enclosure, thought to be as result of the surrounding, windowless walls.

Here, we have an apparent contradiction between virtual and physical environments yet, when we consider it further, the analogies still hold. A direct physical analogy to the ceiling-less space in Sweeney (2008) is the Memorial to the Deportation (Mémorial des Martyrs de la Déportation) Paris by Georges-Henri Pingusson. This built object relies entirely on the fact that we feel claustrophobic not despite the fact that we are able to see the sky but precisely because we can. Being able to see into the far distance of sky without being able to perceive any other context at all actually dislocates the user and engenders a feeling of enclosure and claustrophobia. This conception is intended by the designer in this physical place but it is also the conception generated in the virtual place reported by Sweeney.

It is argued here that it is not simply the measurable height that generates the observation made by Anthes; it is the conception of the space. The variety of factors that encourage 'openness' is huge but essentially, in natural language, the more 'open' it feels, the more 'open' our minds might become. There are obvious parallels and lessons to be learned by both physical and virtual architects in these examples and this may represent the smallest example of future study.

But we do need to remember what is common between these things – we need to recognise that it is the conception formed in our minds that is the thing of relevance. The difference between physical and virtual is typically made by considering only perception and this is insufficient to understand the whole phenomenon.

Neither is it sufficient to consider only the cognition. By this, it is meant that there are no single, predictable mental processes that operate in reaction to perception on their own. There is no part of our brain that deals with 'ceiling height' or 'view of horizon' as single cause and effect operations. We may draw on these (whatever they may actually be) but must also draw on past experience, cultural upbringing, mood, time of day, etc. The entire result is the thing of importance – is the conception.

The ceiling example above is simply a transfer of conceptual events. It may work at a practical level (i.e. there may appear to be a cause and effect that we can put to practical use) but understanding the phenomenon allows us to extend its use to other knowledge domains. We now have a bit of the knowledge of how to affect the phenomenon of 'openness' (at some level and in some way) and this is a very powerful knowledge to have. But we also know that if we want to create the conception that arises from a higher ceiling that there are other ways

We must realise, too, the potential of transfer from virtual to physical. Why not work on a physical world version of the wonderful extending table (Derrington and Homewood 2008)? We know that desk configurations have an effect on attention and work methods in schools, so how can we enable this knowledge in physical and virtual environments? What other wonderful virtual world ideas can we turn into physical reality?

1.4.3 Start with the Conception

What begins to emerge from the above is that it is the conceptions we form (the phenomena) that are the things of potentially greater interest – not the environment, whether virtual or physical. Can we, therefore, start designing with the conception we wish to convey rather than the object(s)?

Three brief and recent examples of this happening are now presented from design practice and education. But before they are, it is important to state that this is in no way new. This is not some new way of considering the design of our physical or virtual realities. Designers have known this, and made use of it, for centuries and good design generates a strong conception (or permits one to emerge). As we saw earlier, the emergence of the conception is incredibly important and it always has been. Whether the good designer was aware of it, or perhaps used other language and terminology for it, they were in the business of the design of conceptions.

U101 Design Thinking – U101 Design Thinking: Creativity for the twenty-first century (Open University 2011) is the Open University's entry-level course for the Design and Innovation Degree. It was designed around the idea of a design atelier, a design studio 'space' where social, peer-to-peer and student-tutor collaboration would be possible and in turn form one of the main teaching and learning objectives. To achieve this, the module makes use of a variety of media in an online blended learning environment – from text, audio, and video information through to forums, shared online portfolios, and asynchronous whiteboard communication environments (Lloyd 2011).

It is the idea behind the course that is of interest here and it is suggested that the conception of the design atelier genuinely infiltrated the entire design of the course. In the atelier, students are expected to engage with the idea of design as a process of thought and action, which is then informed and modified by interaction. The interaction element is of vital significance since it is this that generates the learning feedback with student peers and tutors.

Moreover, the focus of the assessment is on process, not product. The duality of process and object is embodied as a single pedagogy and students are engaging with a conception and not simply a set of instructions or learning tasks. This embodiment of idea and action is at the heart of Donald Schon's idea of 'reflection-in-action' (Schon 1991), a central tenet of all design education. It is also a central requirement of Merleau-Ponty's embodied phenomenology.

The idea of a learning community is certainly not unique in online learning environments. Many rely on the very fact that a 'virtual world' consisting of individuals sharing a single learning goal can work. Many of these also rely on this simply emerging from the elements provided rather than specifying it in the design. What is interesting about U101 is the fact that this community, and the reason for the community, was an explicit requirement from the start and that each activity and online event was designed to support this. It was not couched in terms of conception or phenomenology, but it most certainly started as a simply stated but complex idea.

It is argued that this idea was a conception and that it was also composed of the original intent, the designed learning environment and (perhaps most importantly) the continued recognition and maintenance of this conception by tutors and students. The two essential points to observe here are that the conception is dynamic (not a static design) – it achieves its dynamism from its own story and the stories brought to it by all parties involved. The other point is that the conception is embodied in a phenomenology of idea and action – the activities require thought and the thinking requires activity. This, in itself, is an incredibly powerful conception.

MIRACLE Implementation in the Norwegian Museum of Science and Technology – A direct example of starting with the conception in design is given in chapter three by Jornet and Jahreie. In this example the entire design process was driven by the desire to create 'place', acknowledging the complexity that is embodied in such a term. The authors observe that, by making use of space as the "shared object", a negotiation took place between different points of reference. This negotiation ultimately allowed the emergence of place to occur, through a shared exploration of the stakeholder's ideas.

In doing so, it is argued that the authors suggest that any space (or indeed any interactive object) relies as much on our conception as it does the simple perception of it. This naturally leads to immediate difficulties in terms of having to deal with the entire range of possible human subjective reactions and how these disparate views can be mediated in a shared conception.

Interestingly, the authors recognise and actively take advantage of precisely this difficulty, considering the design process in the project study as a "learning process". This affirms what many designers know intuitively – the process of design is one of incompleteness where discovery and emergence are essential. But in this particular case study it was essential in both defining the shared conception and resolving its designed solution.

What becomes clear from this example are the difficulties involved in expressing and consciously dealing with the conception. The case study suggests one explicit way in which this difficulty is mediated – through the use of representations of space (architectural drawings) as a communication tool. The authors identify this as central to the individual stakeholders' ability to move beyond their own conceptual boundaries and enter into shared conceptions with one another. By sharing a conceptual object around which they can communicate, the parties arguably share (at least partially) a conception of that object. Co-operative, inclusive and open-minded design thinking seems to allow this possibility – in fact it could be argued that it will naturally follow from this type of design process.

Of course, this does require genuine collaboration – not just coordination or cooperation (Pollard 2005). The conception to be designed has to arise in the design process itself and, since there is no simple objective way of measuring the breadth of human response, it is necessarily a wicked (or tangled) design problem (Rittel and Webber 1973). Using as wide a range of design thinking as possible simply makes sense to come close to a problem solution and it is arguably a natural extension of Schon's 'Reflection-in-action' (Schon 1991).

One final observation is that there may have been a further medium for the shared conception, not just the representation of space. It is hinted at in both of the excerpts that drama (or storytelling) is a real consideration and all stakeholders pick up on this. It is suggested here that, like our conceptualisation of place, storytelling is a medium that allows us to go beyond individual positions and move into shared ideas. When we listen to a story we suspend part of our critical thinking, reject less and imagine more. When this happens, new (often shared) ideas emerge.

Building information modelling – In the building design and construction industry, Building Information Modelling (BIM), is changing the way designers work together (NBS 2012). The adoption of BIM in construction disciplines is rapidly increasing and it may represent a significant shift in the approach and attitude to the massive task of designing an object as complex as a modern building (Shelden 2009).

BIM is the process of creating a virtual computer model of a building, effectively constructing a virtual building (sometimes many times) before it is physically constructed. But it is not simply the creation of the physical elements of the model that are relevant – each element also has information attached to it to provide a deeper and more informed database of design elements. It is this extension of the model to other 'dimensions' of information that enables designers to do far more in this virtual environment than previously possible.

Another key intent for this information model is the fact that all members of the design team work in it together, allowing them to collaborate in a single 'place'. It is suggested here that BIM is effectively a virtual world, allowing all stakeholders to work collaboratively – from the client's brief to the designer's model and right through to a final virtual building that can be used to manage the physical building itself.

It is the potential paradigm shift that is of interest in this example since effective BIM requires all stakeholders to share a conception of the process of design and the object being designed as a single entity. The two main features identified above effectively force collaboration in a single environment rather than the current practice of the linear transfer of discrete packets of information.

Effectively, the duality between the process and object becomes embodied to allow both to align much more naturally. As designers we seek to embody the idea and the thing together – not as separate entities. Ideas such as incompleteness and direct (non-specialist) stakeholder involvement are starting to emerge in the debate about how we should go about designing buildings.

There are clear and relevant parallels between this and both preceding examples and it is suggested here that the conception is the thing that allows these parallels to exist. On a simple level, we might consider the shared virtual information model to be a shared spatial environment and, similar to the Jornet and Jahreie case study, this will foster the interaction between parties and breaking down of individual conceptions.

At another level, we might consider the shared environment to be an opportunity to share a story – to communicate and collaborate in an entirely different way.

1.4.4 Conception Considerations

If we start with the conception (or phenomenon), there are several things we must bear in mind.

Phenomena – It is phenomena that are the essence of our relationship to any form of reality. When we make use of any information, the perceptual parts of it represent only a part of the conception we form in our minds. These conceptions are transferrable, allowing a single conception to exist in a wide variety of media and this offers an incredible variety of opportunities for the sharing of knowledge, ideas and methods. Moreover, we should not restrict our learning in only one direction – lessons in virtual design can equally apply in physical design.

Interaction – It is the interaction with (and within) these virtual worlds that is the driver (or enabler) for the conception to be maintained. All participants are able to affect their environment and the sharing of consequence of change is a large part of the process itself. The interaction with and within virtual worlds is just as important as it is in physical reality and this must be offered to users of these environments. Interaction is not simply pressing buttons or reading notes – it is the active engagement with phenomena. It is even possible that the phenomena do not exist without the interaction.

Collaboration – These conceptions make use of social phenomena and in particular collective interactions. The conception is a shared entity embodied not in the virtual world itself, but in the minds of the participants. Differences of conception will arise but these are embodied in the shared event, creating the potential for interaction. Expert and novice share the same space. Not only will novices learn expertise but the expert (with the right attitude) can realise that expertise is not the only way to go about their specialism.

Emergence – The conception is necessarily emergent and dynamic. People are different and are constantly changing. This is an important lesson for virtual world designers – the environment you create does not 'belong' to you and you cannot easily predict how it will be conceived by users. A simple lesson from physical design can be learned here – the spaces that allow the emergence of activity (especially those not imagined by the designer) can often be the most successful.

Design Thinking – To design effectively in virtual worlds (and in physical reality too) we have to recognise the above characteristics and work with and within them. This is very different to a traditional 'expert' based design method. As Lloyd (2011) infers, an architect may design space very well, but this is an 'architectural' solution emerging from that specific discipline. If it does not recognise the dynamic, interactive and emergent capabilities of virtual worlds then it will not enable 'Place'. Design of virtual worlds requires the consideration of the phenomena being generated and this calls for design thinking, not only specialist design.

1.5   Conclusion

When we consider reality in terms of phenomena, we realise that the conception of reality in the mind is potentially more relevant than any 'objective' measurement of it. Reality, as an independent object, becomes far less important than the embodied understanding of it we each have, with the values we attach to it individually and socially. A similar observation can be made when we consider virtual worlds (of all varieties) and even information itself. In all forms of reality it is the conception we generate that is the thing of importance.

From this perspective, the reality conceived is the matter of relevance, which in turn means that we can consider the transfer of conceptions between a range of 'realities'. This cannot be achieved by simply copying objects between realities – it has to be achieved by transferring the possibility of conception.

This then leads to interesting opportunities in design. Making use of the conception as the starting point for the design provides us with an alternative approach and process to design in general. Emergent design becomes explicitly possible and the full spectrum of a design context becomes significant. Specialist design is only relevant as part of a holistic design thinking approach, where the specialism of the designer is as an expert in the process of design

It is these overall conceptual (and collaborative) attitudes and processes that will see genuine alternative reality emerge. Moreover, there are many examples of this already taking place – both from history and in current practice.

In education, the opportunity to start with the conception in either physical or virtual design may offer a completely new way of looking at how we design learning spaces and events. Jornet and Jahreie (Chap. 3, this volume) have shown that this is possible to achieve in a physical space and it is argued that similar approaches can be applied to virtual places too – and not simply virtual worlds that recreate a 3D replica of a physical reality. All learning events can be considered as conceptual phenomena and starting from this point of design offers learning designers a different method and starting point in their design.

But it is necessarily difficult to design from this starting point. The subjective nature of the conception creates a difficulty since we cannot satisfactorily predict the ideas that will form in each student's mind. Instead, emergent, dynamic and interactive design processes are required because the objects we seek to create are themselves constantly nascent.

We can finally return to the question 'Why do we use artificial gravity in virtual worlds?'

It is proposed that we do this not only to provide a simulacrum of the physical world but to provide a phenomenon; something we can interact with to provide us with a *conception* of reality.

Gravity may help us translate physical reality into a virtual world but this is only a small part of what it does in our minds – it also translates a *conception* of the physical world. In many ways, the *idea* of gravity is as important as the physical thing itself. Without gravity in a virtual world, there is no up and down but, more importantly, Bachelard's 'attic' and 'cellar' might not exist – one of the central pillars of psychosocial storytelling would be removed and we would have no reference for the *meaning* of up or down in any of their many senses.

But then what would happen would be the emergence of new conceptions.

References

Addison, A., & O'Hare, L. (2008). *How can massive multi-user virtual environments and virtual role play enhance traditional teaching practice?* Paper presented at the learning in virtual environments international conference, Open University, Milton Keynes, pp. 7–16.

Anthes, E. (2009). Building around the mind. *Scientific American Mind, 20*(2), 52–59.

Attwell, G. (2007). Personal learning environments-the future of eLearning? *ELearning Papers, 2*(1), 1–8.

Bachelard, G. (1994). *The poetics of space* (2nd ed., M. Jolas, Trans.). Boston: Beacon Press Books.

Barker, T., Haik, E., & Bennett, S. (2008). *Factors that hinder and assist learning in virtual environments: An empirical study.* Paper presented at the learning in virtual environments international conference, Open University, Milton Keynes, pp. 27–38.

Berners-Lee, T. (1999). *Weaving the web: The original design and ultimate destiny of the world wide web by its inventor.* San Francisco: Harper.

Brown, E., Gordon, M., & Hobbs, M. (2008). *Second life as a holistic learning environment for problem-based learning and transferable skills.* Paper presented at the learning in virtual environments international conference, Open University, Milton Keynes, pp. 39–48.

Burden, D., Conradi, E., Woodham, L., Poulton, T., Savin-Baden, M., & Kavia, S. (2008). *Creating and assessing a virtual patient player in second life.* Paper presented at the learning in virtual environments international conference, Open University, Milton Keynes, pp. 49–62.

Burton, B. G., & Martin, B. N. (2008). *The use of three dimensional interface within a virtual learning environment and the impact on student collaboration and knowledge creation.* Paper presented at the learning in virtual environments international conference, Open University, Milton Keynes, pp. 63–71.

Carlson, L. A., Hölscher, C., Shipley, T. F., & Dalton, R. C. (2010). Getting lost in buildings. *Current Directions in Psychological Science, 19*(5), 284–289.

Carr, D., Oliver, M., & Burn, A. (2008). *Learning, teaching and ambiguity in virtual worlds.* Paper presented at the learning in virtual environments international conference, Open University, Milton Keynes, pp. 83–93.

Chafer, J., & Childs, M. (2008). *The impact of the characteristics of a virtual environment on performance: Concepts, constraints and complications.* Paper presented at the learning in virtual environments international conference, Open University, Milton Keynes, pp. 94–105

Clark, S., & Maher, M. L. (2001, July 8–11). The role of place in designing a learner centred virtual learning environment. In Computer aided architectural design futures 2001: Proceedings of the ninth international conference held at the Eindhoven University of Technology, Eindhoven.

Dalton, R. C., Bazan, J., Liu, X., Migoski, L., & Yang, D. (2002). *Through a glass darkly: A case for the study of virtual space.* In 90th Association of Collegiate Schools of Architecture (ACSA).

Derrington, M. de J., & Homewood, B. (2008). *Get real – This isn't real, it's second life teaching ESL in a virtual world.* Paper presented at the learning in virtual environments international conference, Open University, Milton Keynes, pp. 106–120.

Doyle, D. (2008). *Immersed in learning: Developing and supporting creative practice in virtual worlds.* Paper presented at the learning in virtual environments international conference, Open University, Milton Keynes, pp. 121–129.

Fingelkurts, A. A., Fingelkurts, A. A., & Neves, C. F. H. (2009). Phenomenological architecture of a mind and operational architectonics of the brain: The unified metastable continuum. *New Mathematics and Natural Computation, 5*, 221–244.

Gardner, M., Scott, J., & Horan, B. (2008). *Reflections on the use of project wonderland as a mixed-reality environment for teaching and learning.* Paper presented at the learning in virtual environments international conference, Open University, Milton Keynes, pp. 130–141.

Glogowski, K. (2006). *Classrooms as third places? Slide presentation* http://www.slideshare.net/teachandlearn/classrooms-as-third-places. Accessed 29th Apr 2013 in Peachey, A. (2010). The third place in second life: Real life community in a virtual World. In Peachey, A., Gillen, J., Livingstone, D. & Smith-Robbins, S. (Eds.) *Researching learning in virtual worlds.* London: Springer.

Grove, P. W., & Steventon, G. J., Dr. (2008). *Exploring community safety in a virtual community: Using second life to enhance structured creative learning.* Paper presented at the learning in virtual environments international conference, Open University, Milton Keynes, pp. 154–171.

Harris, J., & Kamvar, S. (2011). We feel fine. Retrieved August 2011, from http://www.wefeelfine.org/

Heidegger, M. (1995). *Being and time.* Oxford: Wiley-Blackwell.

Hobbs, M., Gordon, M., & Brown, E. (2006). A virtual world environment for group work. *International Journal of Web-Based Learning and Teaching Technologies, 3*(1), 1369–1373.

Hollins, P., & Robbins, S. (2008). *The educational affordances of multi user virtual environments (MUVE).* Paper presented at the learning in virtual environments international conference, Open University, Milton Keynes, pp. 172–180.

Honderich, T. (Ed.). (1995). *The oxford companion to philosophy.* New York: Oxford University Press.

Lloyd, P. (2011) Does design education always produce designers?. In *Conference for the international association of colleges for art, design and media (CUMULUS)* (p. tbc) Paris, France.

Lotto, R. B. (2004). Visual development: Experience puts the colour in life. *Current Biology, 14*, R619–R621.

Merleau-Ponty, M. (1962). *Phenomenology of perception* (C. Smith, Trans.). London: Routledge Kegan Paul.

Milk, C. (2010). *Dreams of black.* Retrieved August 2011, from http://www.ro.me/

Mingers, J. (2001). Embodying information systems: The contribution of phenomenology. *Information and Organization, 11*(2), 103–128.

Minocha, S., & Reeves, A. J. (2010). Design of learning spaces in 3D virtual worlds: An empirical investigation of second life. *Learning Media and Technology, 35*(2), 111–137.

Minocha, S., & Tungle, R. (2008). *Socialisation and collaborative learning of distance learners in 3-D virtual worlds*. Paper presented at the learning in virtual environments international conference, Open University, Milton Keynes, pp. 216–227.

NBS. (2012). *National BIM report 2012*. London: RIBA Publishing. Available online at http://www.thenbs.com/topics/bim/articles/nbsNationalBimSurvey_2012.asp

Norberg-Schulz, C. (1980). *Genius loci: Towards a phenomenology of architecture*. London: Academy Editions.

Open University. (2011). *Design thinking: Creativity for the 21st century*. Retrieved August 2011, from http://www3.open.ac.uk/study/undergraduate/course/u101.htm

Peachey, A. (2010). The third place in second life: Real life community in a virtual world. In A. Peachey, J. Gillen, D. Livingstone, & S. Smith-Robbins (Eds.), *Researching learning in virtual world*. London: Springer.

Pollard, D. (2005). Will that be coordination, cooperation, or collaboration?. Retrieved December 29,2011,fromhttp://howtosavetheworld.ca/2005/03/25/will-that-be-coordination-cooperation-or-collaboration/

Ramondt, L. (2008). *Towards the adoption of massively multiplayer educational gaming*. Paper presented at the learning in virtual environments international conference, Open University, Milton Keynes, pp. 258–268.

Rittel, H. W. J., & Webber, M. M. (1973, December). Dilemmas in a general theory of planning. *Policy Sciences, 4*(1969), 155–169.

Rosling, H. (2006). *Hans Rosling: Stats that reshape your worldview, TED Talks*. http://www.ted.com/talks/lang/eng/hans_rosling_shows_the_best_stats_you_ve_ever_seen.html

Schon, D. A. (1991). *The reflective practitioner*. Farnham: Ashgate publishing Ltd.

Shelden, D. (2009). Information modelling as a paradigm shift. *Architectural Design, Wiley Online Library, 79*(2), 80–83, [online] Available from: http://onlinelibrary.wiley.com/doi/10.1002/ad.857/abstract. Accessed 19 Dec 2011.

Sweeney, B. (2008). *Mathematics in a virtual world: How the immersive environment of second life can facilitate the learning of mathematics and other subjects*. Paper presented at the learning in virtual environments international conference, Open University, Milton Keynes, pp. 298–309.

Trinder, K. (2008). *Fearing your avatar? Exploring the scary journey to the 3rd dimension*. Paper presented at the learning in virtual environments international conference, Open University, Milton Keynes, pp. 348–358.

Truelove, I., & Hibbert, G. (2008). *Learning to walk before you know your name pre-second life scaffolding for noobs*. Paper presented at the learning in virtual environments international conference, Open University, Milton Keynes, pp. 359–365.

Twining, P., & Footring, S. (2008). *The schome park programme – Exploring educational alternatives*. Paper presented at the learning in virtual environments international conference, Open University, Milton Keynes, pp. 366–377.

Velmans, M. (1990). Consciousness, brain and the physical world. *Philosophical Psychology, 3*(1), 77–99.

Chapter 2
Guidelines for Conducting Text Based Interviews in Virtual Worlds

Carina Girvan and Timothy Savage

Abstract Interviews are a staple data collection tool in social science research and in recent decades have been increasingly formalised and systematised. However, due to the specific affordances and constraints of virtual worlds, researchers cannot simply replicate traditional interview techniques in virtual worlds without careful consideration of the specific features of the technology. For example the prominent use of text as the medium for communication, role of the avatar, interview location and inworld objects have implications for all inworld research interviews. Building on the foundation of traditional interviews in educational research and the current literature on inworld interviews, this chapter focuses on the use of text communication tools in both one-to-one and group interviews inworld. Based on previous research by the authors the opportunities, implications, constraints and techniques for conducting text based interviews inworld are discussed. The chapter concludes with a set of guidelines for researchers considering the use of inworld text based interviews.

2.1 Introduction

While educators are challenged by the educational affordances and constraints of virtual worlds (Jarmon 2009), researchers also need to consider both the opportunities and obstacles to conducting educational research in virtual worlds (Moschini 2008). Within qualitative methodologies, interviews provide researchers with a particularly powerful research tool as a means to get 'inside a person's head' (Tuckman 1994) in order to understand their subjective experience. With

C. Girvan (✉) • T. Savage
Centre for Research in IT in Education, School of Computer Science
and Statistics, Trinity College Dublin, Dublin, Ireland
e-mail: girvanc@tcd.ie

M. Childs and A. Peachey (eds.), *Understanding Learning in Virtual Worlds*,
Human–Computer Interaction Series, DOI 10.1007/978-1-4471-5370-2_2,
© Springer-Verlag London 2013

an increasing body of literature on educational research in virtual worlds, it is perhaps surprising that there is not a relative increase in the number of reported interviews conducted inworld.

Interviews about inworld learning experiences, conducted in the virtual world, provide researchers with opportunities unavailable in traditional face-to-face settings, such as travelling with the interviewee to different locations in a learning milieu in order to stimulate recall. However there are also disadvantages to be considered such as the loss of non-verbal cues. Although a number of virtual worlds have integrated voice technology, text remains the primary medium of communication between users. As such, text is potentially a more appropriate medium for conducting interviews inworld.

Text based interviews are not unique to virtual worlds and have hitherto been chosen over face-to-face for reasons such as access to otherwise unavailable participants and cost (Chen and Hinton 1999). Text can be either synchronous or asynchronous and allows both interviewer and interviewee to edit statements before sending. As a result the medium can fundamentally change the nature of the discourse.

While insights may be gained from other text based interview tools such as instant messaging systems, features such as avatars and the opportunity to interview *in situ* provide researchers with unique opportunities, implications and constraints and as such require specific techniques. However the literature lacks clear guidelines specific to the use of synchronous text based interviews in virtual worlds.

This chapter has been developed as a guide for researchers considering the use of use of text based interviews in virtual worlds. Some of the issues raised in this chapter may also prove useful to researchers conducting other forms of inworld interview. The guidelines are broken down into three phases: prior, during and post interview.

These guidelines have been developed from an original research paper (Girvan and Savage 2011) in which the authors explored the opportunities, constraints, techniques and implications of conducting text based interviews inworld to understand learners' experiences. This work was based on an analysis of interviews the authors had conducted inworld in the course of researching different learning experiences in the virtual world *Second Life*. Each interview was conducted following learner's participation in one of these learning experiences. The analysis of this data was then combined with a structured reflection on the authors' experiences as both interviewers and interviewees. In total 20 individual and 10 group interviews were analysed to explore the effect of the interview medium.

To provide a foundation for the reader, this chapter begins by considering the role of interviews in educational research and the current literature on inworld interviews. This is followed by a detailed discussion of the opportunities, implications, constraints and techniques of conducting text based interviews in virtual worlds. Finally the guidelines for prior to, during and post interview phases are presented.

2.2   Understanding Learning Through Interviews

The popularity of interviews across social science research and educational research lies in their ability to generate a holistic understanding of the subjective lived experience of the participants. Educational research interviewers search for an understanding of learning from the perspective of the participants' meaning-making in their own socially situated lives (Brenner 2006).

Interviews generate data, as opposed to simply capturing data, representing the co-construction of knowledge relating to the lived experience of the participants. This focus on the collaborative construction between the researcher and the participants combined with the focus on the lived experience results in a powerful yet complex phenomenon.

There are five characterising features of interviews: purpose, type, form, medium and location. This section briefly presents each feature and is followed by an exploration of these characteristics within the current literature on educational research in virtual worlds.

2.2.1   Purpose

In any research study there are three distinct purposes for choosing to conduct interviews (Cohen et al. 2007). Firstly, and most commonly, the purpose of a research interview can be to collect information pertinent to the broader objectives of the study. Secondly the interview purpose can be to validate, refute or amend hypotheses. Finally the research interview can be used in conjunction with other data collection instruments to develop nascent understandings or delve further into emergent aspects of the phenomena under study.

2.2.2   Type

The purpose of the interview then guides the selection of the interview type. The literature in this area presents differing views on the number of types of interviews (Cohen et al. 2007), however the most common typology is that arranged along the continuum of *structure*, from the structured (or standardised) interview to the unstructured or open interview relying solely on open questions allowing the participant to form their own response (Creswell 2002; Cohen et al. 2007).

2.2.3   Form

One-to-one interviews are the most prominent form of interviews (Kvale and Brinkmann 2009) and are popular in educational research (Creswell 2002). Although time consuming, the one-to-one interview allows the researcher to gather a personal perspective from the participant without fear of ridicule or the impact of group dynamics. Group interviews gather information from individual participants as well as collecting the shared understanding of multiple participants (Creswell 2002). As such they can be seen to represent aspects of a knowledge construction event (Kvale and Brinkmann 2009).

2.2.4 Medium

Whether conducting one-to-one or group interviews, there are several communication media through which the interview can take place. Traditionally interviews are conducted face-to-face or in some cases via telephone, however advances in computer mediated communication tools and environments have opened up the possibility of conducting interviews through synchronous and asynchronous text based communication through tools such as electronic mail and instant messaging. Alternative voice-based communication tools include voice over IP (VOIP) and video conferencing.

2.2.5 Location

The final feature to be considered is that of location. As previously mentioned, interviews traditionally take place face-to-face with both interviewer and interviewee in the same location. However telephone interviews provide an opportunity for interviewer and interviewee to be at a distance from one another. The location of an interview is typically a quiet and comfortable location where the researcher can minimise potential disruptions (Creswell 2002). Whether the interview is conducted in the research setting (in context) or out of context (for example in a private office) will depend on the purpose of the interview. Thus the traditional interview location may be face-to-face or at distance and in or out of context. In addition virtual worlds provide researchers with another choice, whether to conduct interviews inworld or out-of-world.

2.3   Research Interviews and Virtual Worlds

While face-to-face interviews are currently the dominant medium in the literature on educational research in virtual worlds, there are a number of advantages to conducting interviews inworld. Unlike other online technologies, virtual worlds provide researchers with a range of opportunities to conduct interviews afforded through a combination of features, particularly the use of avatars and the variety of communication tools available. For example, Minocha et al. (2010) identified potential participants through serendipitous encounters with their avatars in selected locations throughout *Second Life* and thus selected participants based on their avatar profile information. Having selected a participant they used inworld communication tools to initiate a conversation and invite them to participate in an interview either there and then or at a later time.

Hew and Cheung's (2010) review of the literature on educational research in 2008 identified only five studies that reported the use of interviews, none of which reported using virtual worlds to conduct the interviews. Since 2008 there has been a significant increase in the literature published on the use of virtual worlds in education and with that an increase in the number of studies using interviews. In a review of 208 articles published or made available as pre-print by July 2011, on educational research in virtual worlds, 54 described the use of interviews for data collection.

While interviews are a common form of data collection in qualitative research, the five key components of purpose, type, form, medium and location are often not clearly described in the method section of educational research articles. For example, of the 54 articles on educational research in virtual worlds that used interviews as a data collection method, it was unclear in 30 of the articles as to the type and form of interviews conducted. Of those that reported the form of the interview, semi-structured interviews were the most common, with only two conducting open interviews. In the same 54 articles it was unclear in 31 articles whether the interviews took place in the virtual world or face-to-face and of the 15 that took place in the virtual world only five reported whether they took place in or out of the learning context. Finally, while some studies employed multiple interview media including both face-to-face and voice-over IP (VOIP) such as Skype, the medium of 40 interviews was unreported.

Of the 15 articles that reported conducting interviews inworld, over half did not state whether text or VOIP were used. Of the seven that reported the interview medium, text was the most commonly used. However these articles provide little insight into the process of using inworld text based interviews.

Kirrriemuir (2007) used inworld text interviews as follow-up to questionnaires. He found that these interviews provided little additional information, however he noted that this was likely to be constrained by his then lack of experience of interviewing inworld, technical problems and the long time to type questions and responses. Time was also a constraint identified by Vasileiou and Paraskeva (2010), who found that conducting the same structured interview inworld took almost twice as long by comparison to a phone interview. However Knorr et al. (2011) found face-to-face semi-structured interviews were significantly longer than those conducted through VOIP inworld.

Based on the literature reviewed, Minocha et al. (2010) provide the only notable description and advice on conducting interviews in virtual worlds, based on their experience of conducting interviews in two Second Life research projects. Logistics such as maximum length of an interview, codes of practice, ethics, researcher identity and interview locations as well as some discussion on the use of face-to-face versus voice are presented.

It is important to note that in addition to the consideration of the opportunities, constraints, specific techniques and implications of conducting interviews inworld, there are additional ethical concerns that may need to be addressed when conducting interviews inworld. These include whether to use voice or text using public or private communication channels (Minocha et al. 2010), informed consent, privacy protection and the identity of the participant (Girvan and Savage 2012).

2.4 Why Use Inworld Text Based Interviews?

While there has been an increase in the use of virtual worlds to conduct interviews across research fields, there is limited existing literature on techniques, opportunities, implications and, importantly, the constraints of interviewing inworld. So why might a researcher opt to use inworld text based interviews?

On a practical level the use of text based interviews offers advantages in terms of access to participants, the process of conducting an interview, and the form of the data gathered. However, unlike standard synchronous chat systems, researchers conducting inworld text based interviews need to consider the wider affordances of virtual worlds. These have implications for the preparation and execution of the interview as well as the nature of the data collected.

For example, avatars can support not only a sense of co-presence but also act as an additional communication tool, whilst allowing the user to be 'hidden'. Although some may perceive text to be slower than VOIP, it provides opportunities to limit technical problems, can be a valuable aid to the researcher during the interview and provides a ready-made transcript.

Since 2008 the authors have been implementing qualitative research into educational learning experiences in the virtual world Second Life and have developed their approaches to conducting interviews inworld across media. Our research has shown that inworld text based interviews can be a particularly powerful data collection tool, providing researchers with opportunities that are not available in other media. The use of inworld text based interviews has implications for the interviewer, interviewee and the data collected. There are additional constraints which need to be taken into careful consideration before deciding to use text based interviews. To negate these constraints we have found a range of techniques to be useful and these illustrate many of the points in the guidelines which follows this section. This section presents the conclusions of our research into the use of inworld text based interviews in both one-to-one and group formats, considering the opportunities, implications, constraints and techniques in the use of this approach to data collection.

2.5 Opportunities

While face-to-face interviews are currently the dominant medium in the literature on educational research in virtual worlds, there are a number of advantages to conducting text based interviews inworld. On a practical level the use of text based interviews offers advantage in terms of access to participants, the process of conducting an interview, and the form of the data gathered.

Fig. 2.1 Interviewing in the learning context

Participants themselves may prefer to use text if they have participated in a text based learning activity or wish to protect their identity. Text based communication also allows access to participants otherwise unavailable, including: those with hearing impairments; those unable to travel due to cost, transport or time; and those that prefer to use text to VOIP. For example, this medium allows the participant and the interviewer to be in different locations, requiring only access to the virtual world. Once a time and virtual location have been agreed, all parties can meet for the interview with no concern over travel time or expenses.

Inworld text based interviews allow the data collection to take place in the context of the research location. This provides the opportunity for the interview to be conducted in the learning context allowing both interviewer and interviewee to move to, identify, share and demonstrate objects and activities during the interview. For example, Fig. 2.1 shows a one-to-one text based interview taking place in the location of the learning experience. In this example, the learner is demonstrating the installation they had created as part of a SLurtle learning experience (Girvan et al. 2013), producing a SLurtle from their inventory that they had already programmed to create a wall.

Opportunities such as this may provide researchers with an opportunity to engage in a modified form of stimulated recall in which the researcher identifies a specific object in the environment and participants would be asked to describe their thought processes whilst engaging with it during the learning experience. Inworld but outside of the learning experience location, both interviewer and participant may take items from the inventories and place them in the environment to 'refresh memories'.

Interviews may be conducted through instant messaging in public locations. This allows the interview to remain private whilst interviewer and interviewee move through and interact with objects in the public learning environment. It also allows the researcher to respond to other users who may try to initiate a conversation, whilst maintaining the flow of the interview.

The medium of text also provides the interviewer with a number of opportunities unavailable in traditional face-to-face interviews or inworld VOIP interviews, such as:

- back-up recordings created by participants;
- ready-made transcripts;
- the opportunity to note-take and scroll through the interview transcript during the interview, as shown in Fig. 2.1.

For example, by scrolling back through the text conversation the interviewer is provided with an opportunity to refresh his or her memory of questions asked during open interviews and earlier comments made by participants. Although sources on traditional interview techniques, (e.g. Cohen et al. 2007) would discourage the taking of notes during an interview or using a crib sheet for questions, as interviewer and interviewee are bi-located notes can easily be made and crib sheets used without losing engagement with the interviewee or interrupting the flow of the interview.

While technical problems may be more likely in virtual world interviews, text based interviews provide researchers with additional opportunities to collect data. Participants may be asked to record their text chat using the inworld tools or to copy and paste from the virtual world and email the transcript to the researcher. Chat loggers may also be used as a back-up with permission. In addition, the researcher can save a significant amount of time overall by comparison to audio recorded interviews, as text provides the researcher with a ready-made transcript.

As data gathered through text based interviews provide the researcher with a ready-made transcript, analysis of the data can begin immediately following the interview. This may be particularly useful when conducting research in a limited time-frame, for pilot or exploratory studies, or when using convergent interviewing (Jepsen and Rodwell 2008).

2.6 Implications

While both inworld text and VOIP interviews have been found to provide the researcher with an increase in efficiency (Knorr et al. 2011), inworld interviews should not be chosen just because they are more efficient than face-to-face interviews. As with the selection of data collection tools, research question, availability of participants, participant preferences, depth and type of data analysis, etc. all need to be considered.

The choice of interview type may influence whether a researcher chooses to use text based interviews and if so what techniques to use. Both structured and semi-structured interviews use pre-determined questions. These questions can be typed in advance and quickly copy and pasted during the interview. This may be of particular advantage to less experienced interviewers and reduces the silence that occurs as the researcher types. The medium of text provides researchers choosing to conduct open interviews with the additional advantage of reducing their cognitive load whilst maintaining the flow of the interview. For example, as interviewer and participant are not face-to-face, the interviewer can take and check notes without disturbing the flow of the interview and can re-read responses.

The data collected from text based interviews may have implications for data analysis. Our findings show that while both one-to-one face-to-face and VOIP interviews resulted in a similar number of words elicited from participants, text-based interviews resulted in significantly less words. For example a 27 min face-to-face interview and 28 min inworld VOIP interview resulted in 3,705 and 3,822 words respectively. By comparison a 28 min text based interview resulted in 669 words from the interviewee.

It should be noted that the speed of typing by comparison to producing verbal language is much slower and may additionally discourage participants from being verbose. Self-censorship or editing responses may also reduce the number of words and researchers may wish to consider recording participants' screens to record this data, with permission.

There may be a number of questions that arise from this for data collection as well as analysis. For example where a participant requests to take part in the interview through text while the majority of participants take part in VOIP based interviews, is the data equally valid? Does it provide the same depth? Dependent on the data analysis approach, if text based interviews provide less depth it may be worthwhile to conduct them first, analyse them for emergent codes and themes, then use VOIP or face-to-face interviews to explore these in depth. Similarly this may support convergent interviewing.

Another implication of conducting interviews inworld is the role of the avatar. While Knorr et al. (2011) found during VOIP-based interviews that, despite prompting, there was no interaction between interviewer and interviewee avatars and participants did not initiate any movement, the participants involved in the study had no previous experience of virtual worlds. It is therefore unsurprising that one participant described "Having a person standing in the middle of the virtual world with no real purpose was a little strange". To be able to effectively compare and conduct face-to-face and inworld interviews we believe it is necessary for both interviewer and interviewee to be comfortable with the medium. Inworld this not only includes VOIP or text but also the use of an avatar (see editors' introduction, this volume).

The findings from our own research suggest that avatar interactions were common in text interviews, with participants sharing objects and moving around the environment. As a result the avatar is more than just an embodiment of the interviewer and participant(s) in a 3D environment but another communication mode and further research needs to be conducted to explore the impact of the avatar on the interview process.

Although it is not possible to observe the participant directly, it is possible for the researcher to observe and record the actions of the avatar if prior permission has been obtained. However it should be noted that the avatar is controlled by the participant, therefore the researcher can only observe what the participant chooses to share, which may or may not be misleading. As suggested, it may also be of interest to observe/record participants' screens, particularly in group interview settings, providing insight into what was typed and then edited before sending, or not.

2.7 Constraints

While there are a number of opportunities that inworld interviews can provide the researcher, there are also a number of constraints to which the researcher should be aware. Text based interviews can be perceived as slow, thus discouraging participation. We also found that in group-based text interviews it could be particularly difficult for the interviewer to gain the attention of participants when they began to go off-topic.

Some constraints, such as the lack of non-verbal cues, can be difficult for the interviewer to work with, while others may be turned into an advantage. For example, in group inworld interviews, participants may engage in back-channel conversations through local-chat, IM or, as found in one case, through VOIP. These conversations may be distracting to participants and result in a lack of engagement with the interview. However it may be possible for an interviewer, with permission, to collect these as an additional data set.

Not all participants may be comfortable using text based communication tools and may find the medium 'slow' due to the time taken to type messages. Using text may also discourage learners from participating if they have a perceived language barrier. In addition participants may misread questions, the equivalent of which did not occur in face-to-face or VOIP interviews. For example, in one text based interview a participant began answering a different question to the one asked, stating "oops, didn't read the question" when this was realised.

Our findings show that in both one-to-one and group interviews participants may wish to take a break from the interview. While in a one-to-one interview a participant may request a short break, in group interviews they may not make this request. As a result a particular concern in group text based interviews is the 'invisible whilst present' interviewee. What this means is that although the participant's avatar is present in the interview location, the researcher is uncertain as to whether the participant is there or not. This leaves the interviewer uncertain as to whether the participant is experiencing a technical problem, is listening to others or has left their computer. Depending on the situation different courses of action may be required and there may be an implication for the data collected.

Finally, as text based interviews do not project identifying features such as gender, validating informed consent by verifying that the person giving consent is who they say they are, becomes more difficult. Despite the ethical concern, accepting unverified consent is not uncommon in online educational research

(Kanuka and Anderson 2007). Researchers willing to accept unverified consent therefore need to be aware that participants may misrepresent demographic information, particularly if they have an incentive to do so (Girvan and Savage 2012).

2.8 Techniques

In this section we focus on techniques to address some of the constraints and opportunities discussed, to support researchers whilst conducting interviews inworld. To address the phenomenon of 'invisible whilst present' participants, at the start of group interviews the researcher may indicate that any participant needing to leave the interview for any reason may do so, and should inform the researcher. Depending on the context this may be most appropriate via a private IM to the researcher. While this may not discourage participants from disengaging, it should encourage participants to acknowledge to the researcher that they have left and may thus be noted in transcript annotations.

In one group text based interview we had a participant who suddenly stated "brb" (be right back). The remaining participants continued to talk and when the missing participant returned the researcher had to get them 'up to speed' by informing them of what they had missed and asking any questions they had missed. The result of this can be a loss of interview time as the interview is paused and the researcher has to type. However this may provide a useful review for participants, particularly in open interviews.

When conducting research inworld, a number of alternative researcher strategies need to be employed as interviewer and interviewee(s) are unable to see each other, and thus non-verbal cues are lost. This is particularly true in text-based interviews when they are also unable to hear each other. While inworld tools such as gestures and animations may be used, we have found them to be distracting to participants and sometimes go unnoticed. Instead we use emoticons and emotes. For example, typing "/me" followed by "nods" will be displayed as "[Avatar name] nods" in Second Life. This provides the interviewer with an opportunity to add a form of non-verbal encouragement and demonstrates that the interviewer is still engaged. There was evidence that these techniques were also used in group interviews by participants who had familiarity with these gestures.

Demonstrating engagement is particularly important when researcher and participant cannot see or hear each other and should be remembered when note-taking or scrolling through interview text during the interview. Another approach used to demonstrate that the interviewer is engaged is to comment directly on what the interviewee has said, for example "That's an interesting point, do you think it affected how you worked?"

Whilst the interviewer accidentally interrupted participants across all media, our findings show that interviewer interruptions most commonly occur in text-based interviews in both one-to-one and group settings. This is attributed to the lack of non-verbal cues, as it is not possible to anticipate if someone is about to type.

Our findings show the average utterance length in text based interviews was 10 words as participants would tend to use several short messages. In group interviews this may result in the appearance of participants interrupting each other. As a result it may not always be possible to know whether participants had finished their answer or whether they had become silent because a more dominant voice had moved the conversation away from the point they wished to make. This can also cause additional confusion when analyzing the transcript at a later date. To address this it may be necessary to annotate text transcripts as soon as possible after the interview to clarify any sections that may be confusing later on.

The lack of non-verbal cues, combined with the artificial silence created whilst waiting for someone to type, can result in the text 'flying' (or in other words, appearing too fast) during group interviews. This occurs because several participants are composing their responses at the same time and sending them within a short space of time to one another. Those that use multiple short responses can compound this substantially. This can be difficult to read, lead to several conversation threads, has the potential to exclude participants who are not comfortable with the speed and can cause confusion for the researcher reading the transcript at a later date. If all participants are engaged and the researcher is experienced this can result in a fast flowing conversation with multiple views expressed. Less experienced researchers may wish to use a turn-taking policy. This will slow the pace of the communication and make it clear who is responding to what. This may be achieved by asking participants to respond only when directly asked. While this may also support participants less comfortable with this medium, there are disadvantages such as the silence created waiting for responses and additional time to conduct the interview. Both of these can also lead to disengagement with the interview and increase the possibility of invisible whilst present participants. With experience, the researcher should be able to manage multiple threads and engage those not participating. One technique to achieve this is to recap the points made and ask for an individual's opinion.

From our experience as research participants in one-to-one text based interviews we have found that silence, although a traditional interview tool, can be difficult to use well in this medium. For example in our own interviews we would wait whilst we observed the participant's typing animations or in IM saw messages such as 'X is typing'. However as participants, having given a detailed answer to a question, we have waited while our interviewer has remained silent with no typing animation. This has given us the sense of great unease, wondering whether the interviewer is experiencing technical problems, is away from their computer or is otherwise not engaged in what we had to say.

We recommend that interviewers should avoid using silence during text based interviews as it may lead the participant to believe that the interviewer is uninterested or is experiencing technical problems. As such the traditional interview technique of using silence to prompt the participant to expand on what they have already said is not appropriate. However participants still need to be given sufficient time to think and respond to questions. Both IM and local-chat animations provide the researcher with cues that the interviewee is typing and so participants should be encouraged to turn the typing animation on if previously turned off. As a result it is clear in Fig. 2.2 that the two participants closest to the camera are still typing responses.

Fig. 2.2 Group interview

Group text based interviews were identified as the most likely to contain off-topic utterances and the most difficult in which to gain the attention of participants. In seven out of the eight group text based interviews there was evidence of off-topic utterances from participants. This was contrary to our initial expectations which suggested that off-topic utterances would be least common in text-based interviews. The off-topic utterances were related to in-world distractions such as props and animations, for example an avatar drinking a Martini resulted in the other participants joking and sharing objects. Interestingly humour was most common in text based group interviews. The percentage of off-topic utterances in an interview averaged 9.39 % across the seven interviews with 15.72 % the highest.

Our data show that regaining the attention of participants when they go off-topic is most difficult in group text interviews, over any other medium or form. In one example it took the researcher two minutes to regain the attention of the group and direct them on to the next question. Tactics included the use of capital letters e.g. "NEXT QUESTION" and persistent short messages. It is important in contexts such as this, especially when time is limited, for the researcher to remember that text-based communication is open to misinterpretation. For example while short messages can be used to gain attention they may also fill the screen, which in addition to gaining attention may be perceived as rude. In the case of the two minute attempt to gain the attention of the participants and to move them onto the next question, the interviewer took 50 % of the lines of text and used short messages such as "guys", "if we may....", along with longer utterances such as repeating the question. It is also important to consider the rapport between interviewer and interviewee(s).

In this context the researcher had recruited participants and engaged with them throughout the learning experience which had taken place over several days.

While off-topic utterances such as sharing drinks between avatars may be useful to support group cohesion they can be distracting mid-interview. The researcher should therefore provide an opportunity for participants to engage in such social activities prior to the interview, for example by offering them a virtual cup of tea via the avatar's inventory.

2.9 Guidelines

Presuming that the purpose of the interview, type and form have already been established and inworld text based interviews have been chosen as the medium, the following guidelines are broken down into three phases: prior, during and post interview.

The key considerations prior to conducting the interview focus on the researcher, participants, group interviews, interview location, data collection and ethical concerns. During the interview the researcher has to focus on the implications of using synchronous text based communication as the medium. The speed of text based communication, interruptions, location, engagement, and lack of non-verbal cues are all presented and can be further complicated when conducting group interviews which can magnify these issues. After the interview both data and participants require the researcher's attention.

2.9.1 Prior

Researcher

- The researcher needs to be experienced in navigating and communicating in the virtual world.
- If a slow typist, consider structured or semi-structured interviews as questions may be pre-typed, ready to be cut and paste into the text channel.
- Turn on avatar typing animations, if supported by the virtual world, to reassure participants of engagement.
- Consider the appearance of the interviewer's avatar. Is it appropriate for the context?
- Be aware that participants may check the avatar's profile, which should therefore include relevant professional and personal information. For example a student may state the name of their course and institution.
- Consider creating an avatar purely for research purposes but be careful not to mislead participants.
- Avoid. deception.

Participants

- Ensure that the participants are familiar with the virtual world and communication tools to be used.
- Consider participants' preference for voice or text based communication.
- Decide, and agree with the participants, whether to use real names or avatar names.

Groups

- Decide whether or not to record back-channel communication between participants and how these will be recorded.
- If interviewees are co-located, will they communicate with each other face-to-face? Consider whether/how to collect this data.
- Provide time for group cohesion and social exchange prior to the interview.
- Engage in ice-breaking avatar activities, such as sharing virtual cups of tea, to overcome novelty, build rapport and reduce distractions later.
- Plan for breaks if needed and agree with participants whether and how breaks may be requested.
- Request that participants inform the researcher should they disengage with the interview at any point for any reason.

Location

- Consider whether to use the location of the learning experience, a purpose-built meeting space or neutral inworld venue.
- A private, access controlled area is preferable but if not possible plan how to limit interruptions.
- Ensure that all participants have access to the venue in advance of the interview.
- Provide a comfortable location, e.g. with chairs for the avatars.
- Ensure that both researcher and participant have sufficient permissions to create objects and run scripts as necessary.

Data Collection

- Decide whether public or private communication tools are to be used. This may be dependent on the location or participant preferences.
- Decide whether or not to record observations and how this will be done.
- Ask participants to record the interview (as well as any back-channel conversation between participants) in case of technical problems, using cut and paste or settings in the application.

Ethical Concerns

- If inworld tools are to be used to collect data ensure that these comply with any terms of service of the virtual world and that participants are aware of them and what they will record.
- Any offline tools used to collect data need to be described to participants in advance.

- Ensure that participants are aware when data is and is not being recorded and how it will be recorded.
- If in a public location ensure that data is only collected from those providing consent and consider using private communication tools.
- Consider how informed consent will be collected and validated.

2.9.2 During

Speed of Text Communication and Sequencing

- Recognise that text based communication can be slow and therefore frustrating to participants.
- Have your interview questions ready in a text document to cut and paste into the text channel.
- Use multiple short lines of text when composing questions and to reduce the 'silence' experienced by participants as you type.
- Recognise you may have to remind people of the question, especially if the question is no longer visible in the chat channel due to multiple responses.
- Be prepared to provide participants with a short recap of main points that have been covered during the interview.

Interruptions

- Recognise that interrupting each other is common in text based interviews and expected in group text based interview.

Interviewing in the Location of the Learning Experience

- Use the location to prompt discussion and responses.
- Lead the respondents around the location according to your question context.
- Ask respondents to show you the items or areas that demonstrate their responses.
- Accept that there will be off-topic utterances, commonly triggered by elements in the environment.

Maintaining Engagement

- Use non-verbal cues such as avatar animations, emoticons or emotes to demonstrate engagement.
- In open interviews explain the link between what the participant has said and the question to be asked. Remember to use short lines of text.
- Make notes concurrently with conducting the interview, this can be achieved with an inworld text editor to avoid switching applications. Also useful if asked to recap during the interview by a participant.

Non-verbal Cues

- Consider using avatar gestures but be aware that they may become distracting or go unnoticed.
- Use emoticons and emotes in text.

- Promote engagement by commenting directly on what the participant is saying or summarizing their responses back to them for validation.
- Recognise that the lack of non-verbal cues causes participants to interrupt each other.
- Avoid "silence" as a technique to elicit more information from a participant as it promotes a sense of unease or uncertainty for them.

Group Interviews

- Be aware that your respondents have differing typing proficiencies and that whoever types the fastest speaks the loudest.
- Text can appear too quickly so be prepared to outline key points and request individual responses.
- Monitor who is not responding in group interviews and elicit their opinions.
- With a particularly dominant or quiet participant consider directing questions at individuals within the group or introduce a turn-taking policy.
- Multiple responses in the text channel can become confusing so be prepared to seek clarification as to what question or comment a response may be referring to.
- Be prepared to summarise any missed discussion and directly ask individuals for their response.
- To regain attention in a group interview, use short utterances and take care not to appear rude.
- Decide when to move on to the next question or topic and make this clear to all participants.
- Monitor private messages in case a participant should wish to speak to you privately.

2.9.3 Post

Participants

- Thank them for their time and answer any questions they might have.
- Establish whether and how contact will be maintained, for the reporting of results etc.
- Collect interview and observation data collected by participants.

Preparing the Data

- Copy the text transcript immediately from the virtual world and store securely.
- Read the transcript through and annotate areas that may be confusing at a later stage.
- Synchronise notes and observations with the transcript.
- Anonymise names including avatar names. Be aware that participants may use short forms of names, so a 'find and replace' may not be sufficient.
- Remove any text that came before or after the interview.

2.10 Conclusion

In order to understand a learners' experience, inworld interviews provide an opportunity to use not only the location and objects of the original learning context but to also use the most prevalent communication medium. This provides researchers with opportunities that would have been unavailable to them in a face-to-face interview context. However along with these opportunities there are constraints that need to be considered.

This chapter has presented techniques and guidelines to reduce the constraints and leverage the opportunities of conducting inworld interviews through text. The guidelines highlight key considerations the researcher should make prior to, during and post interview. Researchers can apply many of these points to inworld voice interviews.

When deciding whether to collect data inworld, researchers need to consider how the medium of the interview may influence the discourse between interviewer and interviewee(s). It is through this discourse that data is generated. Therefore the researcher must remain cognisant of the opportunities and constraints of conducting interviews inworld, the implications for data collection and analysis, as well as the techniques which will be required. By keeping these in mind throughout the research process, researchers using text based interviews in virtual worlds will provide a strong foundation to the data collected.

References

Anderson, K. (2007). Ethical issues in qualitative e-learning research. *International Journal of Qualitative Methods, 6*(2), 20–38.

Brenner, M. (2006). Interviewing in educational research. In J. Green, G. Camilli, & P. Elmore (Eds.), *Handbook of complementary methods in education research* (pp. 357–370). Mahwah, NJ: Lawrence Erlbaum Associates.

Chen, P., & Hinton, S. M. (1999). Realtime interviewing using the world wide web. *Sociological Research Online, 4*(3). http://www.socresonline.org.uk/4/3/chen.html

Cohen, L., Manion, L., & Morrison, K. (2007). *Research methods in education* (6th ed.). London: Routledge.

Creswell, J. W. (2002). *Educational research: Planning, conducting, and evaluating quantitative and qualitative research.* Upper Saddle River: Merrill Prentice Hall.

Girvan, C., & Savage, T. (2011). Conducting text-based interviews in virtual worlds. In A. Peachey (Ed.), *Proceedings of researching learning in immersive virtual environments (ReLIVE2011)* (pp. 78–86). Milton Keynes: The Open University.

Girvan, C., & Savage, T. (2012). Ethical considerations for educational research in a virtual world. *Interactive Learning Environments, 20*(3), 239–251.

Girvan, C., Tangney, B., & Savage, T. (2013). SLurtles: A tool to support constructionist learning in second life. *Computers in Education, 61*(1), 115–132.

Hew, K. F., & Cheung, W. S. (2010). Use of three-dimensional (3-D) immersive virtual worlds in K-12 and higher education settings: A review of the research. *British Journal of Educational Technology, 41*(1), 33–55.

Jarmon, L. (2009). Pedagogy and learning in the virtual world of second life. In P. Rogers, G. Berg, J. Boettcher, C. Howard, L. Justice, & K. Schenk (Eds.), *Encyclopaedia of distance and online learning* (2nd ed., pp. 1610–1619). Hershey, PA: IGI Global.

Jepsen, D. M., & Rodwell, J. J. (2008). Convergent interviewing: A qualitative diagnostic technique for researchers. *Management Research News, 32*(9), 650–658.

Kirriemuir, J. (2007). *An update of the July 2007 "snapshot" of UK higher and further education developments in second life*. Bath: Eduserv.

Knorr, R. M., Bronack, S. C., Switzer, D. M., & Medford, L. F. (2011). Methodology of a novel virtual phenomenology interview technique. *Journal of Virtual Worlds Research, 3*(3). doi:10.4101/jvwr.v3i3.1400

Kvale, S., & Brinkmann, S. (2009). *InterViews: Learning the craft of qualitative research interviewing*. London: Sage.

Minocha, S., Tran, M., & Reeves, A. (2010). Conducting empirical research in virtual worlds: Experiences from two projects in second life. *Journal of Virtual Worlds Research, 3*(1), 3–21.

Moschini, E. (2008, November). The second life researcher toolkit. An exploration of inworld tools, methods and approaches for researching educational projects in second life. In *Proceedings of the researching learning in virtual environments conference, ReLIVE08*, Milton Keynes.

Tuckman, B. W. (1994). *Conducting educational research*. London: Harcourt Brace College Publishers.

Vasileiou, V. N., & Paraskeva, F. (2010). Teaching role-playing instruction in Second Life: An exploratory study. *Journal of Information, Information Technology, and Organizations, 5*, 25–40.

Chapter 3
Designing for Hybrid Learning Environments in a Science Museum: Inter-professional Conceptualisations of Space

Alfredo Jornet and Cecilie Flo Jahreie

Abstract This article examines conceptualisations of space in the design of hybrid learning environments. Our focus is the relationship between the task of designing a museum exhibition space and the material and conceptual tools that an inter-professional team of researchers, museum curators and exhibition designers take up, interpret and transform in order to make them serve the team's purpose. Using Cultural-Historical Activity Theory (CHAT) as a theoretical lens, our purpose is to understand how the tools mediate the task. Understanding the relationship between the physical space and social interaction has become a central concern in the design of hybrid learning environments, i.e. spaces where digital and physical elements are combined to foster immersive learning experiences. Research has focused on exploring the ways users experience designed spaces. However, little attention has been paid to how designers negotiate conceptualisations of space in the design process.

Using video recordings of the interactions of an inter-professional team, we explore how material and conceptual tools mediate the conceptualisations of space in the design of a hybrid learning environment in a science museum. In this chapter, we discuss how the notion of transparency and the prototype of a motion-sensing device became powerful tools in the design of hybrid learning environments. We also discuss how the relationship between the tools and the task has to be understood based on the object-motives of each of the different professional practices. It is argued that a design strategy that includes an understanding of the design process as a cultural-historical process allows for innovative implementations in hybrid learning environments.

A. Jornet (✉)
Department of Education, University of Oslo, Norway
e-mail: a.g.jornet@intermedia.uio.no

C.F. Jahreie
Training Department, Østfold County Council, Norway

M. Childs and A. Peachey (eds.), *Understanding Learning in Virtual Worlds*,
Human–Computer Interaction Series, DOI 10.1007/978-1-4471-5370-2_3,
© Springer-Verlag London 2013

3.1 Introduction

In this article, we examine how an inter-professional team negotiates an understanding of a space in the design of hybrid learning environment in a museum setting. Hybrid learning environments refer to the merging of real and virtual worlds to produce new spaces, where physical and digital objects co-exist and interact in real time and across different contexts (Smørdal et al. 2012). Considerations of space are central in the design of virtual worlds, where issues of virtuality and a sense of presence have been the focus of much research (Schultze 2010).

Hybrid environments involve the distribution of computational devices across a physical space, whether these are part of the structure (e.g. interactive walls) or are embedded in it (e.g. mobile devices) (Ciolfi and Bannon 2007). Thus, a regular classroom may be turned into a technology-enhanced setting where students experiment with simulated visual and haptic phenomena distributed across the classroom (Moher 2006). Seen in relation to the design of a museum space, which is the analytic concern of this chapter, technology may mediate engagement by supporting the unfolding dynamics of students' and visitors' exploration, reflection, imagination and emotional attachment (Kaptelinin 2011). Information and communication technologies can be integrated with museum exhibits to support re-contextualisation of the visitors' activities, e.g. by supporting the exhibit with an interactive representation. In the same way the museum space can be re-contextualised by distributing interactive 3-D projections on floors and walls, portions of a larger room may become 'mini-immersive' environments (e.g. Bannon et al. 2005). Mobile technologies, such as hand-held devices, web-based platforms and social networks may connect activities taking place in a museum with later activities taking place in the classroom (Jahreie et al. 2011). In all these examples, spaces with a certain history and established practices are re-contextualised with virtual layers that potentially bring about new kinds of spatiality.

Our interest in exploring conceptualisations of space is motivated by recent phenomenological research in interaction design. These studies have introduced the notions of *place* and *sense of place* to address subjective experiences of presence, participation and engagement in computer-mediated spaces such as virtual worlds and hybrid learning environments (Ciolfi 2004; Dourish 2006; Harrison and Dourish 1996; Schultze 2010; Turner and Turner 2006). While these studies mostly focus on users' experiences of already established spaces, our concern is how the concept 'space' is negotiated in the design process, and how a sense of place emerges during interactions related to projected spaces. Our analytic focus is on how the designers negotiate conceptualisations of spaces that are made materially present through different means along the design trajectory, including a floor plan, a hand-drawn sketch of an interactive exhibit and a prototype of a motion-based 3D game.

Before we review notions of place and space in interaction design, we will outline our theoretical framework. After the review, we discuss implications for the design work and then take a closer look at our empirical case and methodology. The empirical analysis is divided in two. First, we have what we prefer to call a socio-historical analysis in which we account for the negation process in the design work. The second part is an interaction analysis of the ongoing negotiations. In the last part of the chapter, we discuss the research questions followed by the concluding remarks.

3.2 Theoretical Framework

The concept of *negotiations* is understood from the perspective of Cultural-Historical Activity Theory (CHAT). In this perspective, learning and cognition are seen as object-oriented activities that cannot be studied in isolation from the tools used, the historical practices that frame such use and the goals and motives that constitute them. Drawing on CHAT, we consider conceptual issues involved in the design process not as something pre-structured in theoretical knowledge, but as something achieved in the course of activity and interactions.

We recognise design work as a complex learning activity in which actors from various organisational practices, who have different traditions and domains of expertise, must collaborate in order to develop an object, which in this case is an understanding of space in a hybrid learning environment. The design process involves working outside these established organisational practices (Edwards and Kinti 2010), as neither the object to be accomplished nor the means to achieve it are defined in any prescriptive manner. Instead, the different actors must negotiate the nature of the object and how it should be materialised. By focusing on the goals and motives of an activity, CHAT allows us to go beyond phenomenological and situative explanations of how space is experienced and enacted to include the horizons of possible actions for inter-professional teams to understand and design hybrid spaces in museums.

Three notions related to CHAT that are of particular relevance to our study are objects, tools and boundaries. The notion of object is the core concept in CHAT towards which activity is oriented. In this study, the focus is on how the designers negotiate an understanding of space in a hybrid learning environment. The object is in a constant state of transformation and is questioned, interpreted and negotiated during the design process (Engeström 2008). The meaning of the object is an inextricable part of the activity. The notion of object has a dual disposition: material and ideational. The object is realised through activity in which the activity is simultaneously formed by the actors' negotiations of the object (Kaptelinin 2005). In our case, space for hybrid learning environments is materialised in the form of a model of a museum space and a museum exhibit, and space in hybrid learning environments is conceptualised in terms of ideas and suggestions, which are in constant negotiation. In this study, we see how understanding of space is realised through the design work and how the object also brings about transformed practises.

Cultural tools shape the way we learn (Cole 1996; Vygotsky 1978). As objects, tools have a dual disposition as material tools (as models, images, prototypes, plans and timelines) and ideational tools (concepts and language). Tools mediate our actions, and the use of tools helps actors make sense of objects. The relationship between tools and an object captures the dialectical process of learning and development (Vygotsky 1978). Tools are vital when characterising design work and are often provided as part of the design (such as the exhibition plan or model of a museum exhibit). The tools serve to coordinate actions in specific ways and mediate the way team members make sense of the object. At other times, team members pick up tools that were not initially part of the design and make them serve their needs (Lund and Rasmussen 2008). The design of technology-rich environments, such as the one currently studied, affords multiple tools, but the question exists: which tools are actually picked up and put to use in object-oriented endeavours?

Design work involves moments for participants in which individual interests become aligned with those of the team's. Individual interests originate in their primary activities in museum, architecture and research centres. The boundaries within the team become problematic places where different sets of practices come into contact (Kerosuo 2003). The boundary work is seen as an important aspect of inter-professional activity.

Since collective orientations across different professional practices are central in inter-professional work, boundaries are a key concept. Boundaries are part of the activities and have historical layers. They are intrinsic to the professional practices, but become transparent in and through participants' interactions (Kerosuo 2006). In design work, one can imagine that the team negotiates an understanding of the borders of the professional practices. In transcending the boundaries, participants encounter different and sometimes conflicting meanings of the task or object; thus, processes of collective concept formation are imperative. Design work depends on the expertise and knowledge of each of the professions. Therefore, to succeed in the design work, collaboration and negotiation of the object is vital. In such collaborative work, there are continuous breakdowns and contradictions between competing organisational options. As several studies have shown, such tensions and contradictions are productive for design work and may shift the path of the activity (Engeström 1999).

Drawing on CHAT, our concern is the relationship between the object and the material and conceptual tools. In the analysis, we trace instances of explicit and implicit conceptualisations of space in order to explore how these conceptualisations are mediated by different material and conceptual tools and the ways in which the tools become relevant to the teams' shared task. Based on this background, we pose the following two questions:

- How do material and conceptual tools mediate conceptualisations of space in the inter-professional collaborative design of hybrid environments?
- How do conceptualisations of space transform the design of hybrid environments for the inter-professional team?

3.3 Notions of Space and Place in Interaction Design

Notions of spatiality are central to most definitions of virtual worlds (Bell 2008). From a classical approach, an aspect of spatiality in the virtual realm relates to its subjective character: unlike a physical space, a virtual space is not a space in its own right (Heeter 1992). The subjective character of the space is contrasted with the 'objective' features of the environments, such as the degree of representational fidelity or of sensorial richness (de Freitas et al. 2010). This approach, therefore, assumes a separation between the physical and the psychological.

Phenomenological researchers have critiqued the classical approach (e.g. Ciolfi 2004; Mantovani and Riva 1999; Turner 2007). For these researchers, the problem is considered a question of engagement and intentionality in activities. Spaces are always mediated by cultural aspects and become meaningful for action and interaction with others. In line with these critiques, the notion of *place* has been increasingly adopted in interaction design literature in order to address issues of spatiality. Harrison and Dourish's discussions on *place* have been particularly influential (Dourish 2001, 2006; Harrison and Dourish 1996). The concept of place arises from the realisation that our behaviour within space cannot be explained exclusively by the relationship between the physical spatial arrangements of matter around us and the individual's mental processes, rather it necessitates consideration of the social meanings and practices related to them (Dourish 2001). Thus, drawing on the notion of place, space is understood in terms of its physical, subjective, social and cultural dimensions (Ciolfi 2004; Ciolfi and Bannon 2005, 2007).

The implications of adopting a notion of *place* in the design of virtual worlds and hybrid learning environments include a shift in focus from features of the environment that may *convey* a sense of presence to focusing on the ways in which designed spaces may support the development of social activities that are the foundation for developing a sense of place, i.e. being a participant in meaningful action. Within this framework, much current research on virtual worlds pursues an understanding of the processes through which virtual spaces become places of meaningful experience or *third places* for social interaction (Peachey 2008). This conceptualisation attends to the discursive practices that bring about a sense of community (Chap. 5 by Ferguson et al., this volume) and to the nature of the narratives that frame engagement in a given environment (Turner et al. 2005).

3.4 Implications for Design Work

Notions of space and place have mostly been discussed in regard to users' experiences of computer-mediated environments, often with the goal of improving design. The design implications bring about a focus on the interactional processes through which users render spaces meaningful to social conduct; this focus prevents us from drawing simplistic *a-priori* relationships between a computer-mediated environment and users' subjective experiences. Some researchers have developed a framework for designing hybrid spaces in museums based on notions of space as place (Ciolfi 2004; Ciolfi and Bannon 2005, 2007). Drawing on the notion of place, these researchers understand space in terms of its physical, subjective, social and cultural dimensions; museums are seen as 'lived places' where the design of an exhibition accommodates visitors' sense of place and historical aspects of the museum space.

However, defining sense of place as an interactional achievement does not render design work incapable of foreseeing hybrid learning environments as lived-in places prior to their actual population. Ciolfi and Bannon's works discussed above, for example, stress the importance of conducting ethnographic investigations of the practices that take place in a physical space prior to implementation of design in order to get an understanding of the kind of social processes that are to be supported. Yet, little attention has been paid to the question of how a sense of place comes to be in a design process prior to the existence of a given place itself. An exception is Binder et al. (2011), who note that if we assume spaces must be appropriated by the users to become meaningful places, 'then we must assume that this is true for designers as well with regard with their environments' (p. 139). They emphasise the peculiarity of design work in which the object (space) to be designed does not yet exist. The authors use the concept of *landscapes* to emphasise the importance of grasping the double nature of design as both a situated practice and a hypothetical practicing of an imagined place (Binder et al. 2011).

In this chapter, we take up the challenge of understanding the emergence of a sense of place in the course of the design. We analyse the interactions of an inter-professional team that collaborates to design hybrid learning environments across the school and the museum. As we mentioned in the introduction, negotiations of various object conceptualisations are vital for success in inter-professional work (Engeström 1999). Therefore, in addition to negotiating the very nature of learning, designing hybrid learning environments may involve negotiating conceptualisations of the lived space as an object of the ongoing design work and as an imagined or projected lived space in the museum.

3.5 Context Description and Methods

Data for this study were generated from the project Mixed Reality Interactions across Contexts of Learning (MIRACLE) (Jahreie et al. 2011). As it makes use of technologically enhanced physical spaces, MIRACLE aims to increase students' interest in and conceptual understanding of science by connecting science education learning activities in upper secondary schools to activities at a science museum. MIRACLE is connected to an exhibition that is to be designed at the Norwegian Museum of Science and Technology (NSTM) called 'Energy for the Future'. This exhibition is part of a redesign of the whole museum. Energy is one of the main themes in the curriculum for the upper secondary freshmen year. Heat pumps, on which we focus in the first of three iterations, are one of the central sub-themes (Norwegian Ministry of Education and Research 2010–2011). The core tools in the design process in this first iteration are the development of a pedagogical plan, a technological plan and a museum exhibition plan. These plans are developed in parallel, but relate to each other. The participants have responsibilities in different plans, which are discussed and negotiated in the workshops. In the data gathered for this study, the focus for discussion was mainly the exhibition plan, although it was seen in relation to the other two plans.

MIRACLE involves a complex design process motivated by a set of workshops with different relevant stakeholders, such as museum conservators, exhibition designers, researchers, scientific programmers, teachers and animation specialists. Because participants are from three different professional arenas—a science museum, an architecture firm and an educational research centre—we refer to the different participants as curators, exhibition designers and researchers. Researchers include educational researchers and scientific programmers, as they share the same workplace and environment.

The study is based on observations from the first year of the project (October 2010–November 2011). During this period, we conducted five design workshops in which the different partners met to discuss and negotiate different development concepts. Some of the technological solutions in development were tested in a first pilot study. Workshops I–IV were used for the ethnographic contextualising of data. All workshops were video recorded, which produced 14 h of material. The analytic work was conducted in three steps. First, we constructed an overview of the total corpus of data in order to select a subset. Second, we conducted an initial analysis to identify recurring patterns of interaction. In the ethnographic analysis of the socio-historical development of the project, we identified two recurring themes, which are discussed in the following section. In Workshop V, which is documented in 5 h of video recordings, we were able to identify specific instances where the team made sense of the exhibition space, and we selected two excerpts for deeper analysis. In addition, a third excerpt was extracted from the pilot study conducted in November 2011. This latter excerpt was selected because discussions on space took place within a full-size prototype of the projected space. The iteration is documented in 2 h and 25 min of video. Our analysis builds on interaction analysis (Jordan and Henderson 1995). Both Workshop V and the iteration were conducted in English. It is important to note that most of the participants were not native English speakers and that we have retained the original phraseology in the transcripts.

As researchers, we participated with our colleagues in the group studied; therefore, caution is necessary. Our own voice should not be more weighted than the others. In effect, this means we are *not* looking for some kind of normative idea about the right way to design and develop learning activities in science, rather we hope to identify how the team negotiates central themes in the design work. In accordance with methodological standards (Jordan and Henderson 1995), we used our socio-cultural research community to objectify our analysis to make sure we dealt with the different voices equally.

3.6   Empirical Analysis

3.6.1   *Socio-historical Development of Negotiations in Inter-professional Design Work*

The initial analysis revealed two recurring themes present in the negotiations in Workshops I–V. The first was experience versus the reflective aspects of learning. Based on observations from Workshop I, our initial analysis of experience and the reflective aspects of learning as a recurrent topic confirm the findings of a previous study (Jahreie and Krange 2011). The participants focused their attention on the same object, designing learning activities across schools and museums, but there was tension regarding the object conceptualisation. The curators were inclined to perceive learning as an interactive, engaging experience, whilst the architects perceived learning in terms of emotional involvement, and the researchers perceived learning as conceptual understanding. This is not surprising, but what is important is that the different conceptualisations were mostly seen as separate, and the integration of these orientations into a shared understanding remained a challenge (Jahreie and Krange 2011).

A second recurrent tension identified concerns the knowledge domain of energy. Energy as a theme involves both scientific (related to physics) and socio-political issues. Both issues are part of the curriculum (Norwegian Ministry of Education and Research 2010–2011). This topic was repeatedly discussed and negotiated in relation to the heat pump sub-theme during the workshops. In the negotiations, we found that exhibition designers often found the scientific issues of heat pumps to be a problematic topic in the museum space. However, researchers were more concerned with fostering students' conceptual understanding of scientific aspects and paid less attention to the socio-political issues. Finally, museum curators clearly showed sympathy for the idea of including scientific-related curriculum issues, but often criticised the heat pump theme for being too complex to be understood beyond its socio-political dimension in the museum setting. What is interesting in this discussion is that the participants often discussed scientific and socio-politic issues separately; thus, their interrelation in the design layout became yet another challenge.

In this ethnographic contextualisation, we identify different orientations to the two recurring topics. As indicated in our first study of the design process, these differences must be understood in relation to conflicting object-motives between practices (see Jahreie and Krange 2011). Through the lens of CHAT, this situation can be identified as one of contradictions (Engeström 2001) between different conceptualisations of the generalised object of designing for learning activities on one hand, and between understanding how the knowledge domain should mediate the object on the other. Until Workshop V, the participants tended to defend their orientation, which was grounded in both their motive for participating and the division of labour in the inter-professional group.

In the following sections, we examine how tools mediate new conceptualisations of space at the boundaries of the inter-professional team.

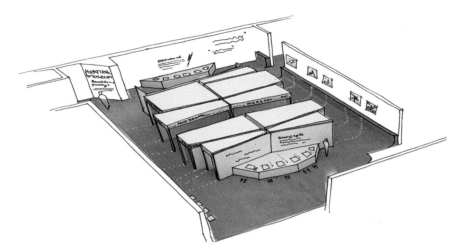

Fig. 3.1 The plan floor presented by the exhibition designers during Workshop V

3.6.2 The Exhibition Plan: Space as a Shared Object

In the first part of Workshop V, the two exhibition designers presented a draft of the exhibition plan. The plan was displayed in a series of PowerPoint slides. The room depicted is square and covers 120 m². It is a small space for an exhibition, which makes it challenging in terms of the architectural design. The solution suggested by the designers involved setting a corpus of modular walls in the centre of the room to form a number of modules (Fig. 3.1).

The modules were intended to house the different exhibits, individuating each one as unique. At the same time, because they are not closed, the modules are still connected to the rest of the room. Apart from a lack of space in the room, the design highlights two other possibilities in the plan presentation. One is related to the inter-activity of the room: 'When you enter an exhibition, you want to meet eyes; you don't want to meet backs. We wanted to focus the exhibition to the core of the space and not to the walls' (exhibition designer). The other involves the challenge of relating the different sub-themes of the exhibition to the overall Future of Energy theme. Thus, a number of solutions were presented to increase the sense of unity. The space dedicated to each exhibit extends beyond the modules up to the external walls of the room, and a single material is used for the entire floor up to the walls. The draft design also includes the possibility of streaming media that is being projected from each module on the external walls, so that what is going on within each exhibit is shared or reflected in the open, shared space.

After a 15-min presentation, the participants discussed the exhibition concept. The matter of how the modules relate to each other, how they are related to the rest of the room and how the room relates to the rest of the museum became a topic of discussion. In Excerpt 3.1, the participants discuss the possibility of having transparent, interactive walls.

Excerpt 3.1

1. **Researcher 1**: One comment. Eh, I liked very much what you said in the beginning with the, eh, not seeing all these backs. When you come into a space, you see only the back heads of people who are working. But still this is a kind of box. Like a black box things set up. Could it be an idea to have some kind of transparent, eh, transparency there? Because you have issues, each, eh…

2. **Exhibition designer**: We are talking about using these corridors (*pointing to the screen*) of course here is a physical corridor where you can walk in, you see people that you've seen before… which is…

3. **Researcher 1**: …Because it could also be an illustration of that it's not only one solution. It's not only sun or only wind, it's a common thing and there are certain different things.

4. **Exhibition designer**: Yeah, and how you connect this one, this one and this one (*pointing to the different cabins*) when you make a transparent window in between and we start using mirrors, where you instead of projectors use mirrors to…

5. **Researcher 1**: Because one thing we thought about is also to have a projection, if you combine this bicycle idea with a projection, it could be interesting if people also are in the other side, so you see kind of semi-transparent projector material that you can look from different sides.

6. **Researcher 2**: A double-sided screen.

7. **Researcher 1**: Yeah

8. **Curator 1**: It's possible on that wall, but not on the other wall.

9. **Exhibition designer**: Which one is that and which one is the other?

10. **Researcher 1**: It is not possible in the walls around…?

11. **Curator 1**: Is this one… (*Pointing at the powerpoint*)

12. **Researcher 1**: Ok, so then it's possible

13. **Curator 1**: And … and this one is facing, facing out into the science center. And this one is facing into a corridor for the engine room for the elevators.

14. **Researcher 3**: Because if you think of this as a kind of an extension of the science center now, it will kind of have the same feeling, what it's in this space …

15. **Curator 2**: It will have, it will be all interactive, but it will have a different form. And it will connect to this big master plan of the future energy… so it will be part of that.

16. **Researcher 3**: Yeah

At the beginning of the excerpt, Researcher 1 refers to the exhibition designer's presentation of the exhibition plan. When someone enters an exhibition, they usually see visitors facing exhibits on the walls and therefore see only their backs (turn 1). Researcher 1 thus acknowledges the exhibition designer's previously introduced idea of designing a space where the focus is on the centre of the exhibition space and not on the walls. However, he is concerned that the design of the space may remain a 'black box', and suggests that one solution might be to design some transparent walls. Since the focus in the conversation was on the modular walls at the centre of the room, it is reasonable to infer that Researcher 1 is talking about transparency as a means with which to connect the modules. The exhibition designer argues that due to the design of the physical corridors, visitors can meet each other and the corridor will therefore prevent a box-like feeling (turn 2). Researcher 1 interrupts the designer and argues that transparency would also be a way to illustrate that energy relates to both solar power and wind power (turn 3). Transparency would then be a means for visitors to connect the different exhibits from each module. With this utterance, the researcher picks up the designer's challenge of integrating the sub-themes related to energy. The exhibition designer seems enthusiastic about the suggestion of transparency between the exhibits. He points to the screen showing the exhibition while explaining that with transparent windows they will be able to design a connection between the exhibits. The exhibition designer is in the midst of arguing for the use of mirrors instead of projectors, when Researcher 1 again interrupts him. The researcher brings a new dimension into the conversation. He suggests that using a projector makes looking at a semi-transparent projection of the exhibit from different sides possible (turn 5). Transparency is not only a solution for integrating the different exhibits, but also for opening the interaction to people outside the modules. The researcher is supported by another researcher who suggests a double-sided screen. Curator 1 then enters the conversation to tell the others on which walls it is possible to have transparent screens (turn 8). In turn 9, it becomes obvious that is not clear to which walls he is referring. Researcher 1 asks if it is possible 'in the walls around', signalling that he is unsure of the walls to which Curator 1 is referring. This shows there is more than one possible interpretation. This interchange represents a turning point, when the focus of the discussion is reoriented toward the walls around the room and not those between modules. Based on the explanation of Curator 1, Researcher 1 concludes in that turn 12 'then it's possible'. Researcher 3 takes up the idea of Researcher 1 and argues that the use of transparent walls makes it possible to see the exhibition space as an extension of the science centre. Curator 2 seems to think it is a good idea because transparent walls are a way to design for interactivity and because the solution is part of their overall plan for the Energy of the Future exhibition.

One main issue concerns the role of material and conceptual tools. In the interaction, we see how the participants take up multiple tools that afford different conceptualisations of the object. First, conceptualisations of space are facilitated by the presentation of the exhibition plan. The material presence of the museum's projected space, in the form of an exhibition plan, affords an interaction where the participants can physically and verbally point to different aspects. In referring to its different structural aspects, the participants simultaneously refer to interactions that some suggested scenarios could afford. Therefore, an exhibition plan has a double nature that mediates the object in different ways. First, the exhibition plan consists of a physical artefact in the form of a PowerPoint slide, which allows indexical referencing in the discussion. Second, the exhibition plan has a projective nature in the sense of being a draft in a design workshop. In this sense, it is understood not as an end product to be interpreted, but as an occasion for inspiration and suggestion. As different participants verbalise these ideas, space for negotiation is opened.

Another issue is that space is inherently treated in terms of affordance for interaction within the projected space and also as a means for solving conceptual tensions within the project. The structure of the modular space facilitates the introduction of the notion of transparency, which in turn generates ideas for how to design for interactivity within the exhibition space. Two aspects are particularly interesting in this respect. First, the idea of a transparent wall between exhibits is related to how to understand the topic of energy (turns 3–4). Transparency offered the possibility for negotiating the nature of the knowledge domain of energy, a topic that represented one of the main tensions for the team in previous workshops. In this sense, the concept of transparency seems to provide opportunities for a more open and integrated discussion of energy as an interrelation of scientific and socio-political issues. Second, the idea of transparent walls between the exhibition and the science centre (turn 14–16) seems to generate new ideas about how to thematically link the different parts of the museum. This would afford an integral participation trajectory within the room and across the museum and a means to solve yet another potential source of tension in the inter-professional team: designing a thematic space within the larger museum.

We also see that the participants use other tools, such as mirrors and technology-based resources, to further generate ideas about how transparency affords interactions within the space: between visitors (turn 1), between exhibits (turns 3–4), within an exhibit (turns 5–6) and between different exhibitions within the museum (turn 14).

The second main aspect we want to highlight is how space evolves as a shared object in the inter-professional team. The exhibition plan and the concept of transparency afforded the negotiation of a shared vision of a possible space, beyond what was represented in the plan. On one hand, we see, not surprisingly, that the exhibition designers introduce a typical architectonic device, mirrors, as a mediating tool, while the researchers are concerned about how digital devices can mediate the space.

Designing a museum exhibit that links a material exhibit with a digital device is introduced by the researchers. This is an important design issue for the researchers. However, even more interesting is that the researchers also introduce a discussion of an overall museum design by considering the new exhibition as an extension of the science centre, which is of interest for the overall re-design of the science museum.

3.6.3 Space as Topic: Tensions Between Tools and Object

After the exhibition designers' presentation, participants from the research group made a presentation in which several possible technological solutions were proposed. Excerpt 3.2 is taken from a group session following that presentation. The team is divided in two inter-professional groups for discussion. The aim is to discuss the proposed scenarios and to come up with ideas about how to combine technology, the exhibits and exhibition activities. The group we follow discusses the heat pump exhibit. The participants' interaction is in part mediated by an image of an exhibit and an associated hand-drawn sketch of an interactive heat pump model. The image and the model are displayed on a laptop visible to all participants (Fig. 3.2). The model is a tool provided by the researchers for the design work.

Excerpt 3.2

1. **Researcher 3**: I am just wondering, you know, what we could do with this thing here (*pointing to the displayed image*) in terms of engagement, embodiment, mixed reality... mmm, ways of unpacking the heat pump.
   [all they stare at the screen in silence for a while]
2. **Curator 2**: "What's going on down there?" (*pointing on the exhibit artefact*). That's the black box. If you can put it up here (*pointing to the heat pump model*), and you have some images, or a way to explain it or show is better...
3. **Researcher 3**: If we discuss not on heat pumps, but on more hybrid spaces that are both physical and digital and mixed... Because that has an architectural issue, I think...
4. **Exhibition designer**: (*long silence*) Yeah, but I don't think it's from that angle. It could be anything. But I think it has to start with...Architecture is mostly sometimes in a way sight specific, as well as sight is not only into space but is also topic. And we have to work with a topic. And how media and architecture interact is not a topic. So you have to start with what issues or what target group, or... are we gonna work from or with.
5. **Researcher 4**: Right, so you are saying that you can't just take any old exhibit and put into that space...
6. **Exhibition designer**: In my world I would like to work with what story are we gonna tell, what are we gonna communicate, why are we gonna do this. And I do not work out of "Ok, I love this chair, and now I am gonna find a room where I can fit this chair in, cause that it's not how I do. Product designers work like that. And that is another angle. And is like the technical and the political...
7. **Researcher 3**: But could that be translated into this one (*pointing to heat pump representation*).

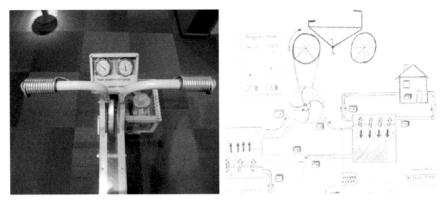

Fig. 3.2 Heat pump exhibition model as screened in a laptop during group session transcribed in Excerpt 3.2

At the beginning of this excerpt, Researcher 3 invites the others to generate ideas about how to facilitate students' 'engagement' with the understanding of the principles behind the heat pump. He mentions resources such as 'embodiment' and 'mixed reality'. Curator 2 fixes his attention on the model of the heat pump. He points to what he defines as the 'black box' in the model and suggests it be 'unpacked' or explained by representing it as a projection in which they can use, for example, images as a way to explain it better (turn 2). Researcher 3 takes up the curators' idea by reframing the question to consider hybrid spaces or mixed realities. By stating that he thinks there is 'an architectural issue', he is addressing the exhibition designer. The exhibition designer replies that from an architectonic perspective, one should focus on the topic of space when designing an exhibition. To be able to solve the problem, they need to work with a topic, and the interaction between technology and architecture on which the researcher focuses is not a topic (turn 4). Researcher 4 backs the designer up and rephrases the designer's comments, stating that the focus should not be the artefact. The exhibition designer acknowledges Researcher 4 by stating that the subject of the communication must be the focus of the architectonic design and not the exhibit or artefact itself (turn 5). The exhibition designer confirms that it is the topic that must be communicated. He explains that, as architects, the intention is not to choose an artefact and then designing an appropriate space to house it. Researcher 3 then asks how that can be translated to fit their heat pump model (turn 7).

In this excerpt, different approaches to students' learning activities in the museum space are discussed. In Excerpt 3.1, a plan for the exhibition in the form of a material tool mediated the interaction between participants. In this group work, there is no material representation of the space. Instead, a model of the heat pump stimulates talk of how to design the museum space. An important aspect in this interaction is tension between the tools and the object. The tension is related to whether the technological means (turn 3) or the topic (turns 4 and 6) should mediate the design of the spatial distribution for this particular exhibit. The researchers are concerned with how to design technological representations and hybrid environments that facilitate learning activities. In their account, the conceptual aspects related to the knowledge domain become relevant for the material distribution of space. Whereas in the exhibition designer's account, the story one wants to communicate through the exhibition is made relevant.

To understand the tension described, we have to examine the impact of historical practices on the current interaction. From this perspective, it is fruitful to understand the interactional tension as a contradiction between two professional practices. The researcher and exhibition designer foreground their knowledge, the former in technology design for learning and the latter in the spatial affordance for communicating a topic in a museum exhibition. Even though we see instances where the researcher tries to integrate the two forms of knowing, they are not able to find a common ground during this interaction.

3.6.4 Being There: Tensions Between Museum Exhibits and Technology

Excerpt 3.3 is from the first iteration that was conducted in a studio at the University of Oslo, where a classroom space and a museum space were set up. The aim was to test some of the technology-enhanced scenarios in development. At that point in the design process, motion-sensing technology was suggested to represent some of the key concepts of the heat pump in an interactive game. A full-size mock-up of one of the modules projected in the exhibition plan and described in Excerpt 3.1 was built to house the motion-based game (Fig. 3.3). The game is designed for two players who must stand within the module to activate it. The players are represented by avatars in a 3D projection on the wall. The players' movements are replicated by the avatars in the virtual space. Players must interact with some of the virtual objects in order to heat up a virtual house. The rationale of the game follows some of the physical principles of a heat pump.

We enter the conversation in Excerpt 3.3 just after a museum curator and an exhibition designer have tried the application. Without leaving the experimental space, the researchers initiate a discussion based on the impressions of the museum curator and the exhibition designer. Just before we come into the conversation, the exhibition designer suggests that including material objects as part of the game would improve the experience in different ways.

Excerpt 3.3

1. **Exhibition designer 2**: and not just weaving around in the air (*waves arms*) but actually touching objects.
2. **Curator 1**: yeah. that's an interesting point because that also bridges the classical museum exhibition and this-
3. **Researcher 5**: digital,
4. **Curator 1**: -game thing that you can do anywhere.
5. **Exhibition designer 2**: mmm,
6. **Curator 1**: if you, if you construct something here in the middle of this room. eh if it's not obstructing this, if it's possible, then you can both get to touch of the physical object, and then you also, you also make the point that this actually brings eh something new and better into the museum exhibition. Because traditional museum exhibitions will just show this (*shapes spaces where he has suggested that physical objects should be placed*). But here you could actually explain it in a way.
7. **Exhibition designer 2**: mmm.
8. **Software engineer**: mmm.
9. **Exhibition designer 2**: and then it leads into a very, an interesting discussion about purpose with the eh, this imaginary virtual space (*pointing to the wall where the game is projected*).
10. **Researcher 5**: yeach?
11. **Exhibition designer 2**: what can you do there that can't be done in reality or with physical objects.
12. **Researcher 5**: mmm.
13. **Curator 1**: (*pointing to game projection*) and I think that-
14. **Exhibition designer 2**: so of course this is, this is an eye catcher and eh an exhibit that will probably draw attention if, at least until every kid has their own-
15. **Researcher 5**: their own kinect,
16. **Exhibition designer 2**: xbox at home, so-
17. **Curator 1**: but they won't, what they won't have in their room is the physical objects here (*shaping the space where the physical objects are suggested to be, again using the same gesture*). for instance, if we have a heat pump, or if we have a turbine or something, we can do also museum objects here. that would be the specific thing about the exhibition, when you both get a hands-on explanation of, of cultural technology and real objects, and you at the same time have the playfulness of this (*pointing to the wall where the game is displayed*) which you of course don't get in our traditional energy exhibition. because they are just a display of death objects. but here you can bring the death objects alive as well.

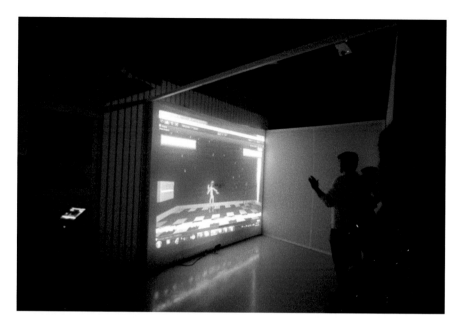

Fig. 3.3 Designers testing the motion-based game during development work

The excerpt opens as Exhibition Designer 2 emphasises his point about including material exhibits in the game, as this gives an opportunity for actually 'touching objects'. Curator 1 adds that it is interesting because it connects 'the classical museum and this...' Researcher 5 interrupts, and says 'Digital...' (turn 3). Curator 1 continues with 'game' and adds 'that you can do anywhere'. It is reasonable to infer that the curator was also thinking about enhancing traditional museum exhibitions with digital technology in turn 2. The exhibition designer seems to agree, and Curator 1 elaborates on how to include material exhibits within the game, illustrating with his hands as described in turn 6. He lists two advantages. The first is the personal learning experience for the visitor: they can both touch something and have an explanation. The other is related to the museum's reputation; it will change the traditional role of museum exhibitions (turn 6). Exhibition Designer 2 and researcher 5 agree (turns 7–8). The exhibition designer discusses the opportunities the virtual space gives, compared to traditional museum exhibits (turns 9 11). He adds that it will be an eye-catcher and will attract significant attention. However, he seems worried that this will just be temporary until motion-sensing devices are common in private homes (turn 14). Curator 1 argues that even though people will eventually have such digital devices at home, the museum will have the advantage of relating motion-sensing devices to exhibits. The digital device will be experienced as 'playful' by the visitors and is a way to bring museum exhibits 'alive'. This reinforces his previous statements.

Of interest in our analysis is how being immersed in a discussion about the object relates to the way the object is approached. The participants discuss space distribution and where to put material exhibits within the space in which they are materially situated. Some of the elements to which they refer are present, such as the wall where the game is projected, while others are absent, such as the material exhibits they might place within the module. In this way, the prototype of the space becomes a tool that mediates the conceptualisation of the object space. The prototype affords the participants an experience of the space in an embodied manner, in which the can act both as visitors and designers. By being placed in the subjective experience of space, new aspects and ideas not yet raised in previous discussions emerge.

A second aspect of relevance is how the inherent tension between the historical role of museums and the emergent role of technology within museums is emphasised and negotiated in the design process. The participants build on each other's statements to elaborate on the possible relationship between the traditional material museum exhibits and digital devices. The advantages of designing for such relationships are discussed on two levels. First, it will improve the visitors' museum experience. In the discussion, the digital enhancement of the physical experience is seen as a means to visualise the knowledge underlying the hypothetic material exhibit. In this way, the prototype of the space (the tool) mediates the object (the conceptualisation of the museum space) as a place for experience, fun and learning. Second, being placed within the tool prompts a discussion of the conceptualisation of space at an institutional level. Designing a museum space where digital devices are used in relation to museum exhibits will be a means to enhance the traditional design of museum exhibitions.

3.7 Discussion and Concluding Remarks

Our aim in this study was to explore how material and conceptual tools mediate the conceptualisation of a museum space in inter-professional design work, and how the conceptualisation of space transforms the design work. We have seen how negotiating and co-constructing a vision of the museum space has encompassed the development of a shared understanding of particular ways of "being there" in an immersive learning environment, as well as the development of general forms of learning in a science museum. In the team's discussions, the physical space was primarily treated as a set of affordances or means for supporting interactivity. Experiential, social and cultural dimensions were acknowledged, as participants discussed social interactions, feelings and expectations related to being within the different imagined spaces. However, the participants took different approaches to the object. These approaches were inherently related to how knowledge is conceived in their individual professions.

In the first research question, our concern was how tools mediated the inter-professional team's conceptualisation of space. Previous studies within CHAT have provided substantial evidence of the importance of using tools, both material and conceptual, as mediating objects to succeed in collaborative work (Ellis 2008; Engeström 2007; Engeström et al. 2005). An important aspect is that a single tool does not mediate the design of hybrid learning environments, but rather a constellation of tools are needed in design work (Engeström 2007). Thinking is done in using the tools, and the analysis shows how different tools afford different object conceptualisations. Furthermore, we have seen that the constellation of tools was both material and conceptual and that some tools were provided as part of the design work while others were picked up by the participants during the interaction (Engeström 2007; Lund and Rasmussen 2008). The analysis shows how the exhibition plan, a tool provided as part of the design, made it possible for the participants to pick up new conceptual tools, such as the notion of transparency, mirrors and projection, in the conceptualisation of space.

What we find interesting is the type of epistemic work the tools accomplish in a given interaction. In the analysis, we saw that the notion of transparency and the prototype of the motion-sensing device became the most powerful tools in the design of hybrid learning environments. These tools opened up a landscape of applications (Engeström 2007). Some of them were outside the initial scope of the project, such as how to transform the museum itself. First, the notion of transparency worked as a means to talk about one of the most debated topics during the design work, how to present the knowledge domain of energy. Second, when the concept of transparency was introduced, it generated ideas about how to link the traditional museum exhibit with a digital device and thematically link the different parts within the exhibition itself and between the science centre and the museum, which until now have been two separate parts within the science museum as a whole.

The prototype of the motion-sensing device was particularly interesting since the negotiation of the hybrid learning environment took place within the actual space. Studies of technologically mediated learning environments typically introduce new digital tools that are ready to use and thus cannot be developed further (Engeström 2007). In the design process, we introduced the technological tools as prototypes, where reconfiguration of the given technologies was an essential part of the design. Instead of getting situation-specific feedback, which is often the case with ready-made technologies (Engeström 2007), the analysis showed that the prototype generated a rich interaction about how to improve visitors' experience with respect to learning and play and about how to improve the design of museum exhibitions in general.

Our second research question was how the conceptualisation of space transformed the design work of the inter-professional team. The ethnographic contextualisation of the first four workshops revealed contradictions within the object and between the tools and the object, and participants defended the boundaries of their respective activity systems (see also Jahreie and Krange 2011). However, in Workshop V, we identified an important turning point when space became a shared object in the participants' interaction. The object's construction has to be seen in relation to the type of epistemic work done with the tools in the interaction. In the analysis, we saw how the notion of transparency and the prototype became powerful tools for the conceptualisation of space. These tools afforded shared ideas about how to present the knowledge domain, how to link material exhibits and digital devices and how to link the science centre with the museum exhibition. In this way, the shared conceptualisations of space transformed the design work of the inter-professional team. Based on the analysis, we can identify two important instances of boundary transformation, which could have caused tension or a breakdown in the team meetings (Kerosuo 2003). The first aspect is related to the design of an overall plan for NSTM. Designing an overall plan for NSTM that links the science centre with the museum exhibitions is not part of the MIRACLE research project, but it is an important focus for the museum curators and the exhibition designers in the future design of NSTM. On this basis, it is interesting to see that the researchers expanded the object by introducing the idea of transparent walls between modules and within an exhibit as a means to link the different exhibitions within the science museum and between the museum and science centre. This re-contextualisation of the museum space may be relevant in regard to how one understands hybrid learning environments in museums, since it gives opportunities for re-negotiating how learning in museums should be understood (see Jahreie and Krange 2011).

The second aspect is the design of technological-enhanced exhibits. Designing technological tools that mediate the museum exhibits is important for the MIRACLE project's motive of enhancing students' science learning between school and museum. This object-motive was accounted for by the researchers in the discussion of trans-parency in Workshop V, and was picked up again by one of the exhibition designers and museum curators in the pilot study 3 months later when they tried out the prototype. What is especially interesting is that the museum curator now sees this as an opportunity to improve museum exhibitions in general, thus generalising the object-motive of the researchers to an understanding of how the science museum may redefine or expand its institutional role of knowledge curation and dissemination.

However, the analysis also showed that not all the tools were powerful enough to extend the negotiation of space. The model of a heat pump, a tool provided by the researchers as part of the design, was discussed by the researchers, but it was not picked up by the exhibition designers or museum curators. To understand this, we need to take a historical perspective regarding the object-oriented activities. How we come to knowledge depends on how we take part in collective activities that evolve over time, and where conceptual and material resources function as collec-tive structural resources (Engeström 1987; Valsiner and van der Veer 2000). The introduction of the heat pump model mediated historical contradictions about how architects and researchers conceptualised the design of the museum space. This contradiction has to be understood based on their professional knowledge of design-ing space and designing digital devices for learning.

In summary, the interactions observed revealed important instances in which the team negotiated shared conceptualisations of space that went beyond boundaries and thus transformed the object-motive of the researchers, museum curators and exhibition designers. While the nature of learning may be an abstract matter, it became tangible when considered in relation to the material features of space. In making such a conflict relevant to the core of the project, new opportunities for transforming the design work emerged.

This study also has implications for how to approach the design of hybrid learning environments. In our review of notions of space in interaction design, we showed that a phenomenological approach to space emphasised the physical, subjective, social and cultural aspects of being in a place. In turning attention towards the ways in which space is conceptualised in design work, we aim to expand the discussion to also include the relationship between spatiality and social interaction. This is accomplished by addressing the ways in which this relationship is also relevant to the projective facet of design, which is devoted to creating spaces that do not yet exist. In line with the landscapes notion of Binder et al. (2011), we contend that inherent in the design process is a multiplicity of possible conceptualisations of hybrid spaces. However, while this notion grasps the double nature of design as both a situated practice and an imagined place, it does not take into account the cultural-historical dimensions of the conceptualisations of the object. As we have seen in this chapter, designing hybrid spaces often involve collaborative work with participants from various professional practices, each bringing a historical way of conceiving the object (Edwards and Kinti 2010). We suggest that the generation of innovative design solutions to support immersive experiences in technology-enhanced spaces can be improved upon with a deeper understanding of the tensions involved within and across the historical practices in the design process. Taking a CHAT framework, we analyse the multi-voiced nature of the design of hybrid spaces by considering the object-motives inherent in different historical practices (Engeström 1995). Having shown how recurrent tensions in design work can serve as catalysts for development, we suggest that the identification of these tensions are productive for the design work, as they may foster innovation in the design process.

References

Bannon, L., Benford, S., Bowers, J., & Heath, C. (2005). Hybrid design creates innovative museum experiences. *Communications of the ACM, 48*(3), 62–65.

Bell, M. W. (2008). Toward a definition of "Virtual Worlds". *Journal of Virtual Worlds Research 1*(1). Retrieved from http://www.jvwresearch.org/v1n1_bell.html

Binder, T., De Michelis, G., Ehn, P., Jacucci, G., Linde, P., & Wagner, I. (2011). *Design things.* Cambridge, MA: MIT Press.

Ciolfi, L. (2004). Understanding spaces as places: Extending interaction design paradigms. *Cognition, Technology Work, 6*(1), 37–40.

Ciolfi, L., & Bannon, L. (2005). Space, place and the design of technologically-enhanced physical environments. In P. Turner & E. Davenport (Eds.), *Spaces, spatiality and technology* (Vol. 5, pp. 217–232). Heidelberg: Springer.

Ciolfi, L., & Bannon, L. (2007). Designing hybrid places: Merging interaction design, ubiquitous technologies and geographies of the museum space. *CoDesign, 3*(3), 159–180.

Cole, M. (1996). *Cultural psychology: A once and a future discipline.* Cambridge, MA: Harvard University Press.

de Freitas, S., Rebolledo-Mendez, G., Liarokapis, F., Magoulas, G., & Poulovassilis, A. (2010). Learning as immersive experiences: Using the four-dimensional framework for designing and evaluating immersive learning experiences in a virtual world. *British Journal of Educational Technology, 41*(1), 69–85.

Dourish, P. (2001). *Where the action is: The foundations of embodied interaction.* Cambridge, MA: MIT Press.

Dourish, P. (2006). *Re-space-ing place: "Place" and "space" ten years on.* Paper presented at the proceedings of the 2006 20th anniversary conference on computer supported cooperative work, Banff.

Edwards, A., & Kinti, I. (2010). Working relationally at organisational boundaries. Negotiating expertise and identity. In H. Daniels, A. Edwards, Y. Engeström, T. Gallagher, & S. R. Ludvigsen (Eds.), *Activity theory in practice. Promoting learning across boundaries and agencies* (pp. 126–140). Abingdon: Routledge.

Ellis, V. (2008). *Boundary transformation in a school-university teacher education partnership: The potential of developmental work research in DETAIL.* Paper presented at the sociocultural perspective on teacher education and development: New directions for research, University of Oxford.

Engeström, Y. (1987). *Learning by expanding: An activity-theoretical approach to developmental research.* Helsinki: Orienta-Konsultit.

Engeström, Y. (1995). Objects, contradictions, and collaboration in medical cognition: An activity-theoretical perspective. *Artificial Intelligence in Medicine, 7,* 395–412.

Engeström, Y. (1999). *Innovative learning in work teams: Analyzing cycles of knowledge creation in practice.* Cambridge/New York: Cambridge University Press.

Engeström, Y. (2001). Expansive learning at work: Towards an activity theoretical reconceptualization. *Journal of Education and Work, 14*(1), 133–156.

Engeström, Y. (2007). Enriching the theory of expansive learning: Lessons from journeys toward coconfiguration. *Mind, Culture, and Activity, 14*(1–2), 23–39.

Engeström, Y. (2008). *From teams to knots: Activity-theoretical studies of collaboration and learning at work.* Cambridge: Cambridge University Press.

Engeström, Y., Lompscher, J., & Rückriem, G. (Eds.). (2005). *Putting activity theory to work: Contributions from developmental work research* (Vol. 13). Berlin: Lehmanns Media.

Ferguson, R., Gillen, J., Peachey, A., & Twining, P. (2013). The strength of cohesive ties: Discursive construction of an online learning community. In M. Childs & A. Peachey (Eds.), *Understanding learning in virtual worlds* (pp. 83–100). London: Springer.

Harrison, S., Dourish, P. (1996). *Re-place-ing space: The roles of space and place in collaborative systems.* Paper presented at the Computer-Supported Cooperative Work CSCW'96, Boston.

Heeter, C. (1992). Being there: The subjective experience of presence. *Presence: Teleoperators and Virtual Environments, 1*(2), 262–271.

Jahreie, C. F., & Krange, I. (2011). Learning in science education across school and science museums—Design and development work in a multiprofessional group. *Nordic Journal of Digital Literacy, 6*(3), 174–188.

Jahreie, C. F., Arnseth, H. C., Krange, I., Smørdahl, O., & Kluge, A. (2011). Designing for play-based learning of concepts in science: Technological tools for bridging school and science museum contexts. *Children, Youth, and Environments, 21*(2), 236–255.

Jordan, B., & Henderson, A. (1995). Interaction analysis: Foundations and practice. *The Journal of the Learning Sciences, 4*(1), 39–103.

Kaptelinin, V. (2005). The object of activity: Making sense of the sense-maker. *Mind, Culture, and Activity, 12*(1), 4–18.

Kaptelinin, V. (2011, January 4–7). *Designing technological support for meaning making in museum learning: An activity theoretical framework.* Paper presented at the HICSS 44,, Hawaii.

Kerosuo, H. (2003). Boundaries in health care discussions: An activity theoretical approach to the analysis of boundaries. In N. Paulsen & T. Hernes (Eds.), *Managing boundaries in organizations: Multiple perspectives* (pp. 169–187). Basingstoke: Palgrave Macmillan.

Kerosuo, H. (2006). *Boundaries in action: An activity-theoretical study of development, learning and change in health care for patients with multiple and chronic illnesses.* Helsinki: University of Helsinki, Department of Education.

Lund, A., & Rasmussen, I. (2008). The right tool for the wrong task? Match and mismatch between first and second stimulus in double stimulation. *International Journal of Computer-Supported Collaborative Learning, 3*(4).

Mantovani, G., & Riva, G. (1999). "Real" presence: How different ontologies generate different criteria for presence, telepresence and virtual presence. *Presence, 8*(5), 540–550.

Moher, T. (2006). *Embedded phenomena: Supporting science learning with classroom-sized distributed simulations.* Paper presented at the human factors in computing systems, Montreal.

Norwegian Ministry of Education and Research. (2010–2011). *St.mld. 22: Motivasjon—mestring— muligheter* [Motivation, requirement, possibilities]. Oslo: Ministry of Education and Research.

Peachey, A. (2008). The third place in second life: Real life community in a virtual world. In A. Peachey, J. Gillen, D. Livingstone, & S. Smith-Robbins (Eds.), *Researching learning in virtual worlds* (pp. 91–110). London: Springer.

Schultze, U. (2010). Embodiment and presence in virtual worlds: A review. *Journal of Information Technology, 25*, 434–449.

Smørdal, O., Slotta, J., Krange, I., Moher, T., Novellis, F., Gnoli, A., et al. (2012). Hybrid spaces for science education. In J. van Aals, K. Thompson, M. J. Jacobson, & P. Reimann (Eds.), Proceedings of the future of learning: 10th international conference of the learning sciences (ICLS 2012) (Vol. 2, Short papers, symposia, and abstracts, pp. 9–15). Sydney: International Society of the Learning Sciences.

Turner, P. (2007). The international basis of presence. In *Proceedings of the 10th international workshop on presence* (pp 127–134). Barcelona: ISPR (International Society of Presence Research). ISBN: 978-0-9792217-1-2

Turner, P., & Turner, S. (2006). Place, sense of place and presence. *Presence: Teleoperators and Virtual Environments, 15*(2), 204–217.

Turner, P., Turner, S., & Carroll, F. (2005). The tourist gaze: Towards contextualised virtual environments. In P. Turner & E. Davenport (Eds.), *Spaces, spatiality and technology* (pp. 281–297). Dordrecht: Springer.

Valsiner, J., & Van der Veer, R. (2000). *The social mind: Construction of the idea.* Cambridge: Cambridge University Press.

Vygotsky, L. S. (1978). *Mind in society: The development of higher psychological processes.* Cambridge, MA: Harvard University Press.

Chapter 4
An Examination of Student Engagement, Knowledge Creation and Expansive Learning in a Virtual World

Brian G. Burton, Barbara Martin, and Jenny Robins

Abstract This chapter examines engagement, creation of knowledge, and expansive learning of undergraduate students using a virtual world. After creating a 3D, didactic, constructivist virtual world, researchers recorded and analysed student conversations within the environment. Using Hara et al. (Instr Sci, 28:115–152, 2000) framework for student engagement and Nonaka and Takeuchi (The knowledge-creating company: how Japanese companies create the dynamics of innovation, The Oxford University Press, New York, 1995) knowledge creation theory the data were analysed. The theory of expansive learning served as a framework for exploring transformations in the environment (Engeström, Sannino, Educ Res Rev, 5(1): 1–24, 2010). Findings revealed that five forms of student engagement amplified the learning process and that a complete knowledge spiral occurred emphasising the four modes of knowledge conversion and hinting at elements of expansive learning (Engeström, Sannino, Educ Res Rev, 5(1):1–24, 2010) occurring. Though limited in time and scope, results further suggest that a highly engaged community of learners with the ability to solve problems critically was created within the 3D virtual world.

B.G. Burton (✉)
Digital Entertainment and Information Technology,
Abilene Christian University, Abilene, TX, USA
e-mail: drburton@burtonsmediagroup.com

B. Martin
Educational Administration Department, University of Central Missouri,
Warrensburg, MO, USA

J. Robins
Library and Information Science in the College of Education,
University of Central Missouri, Warrensburg, MO, USA

M. Childs and A. Peachey (eds.), *Understanding Learning in Virtual Worlds*,
Human–Computer Interaction Series, DOI 10.1007/978-1-4471-5370-2_4,
© Springer-Verlag London 2013

4.1   Introduction

Dalgarno (2002, p 1) argued, "Three dimensional (3D) environments have the potential to harness technological developments and facilitate new levels of learner-learner and learner-computer interaction". Due to improvements in technology and the utilisation of 3D environments on a successful commercial basis (Blizzard 2010), there has been renewed interest in the utilisation of 3D environments as learning tools. 3D immersive virtual worlds allow learners to 'touch' and manipulate items in a virtual universe. Virtual Worlds come with a myriad of features; though, normally most provide three main elements: the illusion of 3D space, avatars that serve as the visual representation of users, and an interactive chat or voice environment for users to communicate with one another (Dickey 2005). Salzman et al. (1999) made a case for the use of immersive virtual reality (VR) for the teaching of complex or abstract concepts: Consequently, these 3D thematic environments were created "with the objective of providing a space where the users can interact" (Kirner et al. 2001, p 62). Created as cyber cafés, university classrooms, chat rooms, and the like, these virtual worlds often become places where students are afforded opportunities to post suggestions, useful resources, and technical advice (Grubb and Hines 2000). These postings and interactions serve as knowledge capital that may contribute to a knowledge spiral within the learning environment (Nonaka and Takeuchi 1995; Nonaka 1991).

Many researchers have undertaken projects to investigate aspects of virtual worlds. Some research has focused on the technical aspects of collaboration such as providing voice with lip-sync (DiPaola and Collins 2003), others have focused on a specific discipline such as mathematics (Elliott and Bruckman 2002) or science (Dede et al. 2004) and others have examined collaboration within a virtual world (Burton and Martin 2010). With this increased interest in 3D environments and a desire to utilise the popularity of such environments for the education of the millennial generation (Dede 2005), the evaluation of such environments for pedagogical purposes is appropriate. This case study was conducted to add to the body of research exploring how a dialectic constructivist virtual world can be used to create a learning environment that encourages student creation of knowledge. This dialectic constructivist virtual world is an online virtual world based in a three-dimensional graphical space that resides on a computer server(s) connected to the Internet, accessed via three-dimensional graphical representations of the users (avatars) (Grant and Huang 2010, p 4). The following overarching research question guided this inquiry:

> Does a dialectic constructivist virtual world contain the essential affordances to support student learning when analysed through the lenses of student engagement, knowledge creation, and expansive learning theory?

4.2   Conceptual Underpinnings

Three conceptual frameworks guided the study: student engagement, knowledge creation theory, and expansive learning theory. Student engagement (Hara et al. 2000) was used to explore how students are interacting using reasoning in a virtual world. Knowledge creation theory (Nonaka and Takeuchi 1995; Nonaka 1991) was employed by the researchers to identify which of the four modes of knowledge conversion were used in a virtual world. Expansive learning theory, which is traditionally used to explain how activities in physical communities evolve (Engeström 2009), provided insight into how a community of learners in an immersive, virtual world developed processes for problem solving.

4.2.1 Student Engagement

Bonk et al. (2006, p 556), when surveying higher education faculty who had taught online, found, "Most respondents saw the potential of the web in the coming years as a tool for virtual teaming or collaboration, critical thinking, and enhanced student engagement", while Henri (1992) identified five dimensions that facilitate assessment of discourses online; the participative, social, interactive, cognitive, and meta-cognitive. In Henri's system reasoning, critical thought, and self-awareness are indicators of the cognitive and metacognitive dimensions. However, since the indicators for each of these five dimensions were not clearly delineated by Henri in her work, the coding system used by Hara et al. (*op cit*) informed the indicators for analysis of student engagement in this inquiry. Five reasoning skills form the basis of the framework used by Hara et al. The first is elementary clarification with indicators such as the ability to identify relevant elements and to reformulate a problem by asking pertinent questions. In-depth clarification, the second cognitive skill, occurs when the participant can define terms, identify assumptions, and establish referential criteria while seeking specialised information and ultimately summarising that information. Inferencing, the third skill, evolves when the participant draws conclusions, makes generalisation, and formulates a proposition. Fourth, judgment occurs when the individual ascertains the relevance of the solutions or opinions and makes a value judgment as to agreement or not. Finally the ability to apply strategies is demonstrated when a participant makes a decision that reflects appreciation, evaluation, and even criticism of the situation. The Hara et al. classification of cognitive skills was used during the analysis of this inquiry, along with knowledge creation and expansive learning theory.

4.2.2 Knowledge Creation

Baumard (1999, p 2) called the knowledge creation process "visible and invisible, tangible and intangible, stable and unstable". Much of the research on organisational knowledge creation has revolved around Nonaka and Takeuchi's (1995) *The Knowledge Creating Company.* Nonaka and Takeuchi (ibid., p 56) stated in a simplified overview, "When organizations innovate, they actually create new knowledge and information from the inside out, in order to redefine both problems and solutions and, in the process, to re-create their environment". Nonaka (1991, p 97) postulated that "creating new knowledge is not simply a matter of 'processing' objective information. Rather it depends on tapping the tacit and often highly subjective insights and intuitions". In order to have an environment that creates new knowledge, individuals must be given time and processes by which to share tacit knowledge. Nonaka and Takeuchi (*op cit*, p 61) have identified this process as the four modes of knowledge conversion. This knowledge conversion is essentially the "interaction between tacit and explicit knowledge" and consist of socialisation, externalisation, internalisation, and combination. In effect, the modes signify a process that begins with shared mental models (Senge 1990) and spirals through different conversions to become knowledge that is explicitly stated and used in everyday practices. Socialisation occurs through the transmission of tacit knowledge as when an individual learns something new through observation, imitation, and practice (Nonaka, *op cit*, p 99). However, socialisation is limiting because no new insights to the learning have occurred because the learning has not become explicit. Conversely, an individual in a learning environment can collect information from everyone (explicit) and from that collective information create new information (explicit) resulting in externalisation of knowledge. The person has in essence synthesised the information but has not created new knowledge.

However, when tacit and explicit knowledge interact, powerful learning can occur. Learners can go beyond just developing an answer for a problem from external knowledge and create innovative ways to solve challenges through the interaction of tacit knowledge and the explicit knowledge of others. This results in the knowledge conversion mode that Nonaka (*op cit*, p 99) labelled internalisation. After this explicit learning has occurred it will then be shared throughout the learning environment, explicit to tacit, and explicit to explicit. Other learners will begin to utilise the new and innovative learning through the knowledge conversion mode referred to as combination. The other learners use the new learning in such a fashion that it becomes a part of themselves and ultimately of the total learning environment. Consequently, as argued by Nonaka and Takeuchi, new knowledge must first begin with the individual's knowledge, then be transformed into group knowledge when certain knowledge creation modes occur (Nonaka). Knowledge creation was the second conceptual framework applied to the data set, followed by expansive learning theory.

4.2.3   Expansive Learning Theory

While Nonaka and Takeuchi's framework of cyclic knowledge creation was one of the learning theories we initially used to analyse the learning process in our virtual world, one of the crucial challenges with the model is the assumption that the instructor provides the project or learning task for knowledge creation. In other words, what is to be learned and created is arguably a management decision that is outside the bounds of a collective student learning process (Engeström 1999). This assumption ultimately leads to a model in which the learning consists of non-conflict interactions, or as Nonaka and Takeuchi (*op cit*, p 45) noted, the creation of 'sympathised knowledge.' Conversely, Ahonen et al. (2000, p 283) argued knowledge creation should be embedded and constructed in collective practices by the learners.

Therefore, we argue that along with the knowledge spiral of Nonaka and Takeuchi, the creation of knowledge and student engagement in a virtual world should be examined through understanding gained from expansive learning theory (Engeström 1987, 2007). The process of expansive learning involves activities that we suggest can be mirrored by students in a 3-D virtual world to create knowledge and engage in learning in new and unpredictable ways. The theory of expansive learning focuses on knowledge building processes of learners whom, when encountering, challenging, and questioning issues, move forward as a community (Engeström 2001). This state of need in an activity, referred to as a contradiction, is the beginning of an expansive learning cycle. Students, by questioning the task given to them in a learning environment, discover contradictions. These contradictions can become explicit only through discussing double binds in an activity. Engeström (1987, p 165) argued that double binds experienced by students can act as agents of change. In effective actions of expansive learning, participants analyse the contradictions and tensions inherent in the learning and create (or model) new solutions for the task or problem. Following the analysing and modelling are the examination and the testing of the new model, which can result in modifications and enhancement of the task. During the performance of the task, contradictions between the old and new ways of thinking about a task occur, followed by a reflection that allows stabilisation and ultimately an evaluation of the problem solving process or learning (Engeström 2007). After evaluation, the generalisation of the new learning or skill takes place. This generalisation can create contradictions between the new tasks, for example between problem one and problem two in the virtual world (Engeström and Sannino 2010, p 8). Quintessentially, the process of expansive learning involves the inquiring and analysing of an existing problem when a stable solution is not possible. In other words, we mean the ability of the students in the virtual environment, when given the problems (activity) they will be able to interpret and expand the definition of the focus or goal of the problem or activity respond to it in increasingly enriching ways.

Engeström and Sannino further posited that the expansive learning theory expands analyses up and down, outward and inward. They noted by moving up and outward, the theory applies to interconnected activity systems (all of the processes involved within a task or problem) with other learning taking place within the environment. However, the theory by moving down and inward, deals with the object of the individual learner. This process of expansive learning represents the sequence of shared learning, during which a new task is created when learners mobilise the existing social and cultural resources to resolve contradictions (Engeström 2007). Expansion is the metaphor that the theory relies on when explaining the learners' erudition of something that is not yet there in the learning environment (Engeström and Sannino, *op cit*, p 2). The learners construct a new object and concept for the collective activity and implement this new object and concept in practice.

Since the research using these three conceptualisations within virtual worlds is limited in scope, our research was conducted to expand upon current understanding. Specifically, in this case study, the 3D virtual world utilising a dialectic constructivist approach was constructed. Next, a project composed of several problems was given to the learners, which provided the organised scaffolding for learning and the opportunity for the learner to create knowledge with other learners to further expand their collective learning.

4.3 Methodology

The design selected for the study was the collective case study approach (Creswell 2007), which allowed the researcher to explore in-depth "how individuals experience and interact with their social world [and] the meaning it has for them" (Merriam and Associates 2002, p 4). This collective case study approach allowed researchers to explore multiple cases of students involved in the virtual world and processes that were "bounded by time and activity" (Creswell 2003, p 15). Relevant themes were then developed from the collection of the emergent data. The researcher is the primary instrument in qualitative data collection (Merriam 1998), including the identification of the sample as well as the modes of qualitative data collection to be employed.

4.3.1 Population and Sample

The purposeful sample of this case study consisted of 28 college students at a small, public college in the Midwest and a small private college in the south-central area of the United States enrolled in computer game programming courses. Both sets of students were in courses designed to teach the fundamentals of game design and development. 75 % of the students were male and 10 % were students of colour. Drawn from a population of 1,600 students attending an open-admission 2-year campus and 4,800 students attending a private, religiously-oriented campus, these 28 students were purposefully selected by their course enrolment. Purposeful sampling was used so that specific subjects were selected to "best help the researcher understand the problem and the research question" (Merriam 1998, p 185). All of the students within the class were given an informed consent letter noting that their grade for the classes would not be affected by their participation in the inquiry and they could withdraw with no penalty at any time. All of the students in the courses consented to participate and 10 % volunteered to be interviewed. In addition, permission from the IRB boards for both institutions was sought and received prior to any data collection.

Within the population of the public campus comprising 1,660 students, 65 % are female, 35 % are male, 47 % are full-time, and 55 % are traditional college students. The population of the private campus comprised 4,800 students, 55 % are female, 45 % are male, 86 % are full-time, and 89 % are traditional college students. While students at the public college typically considered minority are few in number (4 %), the students attending this university are economically and educationally disadvantaged (89 % receive financial aid, 74 % require one or more developmental education course). The private college had a higher diversity of enrolment with 21 % minority. Thus, the sample was not a representative sample of the total population in the two school settings. The 28 students were divided between the public and private institutions with 15 from the public institution and 13 from the private.

4.3.2 Data Collection

Two methods of data collection were used during the course of this research. First, as a part of this research we created a dialectic constructivist virtual world to see if student engagement, knowledge creation, and learning expansion occurred within such an environment. Specifically, the *Torque Game Engine* produced by *Garage Games* was modified to create an environment that enabled learners to interact in a dialectical constructivist environment that facilitated student engagement (Hara, Bonk and Angeli, *op cit*), knowledge creation (Nonaka and Takeuchi, *op cit*) and expansive learning (Engeström and Sannino, *op cit*). Since the target group of participants for this study was students enrolled in computer programming courses, an intended outcome of this project was to improve their programming skills and give them experience in programming and working with a 3D game engine. To that end, the virtual world was created and equipped with male and female avatars, several 3D tank models to which the participants would eventually apply basic artificial intelligence, and a virtual world in which the participants could interact with one another. Additional kiosk stations were placed in the environment to provide directions and clues to the participants as they went about solving the problems.

Participants created their own account, which enabled them to connect to the chat database. After login, the virtual world enabled the participant to then connect to a Master Game Server, which provided a link to the hosted game. All chat messages were saved on the Chat Database and forwarded to all active participants through the hosted game along with student interaction and dialogue, which was recorded by the researchers.

Additional data were collected with a survey and interviews. This survey was distributed after the completion of the project to participants. The survey provided Likert type scale and open-ended questions. Open-ended interviews were also conducted with 10 % of the participants. The goal of these interviews was to provide rich, thick, descriptions of the participants experience during the course of the research.

4.3.3   Data Analysis

The data collected were analysed through three different filters. Utilising the framework proposed by Hara et al. (*op cit*, p 125), student interaction recorded in the 3D virtual world was first categorised into five classifications as follows:

1. Elementary clarification – observation and identification of a problem and its elements. This includes identification of linkages to gain a basic understanding of the problem.
2. In-depth clarification – gaining an understanding of the problem so that it "sheds light on the values, beliefs, and assumptions which underlie the statement of the problem".
3. Inferencing – Use of induction and deduction in the analysis of the problem.
4. Judgment – Making a decision.
5. Application of strategies – "proposing coordinated actions for the application of a solution".

Next, the dialogue between the students was analysed using the four modes of knowledge conversion of socialisation, externalisation, internalisation, and combination. Socialisation essentially occurs when tacit is shared with tacit or when an individual learns some new through observation, imitation, and practice (Nonaka, *op cit*, p 99). Externalisation occurs when an individual collects information from everyone (explicit) and from that; collective information creates new information (explicit). Internalisation occurs when a learner creates an innovative way to solve the challenge. After this explicit learning has occurred it will then be shared throughout the learning environment, explicit to tacit, and other learners will begin to utilise this new and innovative learning through the knowledge conversion mode referred to as combination.

The last analyses occurred using the theory of expansive learning, focusing on any interactions or dialogue of participants that were challenging, questioning, and expanding on issues, especially if done from a collective process (Engeström 2001). We looked for a state of need expressed by the learners through their questioning with the questioning resulting in new solutions. We further looked for learners' creation of new models and the testing of these models to modify or enhance the task. In addition, contradictions of the old and new learning were examined and self reflections were noted. Particular attention was paid to actions by the learners that resulted in expansion of problem solving as Engeström and Sannino (*op cit*, p 2) noted occurred up and down, and outward and inward. In other words, did the learners construct a new object and concept for the collective activity, and implement this new object and concept in practice?

Bogdan and Biklen (1998) noted that data analysis must involve working with, organising, and breaking data into manageable units. The process of coding, or identifying categories, classifications, and themes derived from the participants of the study was useful in the organising of the data and resulted from the use of the three conceptualisations: student engagement (Hara, Bonk, and Angeli, *op cit*);

knowledge creation (Nonaka and Takeuchi, *op cit*); and expansive learning (Engeström and Sannino, *op cit*). This coding was followed by axial coding to aid in making comparisons and connections between and among the identified themes. The final step was summarising (Thomas and Brubaker 2000) designed to promote synthesis of the data, and identification of patterns.

4.4 Discussion of Findings

The researchers examined the student engagement by utilising qualitative data gathered from the chat records of the virtual world. The chats captured from the virtual world provided a rich texture of collaborative data. Of the 682 conversations that occurred during the 2 weeks of data gathering, a majority (62.6 %) were found to be collaborative in nature (see Table 4.1).

Again using the data from the virtual world, the researchers analysed the conversation data through the framework of Nonaka and Takeuchi's (*op cit*) knowledge spiral. The beginning of the knowledge spiral must show the transference of tacit knowledge to explicit knowledge, passing through the four modes of knowledge

Table 4.1 Classifications of conversations

Classification	Conversations
Elementary clarification	201
In-depth clarification	92
Inferencing	35
Judgment	37
Application	62

Note: 174 off topic conversations occurred; 67 incidents of greetings (salutations), and 14 incidents labelled flaming. Classifications determined by Hara et al. (*op cit*) framework. N=682 Initially, the majority of conversations was off-topic or focused on learning the environment, however, participants were able to easily move and communicate within the virtual world (see Fig. 4.1). After approximately two and a half (2.5) hours of working inside the virtual world, there was a dramatic drop in off-topic conversation. At this same point, there was a noticeable change toward student engagements through conversations that were seeking in-depth clarification and application. From the interviews, several comments were made concerning the initial general engagement: As one student said, "Most of it was us helping each other understand the mechanisms of the environment, figuring out what was tied to what." Another student found that the student engagement through dialogue allowed for the "clarification of goals, discussion of problems, fun banter, answered questions that others raised, and some arguments when misunderstandings arose." These conversations also could be interpreted through the lens of expansive theory, in which the students were not only clarifying the activity but also through conversations expanding beyond the initial scope of the problems

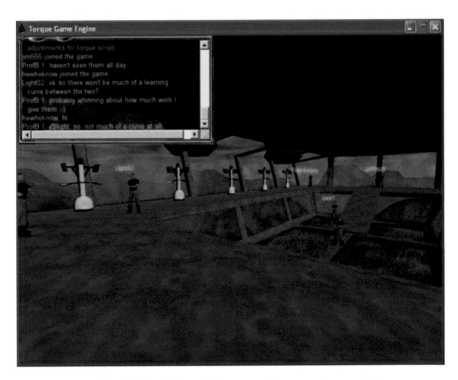

Fig. 4.1 The virtual world allowed for participants to easily move and communicate

conversion: socialisation, externalisation, combination, and internalisation. This process became evident from the chat records recorded in the virtual world. One example of the Knowledge Spiral is illustrated from the following data set:

Student_1: "The Prof says he switched to code on the CLIENT side only for switching between characters"

Student_2: "Yeah but it is set up differently than the tank code"

Student_2: "he is calling to two different cs files instead of one"

Student_1: "Whatever he switched turned off the animations, and I'm not sure the server would EVER see the Ava model..."

Student_1: "...if the server side code doesn't have the new selection methods"

Student_2: "let s throw in blue man to see if the code is defaulting to the player.css"

Student_3: "hey is the problem of not showing the animations and not loading av in the aiplay.cs?"

Student_3: "OMG i got the animations to work..."

Student_3: "all problems are in the aiPlayer.cs"

Student_2: "That s why the[y] have to be in the same file"

Student_1: "No[w] what?"

Student_3: "w[ait] ill change to adam"

Student_3: "ok thats weird"

Student_2: "See you broke it:)"

Student_3: "Whatever the server host chooses gets cast to all other players"

Student_1: "Ava s animations worked for servers AND clients". Adams s animation ONLY works on the Server.

Student_3: "the call backs need to be uncommented and the male needs to be taken out of the aiplayer.cs file"

In this sample of conversations selected by the researchers, the students completed all four of the modes of knowledge conversion: socialisation, externalisation, combination, and internalisation. During the socialisation process, tacit knowledge is shared with other students. From the data, one can see the students start out by sharing what they have learned by experimentation and from others. In Statement 1 and 2 of the conversation, Student_1 and Student_2 discuss what they have learned thus far from others and observation inside the virtual world. This socialisation process ensures that they are both at the same starting point as they prepare to address the avatar and animation problems in the learning environment.

In the externalisation conversion of tacit to explicit, a hypothesis is proposed as to where the problem is located. Statements 3 through 7 represent this move from tacit to explicit. Student_2 notes to Student_1 that two data files are being accessed in the computer program instead of just one, which they had seen in another example. Student_1 makes a hypothesis that this might be the cause of the animation problems. Student_2 (in statement 6) proposes a method of checking to see if this might solve the problem. At this point, Student_3 in statement 7 notes that the problem being discussed seems to be originating from one data file, beginning the transfer to the combination mode.

As the students move into the combination mode, students create a structure for the problem and attach it to one location with the program files. Statements 8 through 14 show the development of the structure and application of the hypothesis developed in the externalisation process. Student_3 initially believes he has solved the problem by making a change to the data files. As he further applies the hypothesis it creates other visual problems within the virtual world, causing Student_2 to tell him, in good-natured fun, that he just broke the system.

During the final internalisation phase of the Knowledge Spiral, the students take what they have learned thus far and apply it. In statements 15 through 17, the three students discuss what was done to create the differences in the virtual world and what files were edited. This creates new observations about the problems that they are addressing, which starts a new cycle of the Knowledge Spiral. Thus the data reveals that the virtual world provides and supports opportunities for the students to practice Nonaka and Takeuchi's (*op cit*, p 69) Knowledge Spiral, which they refer to as "learning by doing". While the students do not completely resolve the problem in this conversation, it does form the bases of future conversations of tacit to explicit knowledge creation that eventually leads to a proposed solution.

Again looking at the sample of conversations using the expansive learning theory, the students first established a state of need, when one student noted (Student_1)

"The Prof says he switched to code on the CLIENT side only for switching between characters" and another responds (Student_2): "Yeah but it is set up differently than the tank code. He is calling to two different cs files instead of one." This line of discussion continues until another student poses a question (Student_3) "Hey is the problem of not showing the animations and not loading av in the aiplay.cs?" This questioning relates to the crucial contradictions of the activity that are apparent to the students in the learning environment. The students have not been given the tools to resolve them, but must rely on each other to formulate solutions. Following the question, the students discuss the issues [tensions] intrinsic in the task and looked for new solutions to the problem when Student_2 noted, "Let s throw in blue man to see if the code is defaulting to the player.css." This was followed by the testing of the new model and resulted in enhancement of the task. Ultimately, the process of expansive learning involves the inquiring and analysing of an existing problem as well as implementing this new object and concept in practice (Engeström and Sannino *op cit*). This was demonstrated when Student_1 stated, "Ava s animations worked for servers AND clients. Adams s animation ONLY works on the Server." The learners successfully discovered and repurposed available resources. This opens possibilities for the creation of new artefacts in the environment that can, in turn, mediate learners' activity. An affordance of 3D immersive virtual worlds is that they not only mimic real life, with its mediating artefacts, rules, community, and divisions or labour, they allow for new possibilities for human interaction and creativity.

4.5 Discussion

In this inquiry, one key finding was, individually, students assumed a myriad of roles to solve the problems. Some began as the leader, then switched to the encourager then perhaps back to the leader, etc. Furthermore, the majority of the students appeared to engage in the content and the context of the learning using the entire dimensions of reasoning skills as postulated by Hara et al.'s (*op cit*) framework. Also according to Hara et al. the frequency of the social cues might be an indicator of the level of learner engagement on the learning task. As one can see from the data set, the frequency of the social cues were high throughout these courses as the students continued to solve the problems, even as the student messages became less formal perhaps due to students feeling success collectively in solving the learning tasks or perhaps they were just more comfortable with each other (Kang 1998).

Consequently, in studies comparing face-to-face to computer-mediated communication (Walther 1996), it has been reported that students do develop social relationships similar to those in a face-to-face class but generally it takes longer. However, the data from this inquiry found that students after just a short time frame settled into an engagement that was focused on solving the problem(s) yet went outside the arena of the virtual world to have phone conversations and hold discussions via emails. One participant noted that "Outside of the [virtual world], more productive communication occurred via text messaging and e-mail chat programs... I received a number of text messages during dinner!" Thus, it can be concluded that a 3D virtual learning environment can enhance the reasoning skills of the participant, if designed in such a fashion that a significant amount of engagement between the participants is provided to resolve the issue. The design of the pedagogy of the virtual world is essential to these myriad applications of reasoning skills.

To assess the extent of knowledge creation between the learners, Nonaka and Takeuchi's (*op cit*) knowledge creation theory was utilised. Those researchers theorised that the active creation of knowledge progresses through four phases, and that while not every instance of socially constructed knowledge may move spirally through each successive phase equally, they are nonetheless consistent with much of the literature related to constructivist knowledge creation. As Wulff et al. (2000, p 150), noted, the instructor can aid the development of collaboration within a constructivist approach by "redistribut[ing] learning control and power by supporting and/or developing interaction-exchange formats, such as synchronous and asynchronous chat sites and display rooms to cultivate social and individual presence". This non-foundational view of learning allows students to learn in a collaborative fashion, rather than with the traditional foundational view in which knowledge is disseminated from the teacher (Bruffee 1999). This was the focus for the creation of this 3D learning environment. The effective learning through constructivism, in which the students attempted to construct meaning in the virtual world around them, occurred in the environment allowing for the creation of knowledge for the learner (Fosnot 1996).

Consequently, a second key finding from this inquiry is that a well-constructed 3D virtual world should be designed around a knowledge creation focus based on expansive learning theory in order to be effective. Within this knowledge creation focus, new knowledge can be categorised and contextualised in an effort to make it accessible and of value to the widest range of students. Moreover, by allowing students to expand their learning and create new artefacts, solutions, or even problems within the learning environment, more meaningful learning happens. Thus it can be concluded some of the design will incorporate the "soft" knowledge of how to engage the students throughout the course in a meaningful, critical thinking process, while allowing students to reflect and discuss in such a way that a knowledge creation spiral is established that reflects the four dimensions, and the students' learning is expanded to incorporate new learning and solutions. Of course just as valuable is the new "hard" knowledge that results in the actual educational tools one uses to create the virtual world (see Fig. 4.2).

4.6 Implications for Practice

The implications for practice focus almost entirely on how the teacher designs the 3D, immersive virtual world, first understandings that dialogue, followed by collective reflection, must exist that allows students to venture beyond the task assigned

Fig. 4.2 The role of
knowledge creation and
expansive learning in virtual
worlds

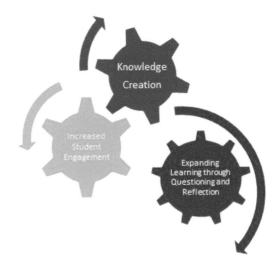

by the instructor and create their own problems and solutions (see Fig. 4.2). The virtual world must be designed to allow the learner's thinking to be observable, and learners must be allowed to engage in questioning and reflection in different phases of problem completion. Designers should include a model of the process of reflection, by providing examples of experts' thinking. Moreover, multiple perspectives can become apparent by providing ample opportunities for collaboration through dialogue and reflection.

Secondly, time and space for student engagement must be in the forefront of design. Designers must create group problem based projects that create contradictions that give students extra motivation to work with others in the class and share ideas. In online contexts, instructors can optimise interaction between learner-instructor (as represented by instructions, explanations, and available artefacts), learner-learner, and learner-content through effective modes of communication (Chen and Willits 1999; Jung 2000). Dialogue is facilitated when it involves an evaluation of the opportunities for exchanges as well as an analysis of the quality of the dialogue that occurs (McBrien et al. 2009).

Next, the designer of the virtual world can provide networking opportunities and the linkage of explicit knowledge. To encourage knowledge sharing and creation in an online or virtual world based course, the instructor helps students develop trust by allowing them to participate in activities that build on personal, social contact. Within the virtual world, the conversation can become collective if there is sufficient time for exchanging ideas. The instructor can establish incentives for those who share their knowledge, allowing capacity building leading to enhanced creative thinking. Finally, the instructor encourages students to admit knowledge gaps and problem failures in order to promote more risk taking within the environment (Fig. 4.3).

Fig. 4.3 The role of virtual
world designer

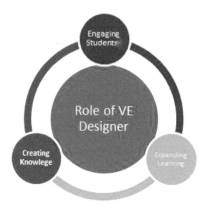

4.6.1   Future Directions for Research

With collaboration now being effectively established within virtual worlds, many
areas remain to be researched regarding impact upon student learning outcomes.
What impact does being able to select and design the *avatar* have upon learning
outcomes? If a student is given an avatar and told that the avatar is very good in a
subject that the student struggles, is learning impacted? Is cheating more or less
prevalent, or even possible, in a virtual world? An additional field of research could
deal with the development of virtual real estate, including kiosks. With online
environments such as *Second Life*, the examination of how such environments
will impact learning is essential to examine. Of course, more research into the area
of student engagement, knowledge creation, and expansive learning theory within a
virtual world is needed.

4.7   Conclusion

Through the use of a collective case study model, a virtual world utilising a dialectic
constructivist approach was constructed and examined in this chapter. While there
has been much written on student engagement, knowledge creation and expansive
learning theory, little research has examined the use of all three constructs in a virtual
world, thus demonstrating the need for such a study. This inquiry established the
potential of using an effectively designed virtual world by designing virtual learning
environments grounded in conceptual frameworks centred on engagement, knowledge creation, and collective reflection allowing students to expand beyond the problems presented in the virtual environment. Education systems are increasingly faced
with a continuous challenge to provide more services and better inclusive educational opportunities to those whom they serve. As technology continues to advance,

it can serve as a catalyst to contribute sound educational experiences in a myriad of settings. Within this chapter, the focus has been to examine three aspects of the learning process, student engagement, knowledge creation, and expansive learning theory within a virtual world. By utilising each authors' construct: Hara et al. (*op cit*), student engagement; Nonaka and Takeuchi (*op cit*), knowledge creation; Engeström and Sannino (*op cit*), expansive learning theory we have made a compelling argument that it is through conversation, interactions, collective reflection that effective learning takes place. Consequently, it is essential that the virtual world be designed to support student learning thoughtfully, effectively, and intentionally.

References

Ahonen, H., Engeström, Y., & Virkkunen, J. (2000). Knowledge management the second generation: Creating competencies within and between work communities in the competence laboratory. In Y. Malhotra (Ed.), *Knowledge management and virtual organizations*. Hershey/London: Idea Group Publishing.

Baumard, P. (1999). *Tacit knowledge in organizations*. London: Sage.

Blizzard. (2010). *World of warcraft*. Retrieved from http://us.blizzard.com/en-us/company/. December 15 2010.

Bogdan, R. C., & Biklen, S. K. (Eds.). (1998). *Qualitative research for education: An introduction to theory and methods* (3rd ed.). Needham Heights: Allyn Bacon.

Bonk, C. J., Kim, K. J., & Zeng, T. (2006). Future directions of blended learning in higher education and workplace learning settings. In C. J. Bonk & C. R. Graham (Eds.), *Handbook of blended learning: Global perspectives, local designs* (pp. 550–567). San Francisco: Pfeiffer Publishing.

Bruffee, K. A. (1999). *Collaborative learning: Higher education, interdependence, and the authority of knowledge* (2nd ed.). Baltimore: Johns Hopkins University Press.

Burton, B., & Martin, B. N. (2010). Learning in virtual environments: Collaboration and knowledge spirals. *Journal of Educational Computing Research, 43*(2), 259–273.

Chen, Y.-J., & Willits, F. K. (1999). Dimensions of educational transactions in a videoconferencing learning environment. *The American Journal of Distance Education, 13*(1), 45–59.

Creswell, J. (2003). *Research design: Qualitative, quantitative, and mixed methods approaches* (2nd ed.). Thousand Oaks: SAGE Publications.

Creswell, J. (2007). *Qualitative inquiry and research design: Choosing among five approaches* (2nd ed.). Thousand Oaks: SAGE Publications.

Dalgarno, B. (2002). The potential of 3D virtual learning environments: A constructivist analysis. *E-Journal of Instructional Science and Technology, 5*(2). Retrieved from http://www.usq.edu.au/electpub/e-jist/docs/Vol5_No2/dalgarno_frame.html

Dede, C. (2005). Planning for neomillinnial learning styles. *Educause Quarterly, 1*, 7–12.

Dede, C., Nelson, B., Ketelhut, D. J., Clarke, J., & Bowman, C. (2004). Design-based research strategies for studying situated learning in a multi-user virtual environment. In *Proceedings of the sixth international conference on the learning sciences* (pp. 158–165). Mahweh: Lawrence Erlbaum. Retrieved from http://muve.gse.harvard.edu/muvees2003/documents/dedeICLS04.pdf

Dickey, M. (2005). Brave new (interactive) worlds: A review of the design affordances and constraints of two 3D virtual worlds as interactive learning environments. *Interactive Learning Environments, 13*(1), 121–137.

DiPaola, S., & Collins, D. (2003, July 27–31). A social metaphor-based 3D virtual environment. In *ACM SIGGRAPH 2003 educators program, San Diego, CA, USA* (pp. 1–2). New York: ACM.

Elliott, J., & Bruckman, A. (2002, June 25–28). Design of a 3D interactive math learning environment. In *Proceedings of the 4th conference on designing interactive systems: Processes, practices, methods, and techniques, London, England UK* (pp. 64–74). New York: ACM.

Engeström, Y. (1987). *Learning by expanding. An activity theoretical approach to developmental research.* Helsinki: Orienta konsultit.

Engeström, Y. (1999). Activity theory and individual and social transformation. In Y. Engeström (Ed.), *Perspectives on activity theory* (pp. 19–38). Cambridge: Cambridge University Press.

Engeström, Y. (2001). Expansive learning at work: Toward an activity theoretical reconceptualization. *Journal of Education and Work, 14*(1), 133–156.

Engeström, Y. (2007). Putting Vygotsky to work: The change laboratory as an application of double stimulation. In H. Daniels, M. Cole, & J. Wertsch (Eds.), *The Cambridge companion to Vygotsky*. Cambridge: Cambridge University Press.

Engeström, Y. (2009). From learning environments and implementation to activity systems and expansive learning. *An International Journal of Human Activity Theory, 2*, 17–33.

Engeström, Y., & Sannino, A. (2010). Studies of expansive learning: Foundations, findings and future challenges. *Educational Research Review, 5*(1), 1–24.

Fosnot, C. T. (1996). Constructivism: A psychological theory of learning. In C. T. Fosnot (Ed.), *Constructivism: Theory, perspectives and practice* (pp. 8–33). New York: Teachers College Press.

Grant, S., & Huang, H. (2010). The integration of an online 3D virtual learning environment into formal classroom-based undergraduate Chinese language and culture curriculum. *Journal of Technology and Chinese Language Teaching, 1*(1), 2–13.

Grubb, A., & Hines, M. (2000). Tearing down barriers and building communities: Pedagogical strategies for web-based environment. In R. Cole (Ed.), *Issues in web-based pedagogy* (pp. 365–380). Westport: Greenwood Press.

Hara, N., Bonk, C. J., & Angeli, C. (2000). Content analysis of online discussion in an applied educational psychology course. *Instructional Science, 28*, 115–152.

Henri, F. (1992). Computer conferencing and content analysis. In A. R. Kaye (Ed.), *Collaborative learning through computer conferencing: The Najaden papers* (pp. 116–136). Berlin: Springer.

Jung, I. (2000). Internet-based distance education: Annotated bibliography. *Educational Technology International, 2*(1), 139–171.

Kang, I. (1998). The use of computer-mediated communication: Electronic collaboration and interactivity. In C. J. Bonk & K. S. King (Eds.), *Electronic collaborators: Learner-centered technologies for literacy, apprenticeship, and discourse* (pp. 315–337). Mahwah: Erlbaum.

Kirner, T. G., Kirner, C., Kawamoto, A. L., Cantão, J., Pinto, A., & Wazlawick, R. S. (2001, February 19–22). Development of a collaborative virtual environment for educational applications. In *Proceedings of the sixth international conference on 3D Web technologies (pp. 61–68) Paderborn, Germany* (pp. 64–74). New York: ACM.

McBrien, J. L., Jones, P., & Cheng, R. (2009). Virtual spaces: Employing a synchronous online classroom to facilitate student engagement in online learning. *The International Review of Research in Open and Distance Learning, 10*(3), 5–10.

Merriam, S. B. (1998). *Qualitative research and case study applications in education.* San Francisco: Jossey-Bass Publishers.

Merriam, S. B., & Associates. (2002). *Qualitative research in practice: Examples for discussion and analysis.* San Francisco: Jossey-Bass.

Nonaka, I. (1991, November/December). The knowledge-creating company. *Harvard Business Review*, pp. 96–104.

Nonaka, I., & Takeuchi, H. (1995). *The knowledge-creating company: How Japanese companies create the dynamics of innovation.* New York: The Oxford University Press.

Salzman, M. C., Dede, C., Loftin, R. B., & Chen, J. (1999). The design and evaluation of virtual reality-based learning environments. *Presence.* Retrieved from http://www.virtual.gmu.edu/ss_pdf/presence.pdf

Senge, P. M. (1990). *The fifth discipline: The art and practice of the learning organization.* New York: Doubleday/Currency.

Thomas, R. M., & Brubaker, D. L. (2000). *Theses and dissertations: A guide to planning, research, and writing*. Westport: Bergin Garvey.

Walther, J. (1996). Computer-mediated communication: Impersonal, interpersonal, and hyperpersonal interaction. *Communication Research, 23*(1), 3–43.

Wulff, S., Hanor, J., & Bulik, R. J. (2000). The roles and interrelationships of presence, reflection, and self-directed learning in effective world wide web-based pedagogy. In R. Cole (Ed.), *Issues in web-based pedagogy* (pp. 143–160). Westport: Greenwood Press.

Chapter 5
The Strength of Cohesive Ties: Discursive Construction of an Online Learning Community

Rebecca Ferguson, Julia Gillen, Anna Peachey, and Peter Twining

Abstract Learning takes place in a social context, shaping and shaped by discourses. In online projects such as the *Schome Park Programme*, these discourses are material-semiotic practices that make use of writing and other manifestations of digital literacies. Discourses include traceable patterns with linguistic features of distinctive forms and functions. Employing a sociocultural perspective of discourse as mediated interaction (Scollon, Mediated discourse as social interaction: a study of news discourse. Longman, London/New York, 1998), we identify use of register and cohesive ties as salient to the practices of learning communities. The study reported here focuses on two groups of teenagers, one a formal learning community based in the USA, the other a larger, online, informal learning community based in the UK. The groups were originally only weakly tied within a network, but aimed to work together within the virtual world environment, despite some different aims. Working with McMillan's (J Community Psychol, 24(4):315–325, 1996) concept of community as characterised by spirit, authority, trade and art, we illustrate how misalignments in register and problems with cohesive ties can be associated with difficulties in the cooperative learning enterprise and we also make recommendations for future practice.

R. Ferguson (✉)
Institute of Educational Technology, The Open University, Milton Keynes, UK
e-mail: rebecca.ferguson@open.ac.uk

J. Gillen
Literacy Research Centre and Department of Linguistics and English Language,
Lancaster University, Lancaster, UK
e-mail: j.gillen@lancaster.ac.uk

A. Peachey
The International Development Office, The Open University, Milton Keynes, UK
e-mail: a.peachey@open.ac.uk

P. Twining
Department of Education, The Open University, Milton Keynes, UK

M. Childs and A. Peachey (eds.), *Understanding Learning in Virtual Worlds*,
Human–Computer Interaction Series, DOI 10.1007/978-1-4471-5370-2_5,
© Springer-Verlag London 2013

5.1 Introduction

> One thing that everyone here has to understand, is that Americans and British people think
> completely differently. (1USTeen)
>   That might be true. (6GBTeen)

Learning is a social endeavour, as meanings that are first negotiated in intersubjective interactions become internalised (Bandura 1971; Vygotsky 1987). Connecting with others gives learners access to expertise and to people who can guide, model, challenge, teach and work with them. These interactions take place within specific temporal and spatial environments, yet understandings of physical features are inevitably perceived through cultural understandings instantiated as discourses. We share with Wertsch (1991, p 8) 'a concern with the cultural, institutional, and historical situatedness of mediated action.' So we view specific learning interactions as always being socio-historically situated, understood by us in terms of discourses we have come across in the past as well as in terms of any newly evolving sense of cultural patterns we discern. As Kumpulainen and Kaartinen (2000, p 432) propose, 'Learning is an enculturation and meaning-making process that occurs through participation in cultural, dialogic activities with peers and more knowledgeable members…' From the perspective of the individual learner, knowledge for the individual is socially constructed in processes that are mediated by language (Gee 1996; Wertsch 1991). This means that the material aspects of learning interactions are inescapably approached and understood through discursive negotiations. Thus discourse functions as a kind of dynamic boundary object between individual learning identity and the patterns of communication, which are always in practice situated, that are imbued with the 'values, beliefs and intentions of […] users' (Hick 1996).

The aim of this chapter is to focus on specific key aspects of discourse and to explore how these came to play a role in constituting instances of degrees of (non)-alignment in a learning endeavour between two communities coming together in a project centred on use of a virtual world. We will begin by outlining our understanding of key concepts. Necessarily briefly, we will develop the relation of discourses to learning as outlined above. We will discuss the oft-debated concept of community in two ways. First, in order to approach an understanding of two groups working both separately and together, we discuss the notion of (online) community as contrasted with network. Second, we establish a durable understanding of community, taken from the work of McMillan (1996), as a framework for analysis. We also introduce two key linguistic concepts: register and cohesive ties. We then move to describing the source of our data for this paper, outlining the context for the debate in the Schome Park Project. Through our analysis according to the frame of Spirit, Trust, Trade and Art (ibid.), we show how discourses as mediated actions arise from differing expectations and misunderstandings and so lead to gaps in intersubjectivity and even conflict. Our final conclusions summarise our endeavours and include recommendations for teaching practitioners and researchers.

5.2 Key Concepts

5.2.1 Learning and Discourses

Interactions that involve opportunities for learning, whether taken up or not, are inevitably instantiated in discourses. This extends to the specifics of the contexts within which we can understand resources. These include frameworks for learning within which we have a role (for example, as learner, teacher or expert); opportunities for the joint negotiation and development of ideas; historical settings within which we can help to develop continuous threads of knowledge, and affective elements such as motivation and confidence that can support our learning (Clark and Brennan 1991; Claxton 2002; Wells and Claxton 2002). Access to these discourses is diverse and uneven; cultural resources that may enable or empower learners are likely to be unequally distributed, a particular challenge for marginalised members of any society (Hick 1996).

In a community that has been set up to support formal learning, where goals and means of achieving them are decided or at least mediated by the teacher (Vavoula 2004), the teacher plays a strong part in recognising, identifying and shaping dominant discourses. Learners are typically socialised from an early age to recognise standard elements of classroom discourse (Sinclair and Coulthard 1975), although this may be more difficult for members of marginalised sections of any community (Hick 1996). In informal learning situations, where goals and means of achieving them are non-specific or are set by the learner (Vavoula 2004), an even greater variety of discourses is likely to be available, and the opportunities for misunderstanding and incoherent exchanges may be increased. Therefore, we suggest that the creation of effective online learning communities is intertwined with the establishment of recognised discourses that foster coherent discussion.

Concern regarding unequal access is an impetus for those teaching and indeed researching literacies in both informal and formal educational contexts to investigate effective practices. However, a significant issue we now turn to is conceptualising communities, especially with relevance to the situation investigated here.

5.2.2 Networks and Communities in Virtual Worlds

In virtual worlds – the learning contexts that we are concerned with here, in common with other contributors to this book – online connections are typically conceptualised either as networks or as communities. It is useful to make a distinction between these concepts, as blurred as they may often be and probably necessarily are in practice. Networked learning has been defined as follows:

> learning in which information and communication technology (C&IT) is used to promote connections: between one learner and other learners, between learners and tutors; between a learning community and its learning resources. (C. Jones 2004, p 89)

Learning networks are made up of actors and the ties between them. These ties can be classified as strong or weak, depending on their frequency, quality or importance. A weak tie has the capacity to act as a 'bridge', the only route between two sets of actors in a network (Granovetter 1973). Online networks can offer learners easy access to large sets of people and resources and a wide range of perspectives and may support both cooperation and collaboration (Haythornthwaite and de Laat 2010).

However, in order for groups of learners to work together successfully, they need to develop shared understanding of what they are trying to achieve, and shared knowledge on which they can build. Such shared, or cumulative, knowledge is built through mediated discourse as social interaction (Scollon 1998) and forms the contextual basis for further discussion (Edwards and Mercer 1989). The temporal elements of context mean that shared history is an important resource; learners can refer back to past discussion, actions or events (Mercer 2000) and can develop a shared understanding of their current actions and their future intentions. Developing and deploying shared contexts, discourses and histories are activities that are associated with communities rather than networks.

There are many types of community associated with learning, including communities of practice, communities of interest and communities of learners (Wenger 1998; Goodfellow 2003; Jones and Preece 2006). They can all be described as having four common characteristics, described in detail by McMillan (1996): spirit, trust, trade and art. Spirit is associated with friendship, and feelings of belonging. It is made possible by boundaries, and ways of assessing whether new recruits will be loyal to the community. Trust is associated with authority, group norms and, ultimately, with justice. Once a community has a live spirit and an authority structure that can be trusted, members discover ways in which they can trade skills and resources in order to benefit one another and the community. Together, spirit, trust and trade combine to form a shared history that becomes the community's story symbolised in art.

In the physical world, a sense of community is strongly associated with place, and pre-Internet definitions of community emphasised location (Bell and Newby 1971). Online, communities tend to be associated with 'cyber-settlements' which offer a minimum level of interactivity and sustained membership, a variety of communicators and a common public space (Jones 1997). Constructing the settlement, though, is just the beginning. Communities need leadership, support, governance, acknowledgement, entertainment and amusement (Jones and Preece 2006), and in an online community these will primarily be constructed through the use of dialogue and the development of a shared discourse.

5.2.3 Coherence, Register and Cohesive Ties

As human beings participate in meaning-making practices, in any domain of literacy, they are characterised by a tendency to make connecting patterns; in other words, to construct coherence (Walsh 2006). In this chapter we make particular use of the idea of register as the key linguistic notion behind interpretation of coherence (Halliday and Hasan 1985). The notion of register combines a recognition that meaning making, in both oral and literacy modes, is constituted in linguistic patterns, and that these are recognized and deployed in particular contexts. That is, this is an approach to language that recognizes language-in-use, i.e. in interactions, as always situated, and thus is theoretically consonant with our sociocultural perspective on learning as outlined above.

Registers 'are the semantic configurations that are typically associated with particular social contexts (defined in terms of field, tenor, and mode)' (Halliday and Hasan 1985, p 43). The field of discourse refers to the nature of the social action that is taking place, the tenor refers to the status and roles of the participants, and the mode refers to what the participants are expecting the language to do for them in that situation. Formality is a key dimension, associated with practices and under-standings of an event by its participants. The same words may carry different meanings depending on register, so in order to understand what is said, we need to understand its register. In the classroom, for example, the words 'When did the First World War begin?' will be interpreted as a request for information if they form part of a student-student register, but as an elicitation of knowledge if they form part of a teacher-student register. Likewise, 'Give me your dinner money' would be an expected request in the teacher-student register, but could be interpreted as a threat in the student-student register.

Coherence in speech, writing and online forums is established, in part, by register. Another way of establishing coherence is through the use of cohesive ties: grammatical devices that bind sentences, utterances and longer passages together (Halliday and Hasan 1985; Ferguson 2009). Cohesive ties connect stretches of language by building relationships between the smaller units. They include the use of conjunctions to link ideas, pronouns to refer back to nouns, punctuation to signal the start or end of ideas, and repetition to recall past input. Other examples are paraphrasing, references, sets of words that are lexically related, and substitution of one word or phrase for another. In asynchronous environments such as the *Schome* forums, where there is no expectation that contributors will be present at the same time, part of the way in which they create coherence is by establishing and marking adjacency between postings. This is important in such settings, as conversational turns are often produced in blocks, with individuals logging on separately and contributing to or beginning several discussions at a time. As a result, topics are discussed in parallel rather than in sequence.

Cohesive ties and register support the development of coherence, but do they support the development of online learning communities? Goodfellow (2003) notes that such communities take time to develop; so opportunities to track and analyse how they are discursively produced are necessarily rare. Despite these difficulties, as online social learning becomes increasingly important and we seek to build learning communities upon and within learning networks (Conole 2008; Walton et al. 2008; Ferguson and Buckingham Shum 2011), it is important to ask:

> What roles do cohesive ties and register play in the discursive construction of online learning communities?

5.3 Data Collection

In order to answer this question, this study draws on data from the encounter of two learning communities, one formal and one informal, within an online learning environment. The data are taken from the *Schome Park Programme*, a project within the *Schome Initiative*, which aims to develop 'a new form of educational system designed to overcome the problems associated with current education systems in order to meet the needs of society and individuals in the twenty-first century' (Sheehy et al. 2007, p 89). The *Schome Park Programme* started in 2007, in the now defunct virtual world of *Teen Second Life®*. Participants who joined in 2007 included individual teenagers from across the UK, supported by adult educators who also considered themselves learners. They interacted on the virtual island of *Schome Park*, and also in the *Schome* forum and wiki. Although the majority of participants had never met face to face, a strong sense of community developed, and members referred to themselves as the *Schommunity*. (For further details of the aims of the Schome Initiative, activities during the phases of the Schome Park Programme and background to the issues studied in this chapter, see Gillen et al. 2012b; Twining 2010.)

Of interest in this chapter is the third phase of the *Schome Park Programme*, which ran from January to June 2008. A particular research aim was to explore the interface/co-existence of the learner-centric approach to education within the *Schome Park Programme* and more traditional schooling. The *Schommunity* as constituted at the beginning of this phase was informal. As in earlier phases, there were no attendance requirements beyond voluntary agreements within collaborative activities, nor any assessed tasks. Teenagers (and adults) participated as and when they chose, with a focus on the development of knowledge-age skills such as leadership and creativity. A formal learning community, a high-school computing class from Los Angeles, joined them in March 2008. The two communities had formed part of a network related to new approaches to education. Within this network, they had been connected by one 'bridge', the weak tie between the *Schome Initiative* director, Peter Twining/1GBStaff (see Table 5.1 for an explanation of pseudonyms used in this article), and the class teacher, 1US Staff. There were significant differences between the two communities: the existing *Schommunity* was informal, mainly based in the UK, familiar with the online environment and primarily interacted online, while the US community was formal, unfamiliar with the online environment and primarily interacted within a face-to-face setting.

The Schome Park Programme generated an enormous dataset including forum postings, virtual artefacts, media assets and records of inworld chat. Our broad analytic approach to this dataset may be described as virtual literacy ethnography (Gillen 2009). Our use of this term here emphasises three features of our approach to researching *Schome Park*:

1. Recognising the significance of understanding diverse literacy practices, as enabled by the different affordances of the communicative domains and as enabling and constraining creativity (see, e.g. Gillen 2012);

Table 5.1 Those who participated in the forum thread, their pseudonyms, roles, and number of postings within the thread

Pseudonym	Role	No of postings
1USStaff	US Staff	3
1GBStaff	England Staff	6
2GBStaff	England Staff	3
3GBStaff	England Staff	3
4GBStaff	England Staff	2
5GBStaff	England Staff	2
6GBStaff	England Staff	1
1USTeen	US Teen	21
2USTeen	US Teen	6
3USTeen	US Teen	3
4USTeen	US Teen	2
5USTeen	US Teen	2
6USTeen	US Teen	2
7USTeen	US Teen	2
8USTeen	US Teen	2
9USTeen	US Teen	1
10USTeen	US Teen	1
11USTeen	US Teen	Co-authored 1
1GBTeen	England Teen	19
2GBTeen	England Teen	18
3GBTeen	England Teen	14
4GBTeen	England Teen	12
5GBTeen	England Teen	12
6GBTeen	England Teen	9
7GBTeen	England Teen	7
8GBTeen	England Teen	6
9GBTeen	England Teen	3
10GBTeen	England Teen	3
11GBTeen	England Teen	2

Note that for ethical reasons concerned with child safety, the real-world identity of the director, Peter Twining (1GBStaff), was in effect transparent

2. Acknowledging, and indeed embracing, the situated nature of our understandings as informed by our longstanding engagement with the *Schommunity* and with the data generated by the community (see, e.g. Sheehy et al. 2010)
3. Reflecting our commitment to the co-construction of understandings through a 'team ethnography' approach, writing collaboratively (Gillen et al. 2012a).

To answer the research question posed by this study, we carried out a thematic analysis of one forum thread, taking as our themes the key elements of community – spirit, trust, trade and art – and considering the roles played by cohesive ties and register in the construction of these.

This forum thread was selected as an exemplar of the extensive discussions and interactions between the two communities that took place during spring 2008.

Re: ⬛ Team Events
« **Reply #6 on:** April 11, 2008, 04:14:32 PM »

my rough draft:

An event/tournament of a sort of LaserTag. There are two teams, everybody on
either team has a popgun, one team has red balls shooting out of the popgun, the
other team blue balls. Each round lasts three minutes, and there are three
rounds. The team with the least collective balls, wins. The tournament will be held
in Schome Park Beta, to allow for enough room for any amount of players, and a
closed arena.

⬛ Logged

Fig. 5.1 Reply #6, a proposal for a LaserTag tournament, posted by 3USTeen as a response to the
request by 1USStaff for proposals for team events

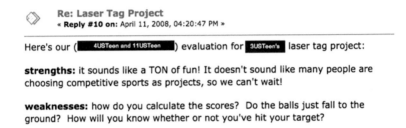

Re: **Laser Tag Project**
« **Reply #10 on:** April 11, 2008, 04:20:47 PM »

Here's our (⬛ 4USTeen and 11USTeen) evaluation for ⬛ 3USTeen's laser tag project:

strengths: it sounds like a TON of fun! It doesn't sound like many people are
choosing competitive sports as projects, so we can't wait!

weaknesses: how do you calculate the scores? Do the balls just fall to the
ground? How will you know whether or not you've hit your target?

suggestions: maybe give us a little bit more detail about how the game works,
and how you plan to run the event. Other than that, awesome idea!

Fig. 5.2 Reply #10, posted by 4USTeen. An evaluation by 4USTeen and 11USTeen, using the
'strengths, weaknesses and suggestions' format, of the LaserTag proposed in Fig. 5.1

It includes the written participation of 28 members of the *Schome Park Programme*
(including two of this article's authors) and, when we began our analysis, it had
been read 12,727 times. It is a long thread (although far from being the longest on
the forum), created over 3 weeks, and including 166 separate posts with a total word
count of 27,871 (to put this number in context, the thread is only 80 words shorter
than Shakespeare's play, *Othello*). It was by no means the only discussion that took
place at the time; while this thread was open there were 1,278 other postings on the
forum, 3 weeks of engagement in the virtual world, and extensive use of the project
wiki. It was selected for analysis here because it represents the main threads of
discussion around the challenges and opportunities presented as the two groups
negotiated an understanding of community.

In the data presented below, note that spelling, punctuation and grammar have
not been standardised, and that the gender adopted by or attributed to participants
in the *Schome Park Programme* may not represent their offline gender. The data
represented within Figs. 5.1, 5.2, 5.3, and 5.4 are screen grabs from the online
forum; the dark blocks within them indicate where we have replaced the names used
within the forum with the pseudonyms listed in Table 5.1.

Re: 1USStaff **Team Events**
« **Reply #7 on:** April 11, 2008, 04:15:54 PM »

Oi. I'm the angel with the black wings and the gun, if you've seen me.

My building project idea is the Moishe Z. Liebowitz Memorial Cathedral. Due to my lack of time in the next two months, mostly because of AP testing and my large role in Ghetto, I've decided on a "rolling building plan." I intend to finish the basic structure of a simple cathedral rather quickly, with very basic textures and no furniture. From there I will add furniture, improve textures, add building detail in more visible areas like the exterior front, and then in less visible areas such as interior corners.

With the exception of the main cathedral, none of these projects will have an exact target date; they'll be implemented in rolling releases leading up to May 26th, the opening day. Optimally the opening day would culminate with a universal service of some kind – all religions welcome, that sort of thing – but I realize that there may be problems with this on both ends of the puddle, so I'm open to something as little as just having people look around.

Here are the four things I need most right now. First, if anyone has links to actual cathedral blueprints I could look at for reference, that would be great. Second, I would love recommendations for textures to use, especially for the windows. Third, ideas for a location are much appreciated. Finally, I want to ear everyone's thoughts on the service suggested. I'd prefer to have it be unaffiliated with any religion, sort of like a Unitarian thing, but it may not be possible anyway. Thoughts?

Fig. 5.3 Reply#7, a proposal to build a Gothic cathedral, posted by 1USStudent as a response to the request by 1USStaff for proposals for team events

Re: 1USStaff **Team Events**
« **Reply #97 on:** April 21, 2008, 05:09:24 AM »

Quote from: 11GBTeen April 20, 2008, 12:21:36 PM
could we not have a gaudi style cathedral instead of a gothic one? it would be far more interesting

First, if you want to talk outrageous prim-counts look to that.

Second, I don't see the difference between two different styles of religious building based on the problems some people seem to have with the project.

Third, and no offense, but people: if I wanted to build a Gaudi or Eastern style church, I would have proposed that.

Quote from: 8GBTeen on April 20, 2008, 12:02:22 PM
What I want to know is why the building is being built? Is it to study the building itself, it features etc?

One, to see if I can.

Two, because I think it'll be useful to have another meeting space.

Three, because that period is of extreme historical interest to me.

Four, because I think this is an issue that the community needs to confront.

Five, because a good deal of my grade in 1USStaff class is riding on this project and I'm starting to approach the point where I won't have time to start over.

Quote from: 2GBTeen on April 20, 2008, 02:17:40 PM
You have missed the argument I gave that religious symbolism in cathedrals biases people's perceptions, tying beautiful gothic architecture down to a particular set of beliefs, and yet it can be much broader than that.

KNEW I forgot something. Sorry.

Perhaps I should be a bit less broad. The architecture of Gothic castles is quite different than that of Gothic cathedrals; do an image search if you don't believe me. As someone mentioned, these were the only real buildings that could be built in that time, and I'd want to do something authentic.

Quote
My artistic appreciation of buildings can be sorely damaged by the associations which they hold.

Do you think this is true of everyone? Or most people, even? I know it's hard to view some things objectively, but isn't that taking it a bit far?

Quote
I do not believe that asking for a secular gothic building is in any way an attack upon religion, but rather an expression of my personal preference, and it seems the personal preferences of several other people, that buildings in schome remain unassociated with religion.

I wasn't talking about that. If you'll notice, I mentioned the parts where people talked about religion like nukes.

Quote from: 1GBTeen on April 20, 2008, 04:00:00 PM
Yes, symbolism can be used, but manbe not religious, for example. Something about a personal hero. eg. Douglas Adams, and 42 pillars or something similar. Just an example.

I hate to tell you this, but if I found a mock synagogue where someone had replaced all the Torah scrolls with the text of Hitchhiker's, I would be pretty offended. Also, I'd have some slight qualms about doing that kind of thing myself. (Second commandment and all.)

Fig. 5.4 Reply#97, a detailed response to posts by several other students (the *shaded areas* are quotations from previous posts), posted by 1USTeen

5.4 Data Analysis

5.4.1 Spirit

The forum thread began with a posting from 1USStaff, headed '1USStaff's Team Events'

> Greetings to all.
> I will be posting events for various members of our team. They would post themselves, but we are a bit short of time and attendance is not always steady.
> Being newbies, I hope I am doing the right thing. Please let me know if I need revisions.
> We would love to have anyone participate in planning the events as well as attending, so feel free to join any group.
> 1USStaff

There is an immediate confusion of cohesive ties here, as names and pronouns are presented ambiguously (1USStaff's Team, all, our team, they, we, group) and the text shifts uncertainly from the first to the third person and from membership to leadership. The next afternoon's postings from the US students suggested a more formal approach was being employed in the classroom; the students were not functioning as a 'team' but were working as singletons or pairs to propose an event in the virtual world and to evaluate another proposal. Figures 5.1 and 5.2 give a flavour of these exchanges, which employ a familiar educational register – the teacher assigns written work and provides a framework or template to support its completion. The pronoun 'we' in these postings clearly refers to the sub-groups within which students were working, rather than to the community. Eight of the ten US students who posted in this thread repeated the same format: they posted a proposal and/or an evaluation, used 'we' to refer to themselves and their project partner, and did not engage with the discussion thread in any other way.

In the context of the *Schome* forum, the appearance of assessed work and of postings that did not form a part of a dialogue was unusual. As the forum thread progressed and debate became increasingly heated, the occasional interjection of postings within a traditional educational register, following a set formula that had been provided by a teacher, was experienced by some as jarring. When 6USTeen posted the following review of a project proposal by 3USTeen,

> That sounds like a ton of fun 3USTeen! How on earth did you come up with such a brilliant idea lol Make sure there is a way to modify the guns and you'll probably need to be a way to inform people of the time as it runs out.

we interpret his positive evaluations as hyperbole, probably tongue-in-cheek exaggerated praise oriented to the education context. However, his posting in the educational register established by 1USStaff appeared, incongruously, in the midst of what had become a fast-moving discussion on religion. A member of the *Schome* community, 5GBTeen, responded,

> I wish to make clear that I am now no longer intending to participate in this project for as long as 1USStaff is busily destroying the whole concept.

This reaction to the previous posting appears somewhat extreme but, in context, it can be understood that the evaluation had not been interpreted by 5GBTeen as merely a difference in register, but as a challenge to the *Schommunity*. Another of the UK teenagers, 10GBTeen agreed with this view,

> In terms of the existence of final projects and suchlike, I tend to agree with 5GBTeen- it isn't at all part of the schome ethos

Here 'the *Schome* ethos' made its first appearance in the discussion, substituting for 'the whole concept' and prompting a query from 1USTeen

> Look, I joined in a bit later than most. What is, in your terms, the Schome ethos, then?

7GBTeen provided a detailed response, referencing a relevant wiki page, and a reformulation of the information on that page, aligning it with the concerns of the ongoing discussion:

> On the schome ethos it basically runs down into some main points
> One being that you are not forced to learn if you choose not to – If I don't choose to go to an event I'm not forced to, If I do then I may
> The main conflicting element of this for the most part is the school philosophy, school lessons nine times out of ten are very structured, you are told what to learn, when to learn it, how to learn it, attendance is compulsory, Learning is compulsory even if the subject is of no interest (school and homework make sure of it)

The thread includes many reformulations of 'the *Schome* ethos', which was in part defined in opposition to the register of postings by members of the US community – *Schommunity* members made it clear that this ethos did not involve final projects, three-line evaluations or graded coursework, which meant it effectively excluded all contributions to the discussion thread by eight of the US participants, and placed the contributions of the others in doubt.

5.4.2 Trust

Two of the US teenagers did engage with the idea of the *Schome* ethos, including 1USTeen. From the start of his engagement with the thread (Fig. 5.3), he employed the same register as members of the *Schommunity*, employing similar ideas, style and terminology. Unlike his fellow students he introduced himself, set out his credentials and engaged with the *Schommunity* by asking for members' help and their thoughts. In his next posting he asked the community to 'green-light this project'. In doing so, he acknowledged the authority of the *Schommunity*, and this produced a tension for him because he then had to try to align the requirements of both communities, one concerned with the ongoing development of knowledge-age skills and one concerned with the development and assessed demonstration of computing skills. (For an analysis of this specific debate in terms of argumentation, see Gillen et al. 2012b.)

When asked why he wanted to build the cathedral, 1USTeen set out five reasons, including:

> because a good deal of my grade in 1USStaff's class is riding on this project and I'm starting to approach the point where I won't have time to start over.

Schommunity members objected to grading but nevertheless engaged in a coherent discussion in which the related terms 'grade', 'mark' and 'A*' acted as cohesive ties. 4GBTeen suggested 'Could this debate not get you a mark – demonstrating different skills?', a view repeated and developed by 3GBTeen: 'For engaging in this debate alone and how well you are presenting your augment etc. alone you should get a A*'. 1USTeen's response, though, was 'Hah, I wish. No, we have to actually make something in second life – it's a computer class.' The US community did not treat its rules, authority and standards as negotiable within the *Schommunity* forum, and no cohesive ties were created between the two communities on these subjects.

5.4.3   Trade

The start of the discussion thread had a networked style to it, with postings apparently offering access to people and resources. 3GBTeen offered to record some cornet music for the concert group, and mentioned access to resources related to laser tag. Yet members of the US community did not respond to these offers – such a response would have meant shifting register away from assessed work and into discussion.

In the forum there was little other opportunity for the trade of material goods, but participants proved willing to offer a wealth of ideas, challenges, discussion and debate.

Figure 5.4 gives an indication of how this worked in practice. This post from 1USTeen made use of the forum's quotation facility to build strong cohesive ties between the postings of different people. No posting was quoted in full, but key sentences were selected for response. The extensive use of selective quotation to keep numerous lines of discussion in play at once would be impossible in face-to-face discussion, and would almost certainly lack coherence in synchronous online discussion. Here, it was deftly employed to manage the exchange of intellectual ideas between several people.

In the space of just one posting, 1USTeen replied to four members of the *Schommunity*, responded to challenges, raised counter-challenges, shared personal interests and beliefs, offered clarifications and modifications, raised questions, provided information about Gothic architecture and introduced new issues. He also built cohesive ties into his posting in the form of numbers that allowed others to respond to separate elements of his arguments – his responses to the idea of building a Gaudi-style cathedral were numbered first, second, third – his reasons for building a cathedral in the first place were numbered one to five. In doing so, he constructed a framework for future discussion – members of the *Schommunity* could, and did, respond to separate points. The posting as a whole was a sophisticated construction that formed part of an extensive exchange of ideas.

5.4.4 Art

Part of that exchange involved the construction of a shared understanding of elements of the history and art of *Schome*. It became clear at various points in the discussion that, although members of different communities were using the same words and referring to the same things, these cohesive ties were not creating coherence because their register was interpreted in different ways.

When 1USTeen introduced himself (Fig. 5.4, above)

> Oi. I'm the angel with the black wings and the gun, if you've seen me.
> My building project idea is the Moishe Z. Liebowitz Memorial Cathedral.

his proposal 'was an in-joke between me and my friends'. His classmates knew that he was an observant Jew, they would have recognised (as the UK teenagers do not appear to have done) that Moishe Z. Leibowitz is a Jewish name, and that there is a comic tension between 'Moishe Z. Leibowitz' and 'cathedral' just as there is between 'angel' and 'gun'. As far as we can tell, the UK members of the *Schommunity* missed these jokes completely.

Later in the thread, 2USTeen commented, 'It is strange to us as Americans that some people might not want to embrace religion into the project', suggesting that the significance and relevance of the topic had also been misunderstood. The two communities had engaged with each other for several weeks before they began to identify these subtle differences in register.

These misinterpretations also existed within the *Schommunity*, and sometimes it was the newcomers who helped the *Schommunity* understand their own art and history. 'The Hawaiian Shirt', a beach bar on *Schome*'s virtual island, was misinterpreted by 1USTeen. 'Isn't the Hawaiian Shirt an expression of native Hawaiian culture?' he asked. 2GBTeen gave a logical, but misleading, explanation for its name

> the Hawai'ian Shirt has no reference, that I know of, to native Hawai'ian culture, and is instead a reference to the relaxed atmosphere linked with a beach hut.

Once the subject had been raised, 3GBTeen could supply a more accurate explanation – it was actually an in-joke, referring to the fashion sense of a former staff member

> It's a… joke/comon knowledge – something that you'd have to have met [the former staff member] to understand.

In the case of the island's 'Japanese Garden' on the island, the UK teenagers in the *Schommunity* referred to it on several occasions as a tranquil, non-religious place to hold ethical debates. The potential for any cultural artefact to be differentially interpreted as contributing to an alternative discourse was vividly instantiated by 1USTeen, who reinterpreted the location by pointing out the Shinto significance of its kami gate.

5.5   Discussion

This forum thread was a focus for the discussion and negotiation of all four key elements of community – spirit, trust, trade and art (McMillan 1996). In each case, cohesive ties and register were implicated in its construction and maintenance. The development of community was closely tied to the joint authorship and understanding of a sustained and coherent narrative. When the thread lacked coherence, as it did when members of the US community posted reviews without linking these to their immediate context, it resembled the activity stream of a social network, where postings of different styles, types and themes share nothing but a temporal link.

All participants used cohesive ties to produce coherence within individual posts. When these internal ties were confusing or contradictory, as in the case of the thread's initial posting by 1USStaff, this appeared to mark uncertainty and an attempt to move from one state to another. The shift from using 'we' to refer to individual communities, or to groupings within those individual communities, to using 'we' to refer to one large community proved to be a difficult move. The *Schommunity* used the pronoun in a seemingly wide sense, but examples such as 'could we not have a gaudi style cathedral instead of a gothic one?' implied that the first-person address referred to those actively engaged in the debate – members of the original *Schommunity* and 1USTeen. In fact, of the 17 members of the US community who authored posts or who were credited as co-authors of proposals or evaluations in the thread, only 1USTeen used 'we' to include himself and the *Schommunity*.

The two communities employed cohesive ties between posts in very different ways. The US community used a formulaic structure (presumably proposed by their teacher) for evaluations, linking their posts – however widely spaced in time – by the use of the headings 'strengths', 'weaknesses' and 'suggestions'. However, only three members of the US community built cohesive ties linking their posts with those of the *Schommunity*. This prompted a shift in the behaviour of *Schommunity* members – they stopped replying to the formulaic project proposals and evaluations, although they still clearly read such postings and made reference to them.

The different registers used by the two communities thus limited communication between the two and reduced the chances that they would unite as one community. This was particularly marked when it came to the issue of authority and community norms. Within this thread, members of the *Schommunity* challenged both UK and US staff and engaged in detailed debate about *Schommunity* norms and standards. Three members of the US community took part in this debate (although not in the direct challenges to staff). However, the register of formal schooling is not designed for the negotiation of norms, authority and standards and there was no apparent shift in lesson planning or assessment, even when the grading of 1USTeen was raised as an issue and alternative assessment methods were suggested. The use of this educational register thus made it almost impossible for the two communities to unite. The *Schommunity* did not have the option of volunteering for coursework and assessment at a school they did not attend; the US teenagers could only adhere to *Schommunity* norms if they were willing to jeopardise their schoolwork and grades.

With respect to trade, it is evident that cohesive ties greatly increased both the possibilities for exchange and the resources available. At the beginning of the thread the proffered resources included information sources, time and digital resources (recorded music). Without cohesive ties linking the communications of the two communities, these resources could not be accepted and these offers ceased. However, when there were cohesive ties between postings, the dialogue in itself formed a valuable resource that brought together ideas, extensions to those ideas, challenges, counter-challenges, questions, explorations and beliefs. The tools available in the forum, particularly the option for clearly delineated quotation, allowed community members to tie posts tightly together, creating a braiding and patterning of ideas that combined to form a complex, multi-authored narrative.

Although an absence of cohesive ties and large disparities in register proved limiting and troublesome for the community, smaller disparities proved more fruitful as community members worked to establish coherence together. The need to consider and explain the '*Schome* ethos', the different understood meanings of the 'Japanese Garden', and the reasons why cathedrals and Hawaiian Shirts could be interpreted both as religious artefacts and as sources of humour, stimulated an interconnected series of rich and complex learning discussions.

5.6   Conclusion

The shift from networked learning communities to a single learning community is difficult to negotiate. Cohesive ties and register are important aspects of discourses that can be mobilised to develop a coherent community narrative by linking the contributions of diverse contributors and thus bringing together the dialogue of separate communities. A shared register and cohesive ties between communications support the development not only of understanding but also of shared organisational structure, standards, goals, art and history. Without cohesive ties, effective communication and negotiation are limited and differences are difficult to resolve.

The analysis presented here focuses on the interaction of just two learning communities, but it has wider implications. Each community has its own practices around spirit, trust, trade and art, which must be renegotiated when it joins another community. Attention to register and cohesive ties offers ways of identifying and avoiding communication problems and also offers ways of increasing a community's cohesion and its potential for knowledge building.

Shared discourses enable individuals to offer resources and services, and to take up others on their offers. Cohesive ties and a shared register also have an important generative role in supporting and structuring the dialogue that resources learning and enables the co-construction of knowledge.

> The opportunity to participate in social activity in situations derived from authentic, everyday contexts and in which social and cognitive elements are intertwined has the power to support meaningful learning, creating knowledge and understanding which can be used for meaning-making and problem-solving in school and out... (Kumpulainen and Kaartinen 2000).

Therefore a recommendation for future practice from this study is to encourage the explicit attention of teachers working in virtual environments towards discourses. To an extent, the teaching role can be seen as socialising learners into particular ways of talking about topics, in order to work towards greater intersubjectivity.

Further, this is not only a linguistic matter for, as we have shown, discourses do not float free of material constructs 'even' in a virtual setting (Gillen and Merchant 2012; Hayles 1990). So paying attention to specific media design features that allow the creation and utilisation of cohesive ties is valuable. In this discussion, the usefulness of formatting tools for numbering or bulleting separate arguments, the creation of clearly delineated and referenced quotation, and easily accessible permanent records of communication has been shown to be vital.

Similarly, for the researcher, attention to the material features of modes for digital literacies is of significant importance. In emphasising a perspective on literacies as mediated action, we have provided further support for Wertsch's (1991, p 8) proposal:

> When action is given analytic priority, human beings are viewed as coming into contact with, and creating, their surroundings as well as themselves through the actions in which they engage. Thus action, rather than human beings or the environment considered in isolation, provides the entry point into the analysis. This contrasts on the one hand with approaches that treat the individual primarily as a passive recipient of information from the environment, and on the other with approaches that focus on the individual and treat the environment as secondary, serving merely as a device to trigger certain developmental processes.

It is extremely unlikely that Wertsch had virtual worlds in mind as a learning environment when writing this, just as McMillan's concept of community was founded on the physical world. But the concept of mediated discourse as social interaction (Scollon 1998) provides us with a lens with which to consider communities, however and wherever the locus of their interactions may spread.

References

Bandura, A. (1971). *Social learning theory*. Morristown: General Learning Press.

Bell, C., & Newby, H. (1971). *Community studies: An introduction to the sociology of the local community* (Studies in sociology). London: George Allen and Unwin Ltd.

Clark, H. H., & Brennan, S. E. (1991). Grounding in communication. In L. B. Resnick, J. M. Levine, & S. D. Teasley (Eds.), *Perspectives on socially shared cognition* (pp. 127–149). Washington, DC: American Psychological Association.

Claxton, G. (2002). Education for the learning age: A sociocultural approach to learning to learn. In G. Wells & G. Claxton (Eds.), *Learning for life in the 21st century* (pp. 21–34). Oxford: Blackwell.

Conole, G. (2008). New schemas for mapping pedagogies and technologies. *Ariadne, 56*. http://www.ariadne.ac.uk/issue56/conole/56

Edwards, D., & Mercer, N. (1989). *Common knowledge: The development of understanding in the classroom*. London: Routledge.

Ferguson, R. (2009). *The construction of shared knowledge through asynchronous dialogue*. Ph.D. thesis, The Open University, Milton Keynes. http://oro.open.ac.uk/19908/

Ferguson, R., & Buckingham Shum, S. (2011). Towards a social learning space for open educational resources. In A. Okada, T. Connolly, & P. Scott (Eds.), *Collaborative learning 2.0 – Open educational resources*. Hershey: IGI Global.

Gee, J. P. (1996). *Social linguistics and literacies: Ideology in discourses* (2nd ed.). London: Taylor & Francis.

Gillen, J. (2009). Literacy practices in Schome Park: A virtual literacy ethnography. *Journal of Research in Reading, 32*(1), 57–74.

Gillen, J. (2012). Archaeology in a virtual world: Schome Park. In R. Jones (Ed.), *Discourse and creativity*. Harlow: Pearson.

Gillen, J., & Merchant, G. (2012). From virtual histories to virtual literacies. In G. Merchant, J. Gillen, J. Marsh, & J. Davies (Eds.), *Virtual literacies: Interactive spaces for children and young people* (pp. 9–26). New York: Routledge.

Gillen, J., Ferguson, R., Peachey, A., & Twining, P. (2012a). Distributed cognition in a virtual world. *Language and Education* (Special Issue: Literacies and Sites of Learning), *26*(2), 151–167.

Gillen, J., Ferguson, R., Peachey, A., & Twining, P. (2012b). Seeking planning permission to build a Gothic cathedral on a virtual island. In G. Merchant, J. Gillen, J. Marsh, & J. Davies (Eds.), *Virtual literacies: Interactive spaces for children and young people* (Routledge research in education). New York: Routledge. 190–207.

Goodfellow, R. (2003). *Virtual learning communities: A report for the National College for School Leadership*. http://kn.open.ac.uk/

Granovetter, M. S. (1973). The strength of weak ties. *The American Journal of Sociology, 78*(6), 1360–1380.

Halliday, M. A. K., & Hasan, R. (1985). *Language, context, and text: Aspects of language in a social-semiotic perspective*. Deakin: Deakin University.

Hayles, N. K. (1990). *How we became posthuman: Virtual bodies in cybernetics, literature and informatics*. London: The University of Chicago Press.

Haythornthwaite, C., & de Laat, M. (2010, May 3–4). Social networks and learning networks: Using social network perspectives to understand social learning. In L. Dirckinck-Holmfeld, V. Hodgson, C. Jones, M. De Laat, D. McConnell, & T. Ryberg (Eds.), *7th international conference on networked learning*. Aalborg: Centre for Learning Sciences and Technologies.

Hick, D. (1996). *Discourse, learning, and schooling*. Cambridge: Cambridge University Press.

Jones, Q. (1997). Virtual communities, virtual settlements and cyber-archaeology: A theoretical outline. *Journal of Computer Mediated Communication, 3*(3). unpaged, Available online at http://onlinelibrary.wiley.com/doi/10.1111/j.10836101.1997.tb00075.x/full

Jones, C. (2004). Networks and learning: Communities, practices and the metaphor of networks. *The Journal of the Association for Learning Technology (ALT-J): Research in Learning Technology, 12*(1), 82–93.

Jones, A., & Preece, J. (2006). Online communities for teachers and lifelong learners: A framework for comparing similarities and identifying differences in communities of practice and communities of interest. *International Journal of Learning Technology, 2*(2–3), 112–137.

Kumpulainen, K., & Kaartinen, S. (2000). Situational mechanisms of peer group interaction in collaborative meaning-making: Processes and conditions for learning. *European Journal of Psychology of Education, XV*(4), 431–454.

McMillan, D. W. (1996). Sense of community. *Journal of Community Psychology, 24*(4), 315–325.

Mercer, N. (2000). *Words minds: How we use language to think together*. London: Routledge.

Scollon, R. (1998). *Mediated discourse as social interaction: A study of news discourse*. London/New York: Longman.

Sheehy, K., Ferguson, R., & Clough, G. (2007). Learning and teaching in the panopticon: Ethical and social issues in creating a virtual educational environment. *International Journal of Social Sciences, 2*(2), 89–96.

Sheehy, K., Ferguson, R., & Clough, G. (Eds.). (2010). *Virtual worlds: Controversies at the frontier of education* (Education in a competitive and globalizing world). New York: Nova Science.

Sinclair, J. M., & Coulthard, R. M. (1975). *Towards an analysis of discourse: The English used by teachers and pupils*. Oxford: Oxford University Press.

Twining, P. (2010). When educational worlds collide. In K. Sheehy, R. Ferguson, & G. Clough (Eds.), *Virtual worlds: Controversies at the frontier of education* (pp. 125–142). New York: Nova.

Vavoula, G. (2004). *KLeOS: A knowledge and learning organisation system in support of lifelong learning*. Ph.D. thesis, University of Birmingham, Birmingham.

Vygotsky, L. S. (1987). The development of scientific concepts in childhood (N. Minick, Trans.). In R. W. Rieber, & A. S. Carton (Eds.), *The collected works of L S Vygotsky* (Vol. 1, pp. 167–243). New York: Plenum Press. (Original publication, 1934, written between 1929 and 1934.)

Walsh, M. (2006). The 'textual shift': Examining the reading process with print, visual and multimodal texts. *Australian Journal of Language and Literacy, 29*(1), 24–37.

Walton, A., Weller, M., & Conole, G. (2008). Social: Learn widening participation and sustainability of higher education. In *EDEN 2008: Annual conference of the European distance and e-learning network*, Lisbon, Portugal.

Wells, G., & Claxton, G. (Eds.). (2002). *Learning for life in the 21st century*. Oxford: Blackwell.

Wenger, E. (1998). *Communities of practice: Learning, meaning and identity*. Cambridge: Cambridge University Press.

Wertsch, J. V. (1991). *Voices of the mind: A sociocultural approach to mediated action*. London: Harvester Wheatsheaf.

Chapter 6
+SPACES: Serious Games for Role-Playing Government Policies

Bernard Horan and Michael Gardner

Abstract This chapter explores how role-play simulations in virtual worlds can be used to support policy discussion and refinement. Although the work described is set primarily within the context of policy formulation for government, the lessons learnt are applicable to online learning and collaboration within virtual environments. The chapter focuses on the most challenging part of the project, which is to provide environments that can simulate some of the complexities of the physical world. Some examples of different approaches to simulation in virtual spaces are provided and the issues associated with them are further examined. We conclude that the use of role-play simulations seem to offer the most benefits in terms of providing a generalizable framework for citizens to engage with real issues arising from future policy decisions.

6.1 Introduction

The EU +Spaces project (Positive Spaces—Policy Simulation in Virtual Spaces) is exploring how information technologies can enable government agencies to measure public opinion on a large scale by leveraging the power of virtual world communities and social networks (Tserpes et al. 2010). The project is building applications that range from simple polling and debating mechanisms to advanced role-play simulations. Many of the challenges for the +Spaces project are shared with immersive education—there are close similarities with the use of virtual worlds for educational 'Serious Games.' The project is employing ideas from

B. Horan (✉)
School of Computer Science and Electronic Engineering,
The University of Essex, Colchester, CO4 3SQ, UK
e-mail: bernard@essex.ac.uk

M. Gardner
Digital Lifestyles Centre, The University of Essex, Colchester, CO4 3SQ, UK

M. Childs and A. Peachey (eds.), *Understanding Learning in Virtual Worlds*,
Human–Computer Interaction Series, DOI 10.1007/978-1-4471-5370-2_6,
© Springer-Verlag London 2013

serious games to provide a framework for engaging with citizens in role-playing simulations, allowing users to explore the implications of government policies under consideration.

This chapter presents an overview of the use of role-playing simulations within the +Spaces project including a brief summary of the results achieved so far. The chapter begins with a description of the +Spaces project, followed by an outline of the challenges faced by the project when attempting to design a mechanism that can simulate example policies. We present our current response to those challenges, based on role-play. After a description of the results of an initial evaluation we conclude with some remarks about the effectiveness of the approach.

6.2 Policy Simulation in Virtual Spaces

3D immersive virtual environments typically allow multiple users to collaborate with one another in an online virtual space. In addition to these environments, the +Spaces project is also exploiting simpler environments that allow users to meet and share information within a social network. Users of social network environments, bloggers and microbloggers all communicate with each other within their respective systems, creating rich patterns of interaction. Consequently, in this chapter, by 'Virtual Space' we mean a general overarching term that covers social networking services and virtual worlds. Included in the social networking services are social network environments such as Facebook, Google+, LinkedIn and Orkut; blogging services such as Blogger and WordPress; and micro-blogging services such as Twitter and identi.ca. The social networking services are small-device or web browser-based, in contrast to virtual worlds which require a dedicated client or web-browser plugin.

The +Spaces project is based on the underlying concept of a Virtual Space as a micro-society: a Virtual Space has many of the same dynamics as the physical world, based on virtual interaction between physical people. Existing Virtual Spaces incorporate the dynamics of social networks that are already widely established, making them ideal testbeds for the simulation of policies.

The project exploits the viral dissemination properties of social networking services to build up engagement with large groups of citizens online. The project is looking at three different ways in which to encourage more participation: online polls, online synchronous and asynchronous debates, and role-play simulations. One of the significant challenges of the project is to provide generalised middleware which can deploy and manage +Spaces applications (polls, debates and role-play simulations) across these different kinds of virtual space simultaneously (Kardara et al. 2011).

We envisage that the reactions governments would see in a virtual space would be participants' real responses to simulated situations, rather than simulated responses in hypothetical situations. We believe these measured user reactions can be extrapolated to derive conclusions for society at large.

The project builds on earlier work, such as that of Castronova (2001), who carried out research into economic modelling using virtual worlds. His research indicated that virtual worlds that exhibit some form of economic behaviour often reflect physical world economic propositions. For example:

- That as the price of a good rises in a market, demand for it falls, and
- If money is injected into an economy, the price level of the goods and services in that economy rises, causing inflation

This confirms the notion that a virtual space (in some contexts) can provide an authentic environment for studying physical world behaviours.

In summary, then, we are not using virtual spaces to create a simulation of society, something that is extremely difficult (if not impossible). Instead we are using environments that are already simulations of reality, miniatures of society, which are richer in characteristics of reality. Thus, the +Spaces project is providing the tools to translate user behaviour in these virtual spaces to their predicted behaviour in physical spaces. Prior to the work reported here, we have already created both 2D and 3D polling environments and a virtual debating chamber, which have been evaluated in a series of field trials.

6.3 Problems of Policy Simulation

The task of simulating policies presents several challenges when attempting to model the physical world. For example how easily can we change a person's regular habits? How can we interpret a user's habit based on the simulation of a policy? To help us explore these ideas, we identified several example scenarios that could be used as the basis for policy simulations. These included:

- Recycling: engaging users in a game that would examine their willingness to recycle. This could involve users exploring the following issues: What is rubbish? Where does it come from? Where does it go? A simulation could involve users having their own virtual homes and activities that produce rubbish of different types, such as organic, plastic, paper, glass, metal. Example policies: 'rubbish tax'—household tax proportionate to amount of non-recycled waste each month; 'rubbish return'—household benefit, in terms of reduced household local government taxes according to amount of recycled waste.
- Transportation simulations: modelling the transportation infrastructure for a particular area such as a town or city. This could be combined with some form of traffic modelling to dynamically vary the characteristics of the simulation (such as congestion, speed of traffic), and allow users to explore some of the implications of transport policy implementation. Example policies: 'Town centre pedestrianisation'—closing some streets in central Athens for pedestrians only; 'Congestion charge'—a zone of a city centre in which vehicles pay a charge to enter.[1]

---

[1] See, for example, http://en.wikipedia.org/wiki/London_congestion_charge

- Marketplace simulations: some virtual spaces (such as *Second Life* and *Farmville*) implement their own economies and currencies that can be used to trade virtual goods and services. A Virtual Space could therefore provide an ideal simulation for economic policies based on a defined marketplace for virtual goods and services. Example policies: 'Sales Tax changes'—apply a tax to all goods and services traded according to either a progressive or regressive perspective; 'Currency 'fragmentation''—introduce extra currencies (one per region) to determine currency exchange fluctuations based on regional financial policies.
- Learning simulations: the SIMiLLE project investigated the technical feasibility and pedagogical value of using virtual worlds to provide a realistic socio-cultural setting and content for second/foreign language learning. The role of the virtual world was to provide a rich simulation environment for learners to practice their language skills in a variety of realistic settings (Gardner et al. 2011).

These scenarios also resulted in the identification of user roles, including:

- the role responsible for considering policies, known in the project as the 'policy maker';
- and the role of the ordinary member of society, labelled the 'citizen.'

It is important to clarify the scope of policy simulations to identify the unique contribution that simulations can provide compared to polls and debates. The policy maker can use a poll to ask a specific question about a policy, whereas the topic of a debate is usually more open but still rooted in a policy's core issue. Citizens give direct answers to polls and in debates they give more qualitative answers. However, when participating in a policy simulation citizens may be unaware that they are answering any question at all.

Policy simulations may also exhibit a Hawthorne effect—if we force citizens to behave in a certain way, they will typically start to adapt their behaviour—thus citizen participants in simulations are likely to change their opinions about the policy being addressed.

There is also the issue of how to encourage citizens to engage in policy simulations. People generally want to engage with a simulation because they are interested in the topic (such as recycling), or they are enticed by the game-playing or entertainment provided by the simulation (such as *Farmville*). A policy simulation, then, has to attract users to participate—this challenges policy makers to design a simulation that entices a broad spectrum of the population.

A key issue for the project was the lack of reusable multi-user simulation models. Most existing simulations, such as the BBC Climate Change Simulation,[2] combine an underlying single-user simulation model (the rules and conditions that affect climate change) with a virtual environment or user interface which enables users to explore and engage with the simulation. Furthermore, like the BBC simulation, many existing simulations are highly complex environments, which contain rich graphics, story narratives and game-playing metaphors.

---

[2]http://www.bbc.co.uk/sn/hottopics/climatechange/climate_challenge/

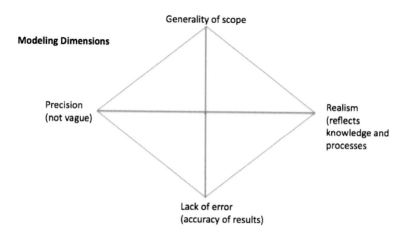

Fig. 6.1 Simulation models

The above simulation scenarios all require the implementation of some form of specialised game-like environment that mimics a physical world setting. This can be difficult to achieve, as it demands the accurate representation of a physical world setting within an artificial environment. Such an environment can be both challenging to model graphically and also complex to model in terms of behaviour, such as transportation congestion or financial systems.

A simulation model is generally measured by four factors (Edmonds and Hales 2003):

- Generality of scope (i.e. broad scope)
- Precision (i.e. not vague)
- Realism (i.e. reflects knowledge and processes)
- Lack of error (i.e. accuracy of results)

A simulation model should aim to combine all of these factors, as illustrated in Fig. 6.1. However, in reality it is difficult to combine all four factors in a single simulation, and policy simulation rarely goes beyond two factors. Generally 'lack of error' and 'generality of scope' are seen as the key dimensions for policy simulation.

Another common problem with computer-based simulations is the 'black-box' nature of their underlying internal models, whereby the models are opaque to the end-user. This opacity may be of benefit in terms of improving the overall usability of the citizens' user interface, but is a major weakness for a policy-making application, where the rules of the internal model will make up the framework for the implementation of any new policy. From a policy maker's perspective the transparency of the internal model is critical to understanding the factors that will affect the successful or unsuccessful outcome of any new policy. Also, by the nature of their implementation computer-based simulations are often specific to a particular problem domain and do not generalise well, if at all.

6.4   Role Play

It was difficult to see how the project could develop a general framework for policy simulation in which each policy did not require its own custom implementation. This observation makes computer simulations appear to be an unfeasible option for the project, as it does not support the dissemination and use of the outputs from the project by third parties, a significant project requirement.

Other experts support this observation. For example, Professor Richard Duke is a pioneer of computer-based urban simulation games and is President of the International Simulation and Gaming Association. His work has moved away from simulations because of their black-box nature—instead, he has adopted a more general approach based on role-playing simulation exercises. Duke believes that this approach provides a far less deterministic outcome, which is both more generalisable and introduces the benefit of an unpredictable element of human choice (Duke and Geurts 2004).

Role-play is regarded as an established technique for engaging individuals in a problem space through a series of structured tasks, which immerses the participants in some of the challenges of a physical environment (van Ments 1999). Role-play has been used for many purposes such as predicting outcomes, war-gaming, team building, and training. It has been particularly useful as a teaching tool in the classroom, allowing students to act out and experience some of the dynamics of a particular problem or issue from different stakeholder perspectives. Aspects of role-play have also been used in online environments such as virtual theatre, gaming, and focused discussion forums.

Within a virtual world, when used as a learning exercise, this type of role-play simulation is often referred to as a 'serious game'. Serious games are frequently used where it would be too dangerous or too costly to attempt a learning exercise in a physical world setting. Examples include safety training on oil rigs and war-gaming exercises. In both of these examples, the key factors are:

- A realistic virtual world environment (reflecting the physical world)
- Multi-user scenarios and collaboration, often with users role-playing different characters (such as paramedic, doctor, patient)
- A rich underlying model reflecting the physical world behaviours available (such as fire fighting capabilities on an oil rig)

The creation of a serious game presents similar issues to those identified for role-play simulations such as the problems of generalising across multiple domains and multiple deployment platforms. However, research in the field of serious games has resulted in potential solutions to these problems. One such solution is PIVOTE: an open source virtual learning authoring system for virtual worlds (Burden and Jinman 2011). PIVOTE provides authors of serious games with a form-based user interface to create a decision tree of game steps. The learning exercises generated by PIVOTE can be seen as isomorphic with the role-playing exercises necessary for a +Spaces policy simulation. We considered that PIVOTE could be used as the means to enable policy makers to specify the role play of a simulation with the additional benefit to deploy exercises onto several platforms simultaneously (including *Second Life, OpenSim* and the web), and that it uses an open architecture based on web services.

However, it is important to note that the key end user role of the +Spaces applications is that of policy maker: a person from a government agency who typically has no expertise either in the creation of virtual spaces or serious games. Thus, it is critical that we provide this user with guidance on how to create role-play simulations. For this reason, we decided not to use PIVOTE for the implementation, as we felt it was too complex an environment in which to ask policy-makers to construct their own role-play exercises.

As an alternative, the project explored the use of role-play templates to help policy makers devise an appropriate role-play simulation in support of a given policy issue. Taking resources from the Australian Flexible Learning Framework[3] as a starting point, we have adapted and developed two role-playing templates for use on the +Spaces platform. These are:

- Galactic wormhole: participants imagine themselves to be 5 years in the future and reflect on positive and negative outcomes of a particular policy,
- Depolarizer: structured game based on the philosophy that many issues that we treat as problems with a policy are actually polarities to be managed,

The two templates share several characteristics, which we have combined, resulting in the following role-play stages common to both templates (also shown in Fig. 6.2):

1. Meet participants in the virtual space.
2. Icebreaker vote—the policy-maker can choose to link the role-play simulation to a previous poll (on the same policy issue). The intention is provide a discussion point where citizen users are asked to predict the outcome of the previous poll undertaken by the general public rather than present their own opinions on the subject. The purpose of the icebreaker exercise is to engage users in the session, without asking, at this point, that they convey any opinion about the policy itself.
3. Icebreaker results—users can compare how close their predictions were to the results from the previous poll.
4. Assignment of roles—depending on the template being used, the users are assigned their role for the role-play by the moderator (or in some cases randomly). In the Galactic Wormhole template, several roles may be specified by the policy maker, and users are asked to take a very positive (utopian) viewpoint, or a negative (dystopian) viewpoint for each role. For the Depolarizer template, users are assigned to either a pessimist or an optimist role. The users are also provided with the instructions appropriate to their role, the template and the policy being simulated.

---

[3]http://designing.flexiblelearning.net.au/

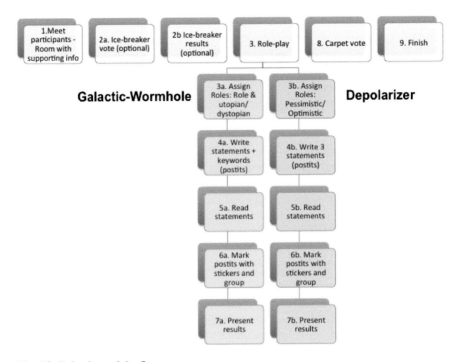

Fig. 6.2 Role-play activity flow

5. Prepare statements—users are asked to write a number of short statements about the policy issue from the viewpoint of their assigned role. (The number of statements is determined by the chosen template.) No open discussion is allowed at this stage, in order to allow all participants to share their input in a systematic manner.
6. Read statements—the users read out and explain their statements and open discussion takes place.
7. Prioritise statements—the users have a number of votes (determined by the template) to prioritise statements, according to their personal preference.
8. Present results—the moderator facilitates a discussion about the results achieved through this process.
9. Vote—the users are then asked to vote on the policy issue from their own personal viewpoint (that is, not from their assigned role).
10. Finish—the moderator wraps up the session with a final discussion.

Thus, our current preferred simulation scenario is to provide virtual spaces in which participants themselves can act out a particular government policy issue through an role-play based on a template. This scenario is a mediated task, facilitated by an online moderator, whereby citizen participants are assigned roles according to the template (such as central government policy maker, civil servant, local government agent, citizen) and then asked to act out a particular role-play

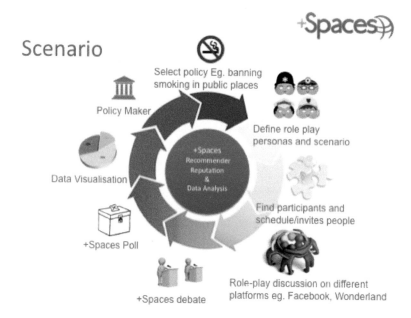

Fig. 6.3 Role-playing simulation scenario

simulation (such as the implementation of a new waste removal service by private contractors). The role-play simulation could take place in virtual spaces that visually recreate the location of the intended policy, such as town hall, local street, or city centre.

Within the context of +Spaces, citizens can be exposed to a simulation activity of this kind, which is then followed by an online poll and debate (using the other +Spaces applications) that can help to capture further quantitative and qualitative information about the user's perception of the main issues arising from the simulation. Such a sequence is illustrated in Fig. 6.3.

The variety of virtual spaces available on the +Spaces platform allows various types of role-playing simulations—textual vs. spoken; synchronous vs. on-going—in which citizens may choose their preferred virtual space for following the role-playing simulation, sharing their thoughts and knowledge. These options also allow the policy makers flexibility in terms of what kinds of role-playing simulation they want to use, and where to use them.

The +Spaces services gather and analyse the events of a role-playing simulation, be that a textual response to a question, a spoken new relevant fact, a gesture supporting or opposing an opinion, or a moderator action such as barring or highlighting a user. These services assist the policy maker both during the role-play simulation and afterwards to make sense of the content, to moderate and steer the role-playing simulation successfully, and to eventually make a decision about the policy at hand based on the role-play simulation.

6.5   Example Policies

In consultation with policy makers in the Hellenic parliament, the project devised several policies for experimentation and evaluation. The goal of the policies was to address as large a constituency as possible, within the constraints of the project resources. The policies included:

- Banning Smoking: 'Do you believe banning smoking in public places will improve public health?' In most EU countries measures have been applied for banning smoking in all public places, even though there have been some difficulties in their implementation.
- Turkey Accession in EU: 'Do you think that it would be a good thing for Turkey to join the EU?' Turkey is willing to be part of the EU but has not conformed to all the chapters of the accession partnership. The accession process is still in progress without much success.
- EU Financial Crisis: 'Do you think that the EU will overcome the financial crisis without having to be dissolved?' The economic and financial crisis and the reactions of the EU to it, such as the EU monetary policy, the austerity measures and the new agreements among EU leaders, is the showcase of how EU responds to global economic crisis for mobilizing new sources of growth.
- Higher Education Privatisation: 'Do you believe that privatisation of higher education will improve your chances of entering higher education?' Higher education privatisation refers to a process of universities taking on characteristics of an enterprise and not a publicly owned body.
- Political Governance: 'Do you believe that forming a "United States of Europe" will improve the well-being of European citizens?' EU transformation may lead to a single constitution, a single government, a single foreign policy set by that government, a single taxation system contributing to a single exchequer, and a single military.

6.6   Implementation of Role-Play Simulations

The 3D version of the role-play simulation is implemented using *Open Wonderland*[4] and the 2D environment uses the *Twitter* service.[5] Figure 6.4 illustrates how role-play simulations appear in the *Open Wonderland* environment: citizens meet at a predefined time and conduct role-playing simulations in a 3D virtual space, facilitated by a moderator and supported by additional inworld tools and objects.

The *Open Wonderland* role-playing virtual space clearly displays the current stage of the role-playing simulation as well as the current topic or policy that is the

---

[4]http://openwonderland.org/

[5]http://www.twitter.com/

Fig. 6.4 Role-play virtual space in Open Wonderland

focus of the session. Only the moderator has access to a control panel that allows him or her to step through the stages of the role-play activities. In Fig. 6.4, the role-play is at the 'Assign roles' stage. A video of a pilot evaluation of the role-playing forum shows how the objects in the virtual world are controlled by the moderator— as the moderator steps through the stages using the control panel, the objects appear and disappear according to their use in the role-play template (Horan and Gardner 2012). Details of the pilot are presented in a later section.

Citizens have the opportunity to prepare reasoned arguments based on an assigned role. When users are ready to contribute their input, *Open Wonderland* provides colour-coded post-its, on which participants enter their input, placed onto a 2D board, known as a 'Statement Wall' (see Fig. 6.5). They can also vote to indicate which statements they consider to have a higher priority, by ticking a checkbox displayed on each post-it.

We have also developed an *Open Wonderland* webcaster module that broadcasts a live scene from inside a *Wonderland* virtual world (Horan 2012). This allows users to view the broadcast session from any Flash and Java-enabled web browser. These remote users are able to observe the live session, and communicate with their colleagues in the virtual world via a local SIP phone that connects with the *Open Wonderland* voicebridge server. In this way it is possible to allow a much greater number of people to participate in live +Spaces sessions. This can also be used to link the live *Open Wonderland* sessions with the *Twitter*, *Facebook* and *Blogger* applications developed by the +Spaces project.

One of the motivations behind the webcaster module was to provide access to those users who merely want to observe (and listen to) the activities instead of

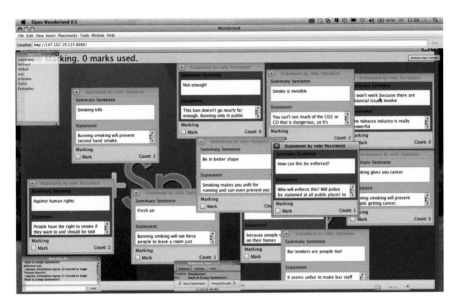

Fig. 6.5 Open Wonderland statement wall

actively participating. In particular, we wanted to enable access to policy makers, who wish to watch a session in which a policy is debated or acted out in a role play simulation and not be able to influence the session.

Participants are invited to take part in the Twitter-based role-playing simulation via their tweets—be that for open discussion or for contributing their structured input. Participants are also able to follow the session and participate through their regular *Twitter* use, or through the +Spaces *Twitter* role-playing simulation page, where they are able to follow the structure of the session, and where their responses will be automatically associated with the relevant and required hashtags.

The *Twitter* role-playing simulation also summarises the session, and clearly displays the current stage of the role-playing session; along with an aggregation of the participants' responses, the user's own role in the session, and the type of response required from the user.

6.7 Pilot Evaluation

Towards the end of the project, we will be undertaking a full summative user evaluation of all the +Spaces services, including the role-play simulation, debate and polling applications. This evaluation will involve policy makers, application developers, and citizens, using all of the virtual spaces supported by the platform (*Open Wonderland, Twitter, Facebook* and *Blogger*) and using some of the polices described above.

However, we carried out an early pilot evaluation of the role-play simulation within *Open Wonderland* as part of our technical testing. This involved six users participating according to the Depolarizer template based on the policy issue of whether Greece should ban smoking in public places. A member of the project team moderated the session, and the participants (students from the University of Essex) were assigned to either 'optimist' or 'pessimist' roles during the course of the session.

The feedback from the pilot was very positive. Overall the participants felt that the process worked very well. They thought that it was clear what they were meant to be doing at each stage of the role-play simulation, and they were able to participate fully in the session. The users felt that it was useful seeing the inworld board with the sequence of the Depolarizer template (the board updated as they progressed through the template). They felt this made it relatively easy to understand the various stages and indicated where they were in the role-play at all times.

They particularly valued the icebreaker stage as an introduction to the policy being addressed. The act of trying to predict how the general public would have voted as an icebreaker was seen to be a useful exercise. Although this was originally conceived as an optional stage, it seems to add a great deal of value to the effectiveness of the overall role-play simulation. The carpet vote mechanism (whereby users move their avatar to place a pole in a carpet that represents a graduated sale of agreement) also worked well as a metaphor for allowing the participants to cast their votes.

It was interesting to note that some of the participants preferred the experience of the role-play simulation compared to their previous experience of taking part in the *Open Wonderland* pilot of the debating application. Because the process in the role-play simulation was much more structured than the debate, the users felt that the role-play simulation was easier to follow than the debate (which was only loosely structured). They also felt that it was easier for the participants to fully engage with the activities because they had a clearer idea of what they should be doing at each stage (that is, they felt that they could participate more fully). From our experience of running the debate pilot, we discovered it was quite difficult to encourage some participants to fully engage in the debate (they tended to stay in the background)—whereas with the role-play simulation the users were far less reticent.

Although the Depolarizer template is a relatively simple role-play compared to the Galactic Wormhole template, the participants all found the optimist/pessimist roles to be very easy to understand. They also felt that because it was deliberately simple (and easy to engage with) that it might be easier to use than the Galactic Wormhole template, hopefully leading to greater contributions from all of the participants. We will be able to report on this further when we run the full user trial.

We identified that some work was needed to optimise the use of the Statement Wall during the stage when the participants make their main contributions based on their assigned role. It was evident that the efficiency of this tool is highly dependent on the number of participants, and the number of statements they are each asked to contribute. For this initial pilot having six participants seemed to work very well. However they felt that having more users might cause problems (they could get bored, or there could be some repetition). So we will need to consider carefully the optimum size of group needed for this type of role-play simulation. It may be that the Depolarizer template might be more suited to smaller groups, whereas the Galactic Wormhole needs larger groups as it has a greater number of roles that need to be assigned.

Some suggestions were also made on how the overall process could be enhanced. For example, after assigning the roles it might be better to allow the two groups time to discuss their ideas separately and then bring them together to share their group comments. Although this might mean that two facilitators would need to be nominated, or provided with the same notional role as the moderator (one for each group), it might make the discussion and ideas flow better, which could be useful especially if the subject being discussed was more complex or required more abstract thought. Also, each group could then use a different Statement Wall to contribute their comments. This leads to the possible conclusion that a "one size fits all" template may not meet the needs for everyone, and that it may be important that policy-makers are able to change the sequence of activities to suit their particular context.

6.8   An Aside on Online Learning

The tools under development by the +Spaces project to provide role-play can also be used in learning activities. Simulations have long been used to support constructivist-learning tasks, particularly based around participatory models of learning (Colella 2000). However, as we have seen above, the 'black-box' nature of simulation models has been recognised as a limitation in their use for teaching and learning, where students can often become frustrated by the hidden nature of the underlying simulation models. There is also evidence that it can result in 'superficial understanding', or 'factually wrong conclusions' about the topic (Turkle 2003). Contributory, 'glass-box' based approaches to discovery learning are therefore encouraged. The +Spaces role-play tools also take this approach. By facilitating online role-plays, we envisage that students can go beyond the superficial understanding of complex topics, to become more engaged with and ultimately achieve a better understanding of the subject matter. Combined with the use of 3D virtual environments, we hope to provide highly engaging immersive collaborative spaces for teaching and learning to take place.

We are at the early stages of developing a more generalizable framework (based on the role-playing applications in +Spaces) to support structured learning activities based on the IMS Learning Design specification (Koper and Tattersall 2005). We envisage that the +Spaces role-play applications can also be used to support classroom-based discovery learning activities, and is highly relevant to the field of immersive education. The implementation of our *Open Wonderland* Learning Design player has provided some encouraging results, and should make it possible for a teacher to design and deploy a wide range of structured learning activities into a 3D virtual world.

6.9   Conclusion

The underlying concept of the +Spaces project is that a virtual space provides a micro-society. The work of Castronova on synthetic worlds and their economies has already demonstrated that user behaviour in virtual worlds can mirror that in the physical world (Castronova 2005, 2008). The objective of the +Spaces project is to engage with users in these virtual spaces and discover their real responses to simulated situations.

Role-playing simulations allow policy makers to examine various aspects of policies and their potential impact, through structured discussions in which participants engage in playing different roles. Through role-playing simulations, policy makers may gain access to fresh thinking and new insights that may only be obtained through brainstorming with people who are invited to view the topic from new perspectives.

Creating computer-based simulations can be very complex, and existing game-based simulations are typically closed environments that cannot easily be re-purposed. It is also difficult to reuse the underlying models to construct a new simulation. For these reasons role playing provides a more tenable and reusable framework for 'simulating' government policy. However, we recognise that there are problems with our approach: the sequence of stages of a role-play—determined by the selection of template—is hard-coded into the software. This lack of flexibility is the price we pay for the benefit of ease of use for the policy maker end users.

From a project perspective the benefits of using a role-play simulation approach are that it emphasises the need for inter-operability across 2D and 3D platforms, across +Spaces applications (polls, debates, simulation), and with other core +Spaces services (recommender/reputation system selecting participants, data analysis service). It will also provide rich data sets for the analysis services in terms of the role-play dialogue and events, and it should provide a more generalisable policy simulation framework.

Acknowledgments This work is partially funded in the 7th framework of the European scientific targeted research project +Spaces, which is co-financed by the European Commission, through theme ICT-2009.7.3 ICT for Governance and Policy Modelling under contract no. 248726 (see http://www.positivespaces.eu). We would also like to express our thanks to our colleagues on the +Spaces project for their support and contributions to this work.

References

Burden, D., & Jinman, A. (2011). Web based authoring for virtual worlds using PIVOTE. In G. Vincenti & J. Braman (Eds.), *Multi-user virtual environments for the classroom: Practical approaches to teaching in virtual worlds* (pp. 170–189). Hershey: Information Science Reference.

Castronova, E. (2001, December). *Virtual worlds: A first-hand account of market and society on the Cyberian Frontier* (CESifo Working Paper No. 618). Munich: CESifo Group. Available at SSRN: http://ssrn.com/abstract=294828

Castronova, E. (2005). *Synthetic worlds: The business and culture of online games.* Chicago: University of Chicago Press.

Castronova, E. (2008). *A test of the law of demand in a virtual world: Exploring the petri dish approach to social science* (CESifo working paper series No. 2355). Available at SSRN: http://ssrn.com/abstract=1173642

Colella, V. (2000). Participatory simulations: Building collaborative understanding through immersive dynamic modelling. *The Journal of the Learning Sciences, 9*(4), 471–500.

Duke, R. D., & Geurts, J. L. (2004). *Policy games for strategic management.* Amsterdam: Rozenberg Publishers.

Edmonds, B., & Hales, D. (2003). Replication, replication and replication—Some hard lessons from model alignment. *Journal of Artificial Societies and Social Simulation, 6*(4). Available at http://jasss.soc.surrey.ac.uk/6/4/11.html

Gardner, M., Gánem-Gutiérrez, A., Scott, J., Horan, B., & Callaghan, V. (2011). Immersive education spaces using Open Wonderland from pedagogy through to practice. In G. Vincenti & J. Braman (Eds.), *Multi-user virtual environments for the classroom: Practical approaches to teaching in virtual worlds* (pp. 190–205). Hershey: Information Science Reference.

Horan, B. (2012). Wonderland webcaster, part two. *Open Wonderland Blog.* http://blogs.openwonderland.org/2012/05/14/wonderland-webcaster-part-two/

Horan, B., & Gardner, M. (2012). Role-play simulations in Wonderland. *Open Wonderland Blog.* http://blogs.openwonderland.org/2012/05/07/role-play-simulations-in-wonderland/

Kardara, M., Fuchs, O., Aisopos, F., Papaoikonomou, A., Tserpes, K., & Varvarigou, T. (2011). A service oriented architecture enabling policy simulation in virtual spaces. In *Games and virtual worlds for serious applications (VS-GAMES), 2011 third international conference* on 4–6 May 2011, pp. 236–243.

Koper, R., & Tattersall, C. (Eds.). (2005). *Learning design: A handbook on modelling and delivering networked education and training.* Berlin/New York: Springer.

Tserpes, K., Jacovi, M., Gardner, M., Triantafillou, A., & Cohen, B. (2010). +Spaces: Intelligent virtual spaces for eGovernment. In *Intelligent environments (IE), 2010 sixth international conference* on 19–21 July 2010, pp. 318–323.

Turkle, S. (2003). From powerful ideas to PowerPoint. *Convergence: The International Journal of Research into New Media Technologies, 9*(2), 19–25.

van Ments, M. (1999). *The effective use of role-play* (2nd ed.). London: Kogan Page.

Chapter 7
Avatars, Art and Aspirations: The Creative Potential for Learning in the Virtual World

Simone Wesner

Abstract The Creative Industries regard the virtual world as a potential aid for fostering creative approaches. The Experimental Learning Framework (ELF) was a 3 year research project that analysed the capacity of Second Life for learning and teaching in project management, aiming to understand virtual learning environments in relation to physical world experience. This chapter focuses on the avatar as an embodiment of a physical person. It analyses avatar design and its workability and avatar awareness, which are discussed within the framework of reflexive methodology. Two research outcomes are presented. Firstly, creative avatar applications resulted in fostering creativity as part of the independent learning process. Secondly, the enduring comparison between physical and virtual worlds as triggered by the avatar-supported analytical thinking skills.

7.1 Introduction

The use of virtual worlds has become a familiar feature in University education, developing an increasing public awareness of technology-based learning environments. As a result, this exploration of virtual alternatives has been matched by policy interest and met strategic interests of university departments. A variety of disciplines and departments including medicine, psychology and an increasing number of UK creative industries courses and departments have firmly moved parts of their learning provision from e-learning to v-learning. The creative and media industry itself, in particular those areas concerned with advertising and design, have identified virtual worlds as potential business opportunities because virtual worlds and in

S. Wesner (✉)
Centre for Research in Cultural Industries Management, London Metropolitan University
Business School, London, UK
e-mail: s.wesner@londonmet.ac.uk

M. Childs and A. Peachey (eds.), *Understanding Learning in Virtual Worlds*,
Human–Computer Interaction Series, DOI 10.1007/978-1-4471-5370-2_7,
© Springer-Verlag London 2013

particular virtual games ensure interactive engagement and participation to a far greater extent than other digital media (Wight 2011).

This move towards v-learning provision may not be happening as fast as the Gartner group predicted for the whole internet population in 2008, stating that 80 % of Internet users would participate in virtual worlds by 2011 (quoted in Hendaoui et al. 2008, p 88), but the UK virtual education landscape is growing by widening its appeal into non-computing and non-technology-related areas. The Creative Industries aim by their very nature to embrace new and innovative approaches to training and the sector has regarded the virtual world as a potential aid for fostering creative approaches while providing new learning opportunities (Dickey 2003; Livingstone et al. 2008).

Second Life (SL) enables users to transfer knowledge into practical project work while research into SL claims high value for learning (Warburton 2009; Antonacci and Modaress 2008; Fallon 2010). In particular the immersive aspect of the learner's engagement is regarded as helpful in solving real-life problems in the virtual environment and has been identified as a motivating factor (Doyle 2010). *Second Life* remains one of the most popular software programmes of its kind used in higher education (Duncan et al. 2012). The majority of universities in the UK have made use of SL in order to facilitate their learning and teaching practice (Herold 2009), despite recurring announcements from the online community that *Second Life* is obsolete (Kirriemuir 2012) and in defiance of growing customer dissatisfaction, which is linked to technical and funding issues affecting higher education provision (Conrad 2011).

Regardless of the continuous search for alternative educational virtual applications, *Second Life* provides a useful platform that encourages participants to create their own virtual content. It is part of a wider group of multi user online virtual environments that operate in real time via the motional use of personalised avatars. Linden Research SL, launched in 2003 and known as Linden Lab, allocates server capacity to the owner and provides a virtual space that is sectored into regions, which are then divided into islands (Molke-Danielsen 2009, 15). *Second Life* operates without geographical borders and anyone with a computer and reliable internet access is able to participate.

7.2   The ELF Project

The creative potential of SL as identified in educational practice has attracted wide research interest (Salmon 2009; Hew and Cheung 2008; Jennings and Collins 2007; Minocha and Reeves 2010), while research into development and application of transferable skills related to creativity has been underrepresented (Bessiere et al. 2009; Doyle 2010). The Experimental Learning Framework (ELF) addresses both skills development and application. Over the last 3 years (2009–2012) ELF investigated the potential of *Second Life* for creative industries project management training. It aimed to test the capacity of SL for learning and teaching in project management

Fig. 7.1 The Nordstar gallery in Second Life

while fostering an understanding of virtual learning environments in relation to physical world experience (Wesner 2011).

Creative Industries students planned, implemented and evaluated projects within the avatar based environment of the virtual world, and the research project investigated if the resultant experience could be transferred into their physical world skills base. Although the research focused on skills transfer from virtual to physical world applications, it considered in particular its creative potential for management solutions.

In practical terms it provided graduate level students from a variety of Creative Industries courses such as Music and Media Management, Arts and Heritage Management, Events Management and Cultural and Creative Industries with the opportunity to design and implement virtual creative industries management projects from start to finish. Additionally, a lecture, workshop and seminar programme supplemented traditional classroom teaching. Occasionally, individual or group tutorials were arranged to counter severe weather conditions, to cater for travel cost-conscious students and to offer non-location based access to tutors. The ELF project was based at Collyer, London Metropolitan University's SL islands, which amongst other buildings housed the Nordstar gallery (see Fig. 7.1), a dedicated art space where the majority of activities were implemented. The gallery was developed in collaboration between the first cohort of students, a computer science student and academic staff. The building was the result of intensive discussion about functionality and design of art buildings in a virtual world. Incidentally, the majority of Minocha and Reeves (2010) design principles for 3D learning space were incorporated in the design of the Nordstar gallery, increasing the likelihood of space having impacted on the outcomes of the ELF study.

Project-based learning experiences have long been considered as one of the most effective tools in Creative Industries education. However, exercised in the physical world they require long term involvement, field experience, are often not cost-effective and carry a high risk of failure. Many courses therefore opt for placement-oriented practical experience instead (Bric 2009). In *Second Life* none of the above mentioned obstacles are relevant. Projects are implemented within the semester schedule, with a minimal budget and without the need for prior experience.

As with a physical live event, students work according to a project plan that explains the idea and its embedded conceptual framework, develop a mission and objectives as well as a strategy (including resource allocation, staffing, marketing and financial management). Students design their projects independently but are advised to work within the parameters of the *Experimental learning framework* research design which follows four stages: foundation, participation, creation and multiplication (see Table 7.1). During the foundation stage students familiarise themselves with SL while creating an avatar and finding their way around. Typically they set up their account in SL, choose a name, body and clothing for their avatar and learn to walk and fly while either attending generic SL tutorials or studying the self explanatory introduction tools provided in SL.

Additionally, a small exercise tool was set up above the Nordstar gallery to facilitate basic coordination and avatar movement (see Fig. 7.2). During the participation stage emphasis was directed towards communication and participation within a set environment. Students attend seminars, lectures and workshops at the Londonmet SL campus. The majority of subject field related activities such as seminars on events and exhibition design take place at the Nordstar gallery seminar area (see Fig. 7.3). Discussions and group work is facilitated but students are encouraged to meet and work outside the formal settings as much as possible. At this stage project planning is nearly complete and students start the implementation phase. The majority of management projects involve extensive communication with other organisers, audiences and artists that covers initial contact, commissioning of products and staff recruitment. This takes the students directly into the creation phase where project events are set into motion. Depending on the type of project, the gallery houses the event or alternatively students design and build their own event space on the island. The virtual application offers building possibilities that could not be achieved in physical world situations. Many projects culminate in a particular event such as an exhibition opening, special viewing, concert, special performance or art procession. Towards the end of the project duration an event evaluation including a self-reflective exercise was carried out, leading to multiplication, the final stage of ELF, where experiences and data are exchanged, analysed and over time increased through a multiplier effect for future student benefit.

7.3 Methodology

The project worked with a progressive design, which gradually built up from one stage to the next to extend the range and depth of the investigation and to maintain the experimental character of the study following the same four project stages:

Table 7.1 Research framework: connecting research design and analysis with learning tools and student project activities

Project and design stages	Research activity	Research methods	Analysis	Learning tools	Participant/student activities
Foundation	Data collection	Participant observation Questionnaires Focus groups (cohort 30–45 participants each year for three years)	Coding of field notes and correlations for questionnaires	Exercise tools above the gallery and generic SL tutorials Self explanatory introduction tools provided in SL	Creating an avatar, set up account in SL, choose name, body and clothing for their avatar, learn to walk and fly project idea developed including background and conceptual framework
Participation	Data collection, design revision	Questionnaires and focus groups	Text analysis transcriptions,	Lectures seminars and workshops in virtual gallery	Communication with fellow students and participation in open SL events Refining of project idea and developing project plan
Creation	Data collection and analysis of data, design revision	Participant diary, researchers' memos	Text analysis with initial focused and axial coding	Building and space provision	Project implementation (setting up of event or exhibition in SL) Event evaluation with self-reflective exercise
Multiplication	Publication of results, research platform	Interviews, student assignment, module feed-back forms	Same as above	Use of dedicated SL groups and open forums in SL	Experiences and data are exchanged and analysed in relation to real experience for future project use through the multiplier effect

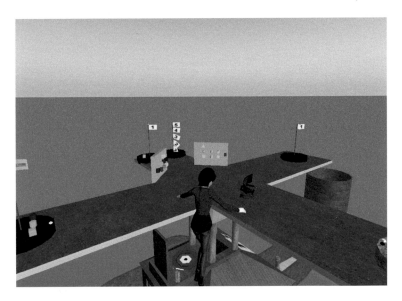

Fig. 7.2 Exercise area above the gallery

Fig. 7.3 Project meeting place Nordstar gallery

foundation, participation, creation and multiplication as the participant progresses in their individual project (see Table 7.1). The crossover of research design stages and project work activity stages is deliberate and made it possible for both researcher and participant to work to similar timeframes. The progressive design helped to ensure that a variety of paths were explored without focusing on a constant re-design of the project.

7.4 Reflexivity

Additionally, in this chapter the Webster-Wright's approach is followed by drawing on reflexivity as a specific methodological strategy (Webster-Wright 2010, p 81) that is applied to grounded theory, which aims to balance the use of descriptive methods and the complexity of uncertainties and self doubt within the research design (Alvesson, quoted in Webster-Wright, ibid., p 80). In this project reflexivity is used to establish a control mechanism which intervened when the project was in danger of drifting away from content and expertise. Reflexive research contains interpretation and reflection as the two basic characteristics, which the majority of research projects would claim to contain. However, while the research in general incorporates both aspects at some stage in the design and often towards the end in the form of evaluation, the reflective approach locates interpretation at 'the forefront of the research work' (Alvesson and Sköldberg 2009, p 9). It is based on the understanding that 'all references to empirical data are the result of interpretation' In this sense, awareness is raised of theoretical assumptions, language and pre-understanding, which was considered as very appropriate when researching international students acting in an international setting. Reflection, the second characteristic, attempts to focus on the inside of the researcher and the research community and pays attention to cultural links and their attached narratives. Considering that the researcher acted in the dual role of participant and researcher in the same investigation it was felt that a critical self-exploration of one's own interpretation, not just of the empirical material but also of the process and the construction, was necessary while interpreting the interpretations (Alvesson and Sköldberg, ibid.).

7.5 Interpretation

In the research process the following levels of interpretation have been applied: Interaction with the empirical material or occasionally interpretation was carried out during participant observation and during interviewing. In a more systematic approach a second interpretation checked findings against education theories such as transformative learning (Mezirow 1991; Mezirow and Taylor 2009) and constructivist pedagogy relating to interactivity (Jonassen 2000). The final level of interpretation was concerned with the text production of the researcher analysing if, for example, any claims to authority dominated the writing while addressing the selectivity of represented voices.

7.6 Methods and Data Analysis

The project applied a variety of methods and the most suitable were selected in each phase considering practical implications such as student availability and student interests as well as content and methodological concerns. During the foundation and communication stage participants were asked to complete a questionnaire and participated in two focus group discussions each. The first focus group took place in the virtual environment while the second was held in a physical world seminar room. Participants who choose to complete their assignment in SL were also asked to write a diary. Module feedback forms were added later to the research method since participants were able to comment on those forms about their experience. Additionally, student assessments were analysed, while the practical implementation of the projects also became part of the research process, as were the written assignments. Semi structured interviews were carried out after the participants had undertaken practical work in a physical world cultural organisation during a placement or an internship. The researcher kept a diary, which included notes and memos covering her own reflections during the whole research process. Participants were observed at all four stages in SL and during the introductory session in the computer labs. The cohort of participants was enrolled in a 1 year MA within the Creative Industries course portfolio (Music and Media Management, Events Management, Arts and Heritage Management and Cultural and Creative Industries) and three consecutive years (2009–2012) were investigated. Data were analysed using inductive reasoning while applying content or thematic and structural analysis, as practised in grounded theory (see Table 7.1). Three steps of initial, focused and axial coding techniques were applied to the interviews, diaries, memos and partly to the focus groups (Charmaz 2006) while simple correlations were harnessed in the questionnaire analysis.

7.7 Results

This data analysis of ELF shows that immersion into the augmented environment had a favourable impact on the empathetic experience of the learners and as students commented: It is *"…a fun way to gain experience"*, *"….in a playful environment"*, while enjoying the freedom to explore and *"being able to go at my own pace"*. *"SL is different, a good tool to stimulate and learn"*.

The opportunities to participate in building creation (from design to production) and filling them with life (simulation) are perceived to be a valuable training ground for physical world situations, despite the fact that a different form of reality is created. One participant stated *"using Second Life is like learning to ride a bike"*. In particular, the exhibition design and its practical application are valued as hands on approaches that show results immediately. The 3D- and 2D-dimensions of art works are experienced in relation to space and location and could be discussed and changed on site within minutes. The majority of students pointed out that the understanding of dimensions helped in physical world design processes while gaining confidence in their abilities. As a result more experimental exhibition designs were implemented in both virtual and physical world environments. For example, one student organised an exhibition project that showed art works by artists who exclusively produced artwork in *Second Life* and placed them in the Nordstar gallery.

The sculptures were amended in size and proportion to the location built for the exhibition, which would of course have been impossible to achieve in a physical world situation. However, later the same student successfully applied her understanding of dimensions (Which object is suitable for which room? Which art works need more space than others and why?), while on placement in a London gallery.

Social interaction with the avatar public (the participants in the event) proved to be challenging. As in a physical world environment, audience development in *Second Life* is based on audience research in which data such as age, gender and interests are analysed in order to define and segment the appropriate target group. However, the catchment area has no geographical boundaries and marketing needs to be directed towards an international audience that might be interested in attending visual arts events. Timing remains one of the most crucial aspects since *Second Life* operates as a synchronous application. One student working from Cyprus scheduled an exhibition opening for a Saturday afternoon which translated into a Saturday night for the UK. This arrangement excluded most fellow UK students since they were engaged in physical world social activities while a number of academics from North America joined during their lunch break and some Australian visual arts enthusiasts stayed up late to attend. In this sense, finding the most suitable time for an international audience proved to be challenging. Students paid particular attention to targeting the right group of people for their events. The early projects in particular could not rely on box office data sets for the gallery and therefore tended to rely on word of mouth and friends' networks. However, a less targeted advertising campaign with banners on the main opening page of SL produced a new audience (newcomers, not normally gallery visitors in the physical world) that would not initially have been targeted by the students but developed into a reliable group of interested visitors to the gallery.

Although the general experience for the students using SL was encouraging, not all students felt comfortable during the first initial sessions, concluding that their uneasiness might be related to their general dislike of computers and Information Technology. As one participant summarised: *"Sorry to completely rant about Second Life: I am just not a computer person and I don't feel comfortable at all with it"*. This indicated that clear guidance remains essential during the foundation stage and that computer literacy cannot be naturally assumed.

Some students reported that if the first technical barrier (downloading the software, setting up an avatar) was overcome they felt enthusiastic about continuing and exploring the software further. It is essential to provide initial technical support and foster an open-minded atmosphere among all participants towards virtual world projects to be able to go on to discover their full potential (Hollins and Robbins 2009).

Overall, the research produced a number of results and I will elaborate in more detail on two outcomes in particular. Both are related to the avatar and its appearance and handling. In recent years avatars have become a familiar feature in the creative industries, including appearances in films and exhibitions outside the virtual environment. Research interests developed in similar ways, covering issues such as identity (Peachey and Childs 2011) and communication (Blascovich and Bailenson 2011).

The outcomes discussed in this chapter touch on the issues mentioned above but the focus remains on the empirical character of the study and on the grounding of the results in the data. The first result is covered under the banner of "fostering creativity" and relates to the creative process, which at the onset of the research was to a certain extent expected not as a result but as a topic for investigation. A second outcome is discussed here under "physical world metaphor" and was originally treated as a side product and surprised the researcher but consequently has inspired a vigorous debate among project participants.

7.8 Fostering Creativity

The software *Second Life* invites users to browse, to explore locations, as learning by trial and error is the main feature of initial investigation and communication. Most of the initial learning takes place independently on an individual level, and many tools in SL have been developed to support these types of learning. In the project simple orientation tools were created above the gallery space, to be used in the orientation phase. Additionally, students were encouraged to go via the orientation island and explore SL according to their project needs.

As the avatar itself represents a projected model of oneself it could be seen as a key element for successful learning transactions when transferred into an educational space (Garrison and Anderson 2003, quoted in Warburton 2009). At all stages of the ELF project 90 % of students spent considerable time developing, polishing, changing and experimenting with their avatar appearance and only once the avatar looked as intended or met students' satisfaction did they engage further with SL. Often students felt that the avatar models provided in SL did not reflect their understanding of self-embodiment and set off instantly to correct their appearance,[1] behaviour resembling that of getting ready to go out in front of the mirror in the physical world. If initial satisfaction with appearance could not be achieved due to technical difficulties or for other reasons, individual users expressed reactions of suffering and in some instances an impact on physical well-being. The reaction regarding embodiment was not recorded when participants choose other non-human like avatars such as animals and robots. For example appearing in the shape of a dog did not trigger instant reconfigurations of avatar appearance and participants seemed to be content with the dog model presented by Linden Lab. Initially, those responses were interpreted as typical teenage/young adult behaviour that stresses the importance of self awareness as part of adolescent development, as expressed via clothing, hair styles and accessories and as observed in the physical world seminars

---

[1] At the beginning of the ELF project avatars could be created from a basic model given by Linden Lab while registering with SL. Now, a selection of detailed, ready-made avatars are offered by the software programme. Users are meant to choose one with the option of altering their appearance later.

beforehand. However, further into the investigation it became clear that reactions went beyond typical fashion statement and fulfilled a vital function within the learning process. If a satisfactory appearance was achieved as expressed in the 'feeling right' statement, a sense of individual achievement and confidence was created by the participant, which had a favourable impact in regards to their learning motivation. Harel and Papert (1991) from MIT Media Lab have argued strongly for the positive impact of a self-developed knowledge structure on learning motivation and their ideas about constructionism have been identified as underlying theoretical concepts in a number of research projects related to computer based learning (Fominykh 2010; Antonacci and Modaress 2008). In summary, their main argument was that individuals would learn best while making and doing. The avatar, as an embodiment of oneself, could be regarded as the first learning framework that offers a highly individualistic approach where people could design and construct their own appearance. In later stages of the project students extended the work on their own appearance, for example presenting floating and circulating art objects attached to their avatars. One student concluded that the avatar provides 'more freedom to be expressive' in comparison to the physical world where appearance is driven by peer group pressure and other cultural norms. Those interventions demonstrated that when a structural framework in the form of an avatar is established, creative thinking is also applied to the personalisation of virtual appearance. Here, creativity is understood as a process that produces something new and at the same time creates value while redefining and transforming context (Bilton and Cumming 2010).

Weisberg's CHOICES model of creative thinking explains the creative process. He argues that nothing extraordinary is to be found in the creative processes and that instead ordinary processes produce extraordinary outcomes. He divides creative thinking into six different components that are summarised in the acronym CHOICES. H stands for habitual thinking, which is often based on domain-specific expertise. Creative thinking uses ordinary (O) cognitive components and this is achieved via small incremental (I) steps. It is a conscious (C) rather them unconscious process and the creative outcomes are based on references of pre-existing products (E for evolutionary). The final component proposes that creative thinking is sensitive (S) to external events, hence incorporating the changing environment. It indicates that among other factors sensitivity to new information/environments while explored within the familiar context of the subject could trigger/foster creative abilities (Weisberg 2010). If this is translated to the ELF project students produced novel solutions and innovations (attaching rotating objects to underline their appearance, as mentioned above), which they would not be able to do in physical world situations. In this case they used their avatars as a new form of presentation while handling familiar managerial processes in an often new and unfamiliar virtual environment. Some students went as far as changing their appearance according to the task they undertook and others would try out clothing that they would consider to be culturally inappropriate if worn in the physical world. For example one girl exchanged her physical world head scarf for a mini skirt in SL. Surprisingly, none of the participants purchased outfits, gadgets or other items for sale in SL to wear or use with their avatar. All students opted to use their creativity rather than their purchasing power to alter their appearance. This could be interpreted as a choice that demonstrates an initial creative potential of the participants that then fostered creative thinking further during avatar creation.

Students happily used two contradictory frames of reference as outlined in the creative process. They built a structure expressed by the avatar and redefined themselves in the virtual environment as something new. As a result students established a positive learning experience for themselves based on creative thinking while using the avatar. This initial situation was re-established every time they engaged with the software.

7.9 Physical World Metaphor

The second outcome relating to the avatar addresses learning issues but emphasises primarily skills development rather than the learning process. Previous research has shown that avatar appearance and operation does not have a direct correlation with reality and therefore the direct responses to reality are flawed and incomplete, despite the fact that the embodiment may cause a strong sense of being in the virtual world (Bessiere et al. 2009). Even if the avatar closely resembles the person behind its creation it could hardly be regarded as representative of a physical human being. This becomes most obvious when comparing body control of the avatar and the physical person. In the physical world gaining control of one's body is a result of a lifetime of experiences, but in the virtual world avatar body movements such as waving, smiling and laughing are realised with one or several mouse/arrow key clicks. As a result, a clear distance is created between physical world experience and virtual reality, which the participant needs to negotiate while using the software. Initially, students regarded this as confusing and irritating in the foundation stage of the project. In the participation and creation phase it was hardly mentioned but it became a prominent discussion topic in the multiplication stage, in particular during the evaluation of the students' projects. The transfer including the creation of the distance from physical to the virtual dimension was reflected as a potential space that fostered the constant comparison between the two worlds and therefore encouraged students to think in different dimensions. As a result, students' project ideas changed and reflection was used as a tool to describe what they experienced while operating the avatar. Students would no longer be satisfied with simply developing and implementing a project that resembled the physical world in the virtual world. Instead they would create a theme in their projects, around their experiences of the discrepancy between physical and virtual. For example, one student developed a project that had avatar appearance as its main topic. She invited friends and fellow students to take part in a procession of avatars that would explore Collyer Island in an evening performance while walking, flying or roller skating from one building to the next. Members of the procession were asked to maintain their position in the float but had to change their appearance in 5 min. intervals. Therefore, participants came either prepared with several outfits stored in their library in advance or would change spontaneously. In this project the idea was to address the avatar theme in a playful manner but at the same time to highlight the students' own observation of the importance of dressing up in a SL environment.

Additionally, the new project ideas allowed for critical investigations which span from questioning the use of the avatar to an overall criticism of the software programme, addressing the political and philosophical context of SL within the framework of creative industry project management. Students did not address the technical barriers but analysed reflectively the potential and limitations of SL, for example when presenting street art, which has become an established art form in the physical world. In SL graffiti art loses its critical potential since the owner of the objects/building needs to give permission before the item could be shown. As an alternative, the avatar itself could represent the art but then the identity of the avatar is revealed at the same time, which would negate the concept of remaining incognito in street art. It was observed that this type of criticism was of a different nature than the start-up frustration often described when SL projects get off the ground (as mentioned above) and users face initial technical difficulties. It could also not be compared to the scepticism that participants with low virtual literacy in particular aired before training in SL was offered. The avatar was identified as a medium that appeared real but at the same time acted as a constant reminder of the distance to physical world project management. Surprisingly, the constant comparison of physical and virtual and vice versa ensured that reflective and analytical thinking was applied appropriately, resulting in sophisticated approaches to project management while advancing conceptual thinking and incorporating both into the project ideas. The students therefore made a contribution to enhancing the subject field of creative industries project management. In this sense analytical thinking is seen here as a skill that, when applied and used over a longer period of time, becomes absorbed into an individual's general tool kit and knowledge pool and remains accessible for use in physical world project management. In turn their achievements impacted positively on their aspirations of what they wanted to achieve in higher education and in the working/business environment. Additionally, artists who acted as one of the main client groups during the project work, noticed that the level of students' reflection resulted in stimulating discussions and in a better overall understanding of their artistic ideas.

Since this outcome was not part of the initial skill set that the researcher envisaged at the beginning of the project, no test had been designed to measure analytical thinking at the start of the project. It may in any case be impossible to capture these data. Consequently, it remains in doubt whether the avatar is the only trigger for such a result. Bearing in mind that numerous other social and environmental influences (such as being exposed to university education) might have been at work at the same time, these results have to be treated with caution.

There is also a correlation between the reflexive approach of the research and the fostering of analytical skills in the student project population, which may be interpreted as a further trigger for the result described. However, the ELF project's main finding in the area of physical world metaphor is the following: Even if the exact extent of the skills development could not be measured there are indications that handling the avatar triggers and supports the development of analytical thinking skills in terms of comparison and self-reflection. Outcomes, the nurtured creativity and the metaphor approach show that learning and skills development is supported by the avatar creation.

7.10   The Ontological Dimension

Surprisingly, the reflective philosophical interpretations of new media technologies was discussed as early as the 1990s even though this was in much more general terms. Beck, Giddens and Lash (1994) argue that modernity becomes reflexive as a theme and a problem for itself. The risk society (Beck 1994) produces a reflexive response to rapidly changing information and with associated forms of learning such as reflective learning and learning by doing, information is transformed into knowledge (Dyke et al. 2007).

Consequently, new media technologies are reflexive technologies that allow social agents such as people and organisations to be self-aware and self-reflective about their social position, resulting in *reflexive living*. Lash (cited in Han 2010) situated this existence between the dichotomies of destabilisation, discontinuity and movement as common agents of societal change. In discussing the outcome of this research familiar attributes have been applied. Avatar awareness and its embodiment as handled by the participants could be interpreted as one example of what Lash defines as non-linear or reflexive living. In 2012 this remains a common experience when people are exposed to new media technologies. Therefore, the emphasis and effort that is directed towards the acquisition of skills, knowledge and the interpretation of the process by the participants becomes a *natural* phenomenon. In this sense the outcome that creativity is fostered and analytical thinking developed and applied could be regarded as logical and expected.

However, caution is advisable when discussing the ontological meaning of the terminology. Since original ideas of reflexive modernity were understood as more of a *reflex* and less as *reflection* about changes and societal conditions at the time, it is arguable that over time terms have changed. In the 1990s, the technologies available to authors were less immersive and as a result their experience was more remote. The experience of the virtual world today engages the user *within* the technology, creating a much more personal and all-encompassing experience. Following Han's approach, knowledge is altered by reconfiguring the relationship between the human and the virtual worlds. Interestingly, this proposes a new line of enquiry and interpretation, which would go beyond the remit of this chapter and the reflexive approach. It might encourage a discussion of virtual worlds from within, using a *new* terminology and accepting virtual worlds as a *reality of their own,* rather than trying to fit the limited understanding and interpretation of one reality to the virtual world.

Additionally, this research indicates that further theoretical implications in particular relating to risk and challenges of avatar behaviour would need to be investigated. For example, Yee et al. (2007) have summarised concerns relating to the avatar presence as expressed in the media effect tradition in which behavioural scientists measure and analyse the level of individual change that is occurring while switching from virtual to physical world and vice versa.

The findings presented in this chapter are explained as two independent entities, but they remain closely related to each other and to their creative industries context. Creativity and analytical thinking are often regarded as a matching combination and seen as part of the same process (Weisberg 2010). In general, this study supports those findings but distinguishes between process and outcomes in order to disentangle the relationship between the two in a learning framework. Furthermore, the findings show that individualised and personal forms of engagement such as that via the avatar in the virtual world can motivate learners and therefore help change their perceptions of themselves and their digital environment. At the same time the findings support rather than contradict conventional views of knowledge accumulation. In this sense the study outcomes could be read as part of the continuing search of the facilitator's ambition to ensure that students' aspirations are developed.

Students valued the skills gained as generally applicable with no distinction drawn between the university context and the creative industries business environment. They argued that their aspirations became more ambitious over the duration of the project and that they exceeded their own expectations within both contexts. Judging by the positive student experience the findings speak for a wider application in project management. However, it has to be noted that both outcomes have been discussed in isolation from other results of the ELF project for this chapter but they remain as part of the wider identified skill set, which will be taken into consideration in future.

Overall, the findings of the 'Experimental learning framework (ELF)' project show that *Second Life* can provide a valuable learning alternative in Creative Industries management training. Additionally, it should be considered that projects can be planned, implemented and evaluated from start to finish with very little impact on the physical world environment. Projects require a fraction of the funding of physical world projects and could be run from any location in the world that allows internet access. Learners are able to transfer their experiences into non-virtual work applications. As a result, new internationally workable management solutions are tested and developed that will help to define the creative industries for years to come.

References

Alvesson, M., & Sköldberg, L. (2009). *Reflexive methodology: New vistas for qualitative research.* London: Sage Publications.

Antonacci, D. M., & Modaress, N. (2008). Envisioning the educational possibilities of user-created virtual worlds. *AACE Journal, 16*(2), 115–126.

Beck, U. (1994). The reinvention of politics: Towards a theory of reflexive modernisation. In U. Beck, A. Giddens, & S. Lash (Eds.), *Reflexive modernization.* Cambridge: Polity Press.

Beck, U., Giddens, A., & Lash, S. (1994). *Reflexive modernization: Politics, tradition and aesthetics in the modern social order*. Cambridge: Polity Press.

Bessiere, K., Ellis, B. J., & Kellogg, A. W. (2009). Acquiring a professional "Second Life:" Problems and prospects for the use of virtual worlds in Business. In *Proceedings of the 27th international conference on Human factors in computing systems* (pp. 2883–2898). Boston: ACM Press.

Bilton, C., & Cumming, S. (2010). *Creative strategy*. Chichester: Wiley.

Blascovich, J., & Bailenson, J. (2011). *Infinite reality: Avatars, eternal life, new worlds, and the dawn of the virtual revolution*. New York: Harper Collins Publishers.

Bric, A. (2009). Teaching arts management: Where did we lose the core ideas? *Journal of Arts Management, Law & Society, 38*(4), 270–280.

Charmaz, K. (2006). *Constructing grounded theory: A practical guide through qualitative analysis*. London: Sage Publications.

Conrad, M. (2011). Leaving the lindens: Teaching in virtual worlds of other providers. In *ReLIVE11 conference proceedings: 28*, Open University, Milton Keynes.

Dickey, M. D. (2003). Teaching in 3D: Pedagogical affordances and constrains of 3D virtual worlds for synchronous distance learning. *Distance Education, 24*(1), 105–121.

Doyle, D. (2010). Immersed in learning: Supporting creative practice in virtual worlds. *Learning, Media and Technology, 35*(2), 99–110.

Duncan, I., Miller, A., & Jiang, S. (2012). A taxonomy of virtual worlds usage in education. *British Journal of Educational Technology*. http://onlinelibrary.wiley.com/doi/10.1111/j.1467-8535.2011.01263.x/full. Accessed 09 May 2012.

Dyke, M., Conole, G., Ravenscroft, A., & Freitas, S. (2007). Learning theory and its application to e-learning. In G. Conole & M. Oliver (Eds.), *Contemporary perspectives in E-learning research: Themes, methods and impact*. London: Routledge.

Fallon, G. (2010). Using avatars and virtual environments in learning: What do they have to offer? *British Journal of Educational Technology, 41*(1), 108–122.

Fominykh, M. (2010, March 15–17). Learning in technology-rich environments: Second Life vs. moodle. In *Proceedings 9th international conference on Web-based Education (WBE)*, Sharm ACTA Press, El Sheikh, Egypt, pp. 266–273.

Han, S. (2010). Theorizing new media: Reflexivity, knowledge and the Web 2.0. *Sociological Inquiry, 80*(2), 200–213.

Harel, I., & Papert, S. (1991). *Constructionism*. New York: Ablex Publishing Corporation.

Hendaoui, A., Limayem, M., & Thompson, W. S. (2008). 3D social virtual worlds, research issues and challenges. *IEEE Internet Computing, IEEE Computer Society, 12*(1), 88–92.

Herold, K. (2009). Teaching media studies in Second Life. *Journal of Virtual Worlds Research – Virtual Education, 4*(2), 4–17.

Hew, K., & Cheung, W. (2008). Use of three-dimensional (3-D) immersive virtual worlds in K-12 and higher education settings: A review of the research. *British Journal of Educational Technology, 3*(6), 959–1148.

Hollins, P., & Robbins, S. (2009). The educational affordances of multi user virtual environments. In Don Heider (Ed.), *Living virtually: Researching new worlds* (pp. 257–270). Oxford: Peter Lang.

Jennings, N., & Collins, C. (2007). Virtual or virtually U: Educational institutions in Second Life. *International Journal of Social Sciences, 2*, 180–186.

Jonassen, D. H. (2000). *Computers as mindtools for schools: Engaging critical thinking*. Columbus: Prentice-Hall.

Kirriemuir, J. (2012). *Snapshot 10.5 – Zombies Can't Fly: The continued use of virtual worlds in UK education*. http://virtualworldwatch.net. Accessed 17 May 2012.

Livingstone, D., Kemp, J., & Edgar, E. (2008). From multi-user virtual environment to 3D virtual learning environment. *Alt-J, Research in Learning Technology, 16*(3), 139–150.

Mezirow, J. (1991). *Transformative dimensions of adult learning*. San Francisco: Jossey-Bass.

Mezirow, J., & Taylor, E. W. (2009). *Transformative learning in practice*. Chichester: Wiley.

Minocha, S., & Reeves, J. A. (2010). Design of learning spaces in 3D virtual worlds: An empirical investigation of Second Life. *Learning, Media and Technology, 35*(2), 111–137.

Molka-Danielsen, J., & Deutschmann, M. (2009). *Learning and teaching in the virtual world of Second Life*. Trondheim: Tapir Academic Press.

Peachey, A., & Childs, M. (2011). *Reinventing ourselves: Contemporary concepts of identity in virtual worlds*. London: Springer Series in Immersive Environments.

Salmon, G. (2009). The future for (second) life and learning. *British Journal of Educational Technology, 40*(3), 526–538.

Warburton, S. (2009). Second Life in higher education: Assessing the potential for and the barriers to deploying virtual worlds in learning and teaching. *British Journal of Educational Technology, 40*(3), 414–426.

Webster-Wright, A. (2010). *Authentic professional learning, making a difference through learning at work*. Berlin: Springer.

Weisberg, R. (2010). The study of creativity: From genius to cognitive science. *International Journal of Cultural Policy, 16*(3), 235–253.

Wesner, S. (2011, September, 21/22). Avatars and aspirations – Fostering the creative potential of project management education in the creative industries. In *ReLIVE11 conference proceedings*, Open University, Milton Keynes, pp. 175–182.

Wight, R. (2011, September 21/22). o.T. – Keynote address to the researching learning. In *Immersive virtual environments conference (ReLive11)*, Open University, Milton Keynes.

Yee, N., Bailenson, J. N., Urbanek, M., Chang, F., & Merget, D. (2007). The unbearable likeness of being digital: The persistence of nonverbal social norms, online virtual environments. *The Journal of Cyber Psychology, 10*, 115–121.

Chapter 8
Second Language Acquisition by Immersive and Collaborative Task-Based Learning in a Virtual World

Margaret de Jong Derrington

Abstract The methods by which English as a Second Language can be taught and learnt in a Virtual World (VW) are explored in this study of an online community of language learners from around the world. Theories of language acquisition are invoked and the affordances required for current methods of teaching and learning a second language in the physical world (PW) and online in *Skype* and VWs are compared and discussed. There are descriptions of the resources created and used by the ELIP~Homewood (E~H) group in their *OpenSim* world and accounts of their activities there and in *Second Life* (SL). The E~H Grid has been running since July 2010 and in some ways the project is just beginning as the students themselves design and create new places, buildings, objects and resources for their own enjoyment and learning and as their world evolves in a Language Learning project which meets many of the principles of immersion and of naturalistic, acquisition oriented and task-based language learning.

8.1 Introduction: ELIP, Homewood, and Language Learning

The Internet and Virtual Worlds have long been recognised for their capacity to facilitate learning and practising a foreign language. There are several language schools in *Second Life* (SL); Derrington and Homewood (2008), and others (Molka-Danielsen et al. 2007; Morton and Jack 2005; Peterson 2005; Chen and Su 2011) have described language learning projects which take advantage of the immersive qualities of virtual worlds, of the rich variety of the setting and of access to native speakers of target languages to facilitate the learning of foreign languages, especially English. Indeed Linden Lab claimed (Team Engage 2009) that language

M. de J. Derrington (✉)
Department of Education and Professional Studies, King's College London, London, UK
e-mail: margaret.derrington@kcl.ac.uk

M. Childs and A. Peachey (eds.), *Understanding Learning in Virtual Worlds*,
Human–Computer Interaction Series, DOI 10.1007/978-1-4471-5370-2_8,
© Springer-Verlag London 2013

learning was the most common educational activity in SL and in 2010 an online special interest group of virtual language educators sharing experience of language learning in Virtual Worlds boasted over 180 members (RezEd 2010).

After investigating language learning and evolving pedagogies in SL (Derrington and Homewood 2008) the Homewood Project was set up to create a VW for learning English as a second language (ESL). *OpenSim* software was used on the server to host a grid of 20 islands and students were advised to use the *Hippo Viewer* to enter the world. A website was set up on which students could create an account and read instructions to help them download and install the client software and set it up to enter the Homewood Grid (Derrington 2011).

8.1.1 The 'English Language Improvement and Practice' (ELIP) Group

English Language Improvement and Practice (ELIP) had originated in *Skype* as a group of 'serious' students who want to improve their English for various very different reasons by chatting together in voice and text. There are many opportunities to practise English on social media by chatting with native speakers and other learners but these students were becoming both confused and irritated by native speakers using mobile text language, and poor spelling and grammar which they felt hindered their progress.

They also wished to distinguish themselves from people they felt were learning English for social networking rather than using online social networking in order to learn English, and to avoid those who 'were not serious students' and wanted chiefly to flirt. A small subgroup of mainly Saudi women wanted an exclusively female group where they could speak aloud and be sure that no man could hear their voices, a religious requirement. So the ELIP~LOL (Ladies Only Lessons) and ELIP~Mixed Invitation *Skype* groups were formed. These groups have continued for nearly 4 years, with a fluid membership of around 100 members in the mixed group and an overlapping more stable membership of about 50 in the ELIP~LOL group.

Members of the group adhere strictly to rules which set out the group's netiquette but go further requiring them to eschew lazy typing, like 'i' instead of I, and texting shortcuts like 'cu' and 'thx'. In the text chat they must correct their typos and other mistakes in English, both in order to help themselves to learn and to avoid seeing and becoming familiar with incorrect rather than correct English. They attend English lessons that concentrate on pronunciation and intonation in the *Skype* conferences with the group's qualified native English teacher, a volunteer who also answers queries and corrects mistakes in the text conference.

These students come from different countries and time zones all over the world and are generally introduced to the group by friends already there. They use various methods to improve their English. Some are enrolled in local colleges and universities and following English courses with local non-native teachers or learning English as part of a university course, but most of them are learning English by various informal methods online. They use online websites like Livemocha (2012) and Kantalk (2012) which promote language exchange and informal amateur coaching, and interactive websites which have tuition, exercises and assessments. A few of the students have learnt their English entirely from online resources. Many of the group listen to BBC Radio 4 and in the group discuss the programmes they hear; the most popular are 'The Archers' (BBC 2012a), a long-running radio soap opera, panel games and the many regular book serialisations. Small groups of students meet regularly online to read English books together. Recently a number of them have begun to write blogs in English and ask each other to read their blogs and help to correct the mistakes they have made.

Several of the ELIP members are non-native English teachers at schools and colleges in their own countries and use ELIP among other internet resources as a way of keeping their own English fluent. The others have various different reasons for learning English, for employment or academic purposes, as an international language for commercial or leisure communication purposes; but many of them profess to be learning English purely as a leisure activity. Whatever their studies elsewhere, their activities in E~H are entirely voluntary. They come and go as they please and take part in whatever activities they choose as and when they please either because they find these activities improve their English or merely because they enjoy them.

8.1.2 Homewood: The Group's OpenSim Virtual World

Several members of the ELIP group had previously been in SL, a few of them were frequent visitors. As with other online resources, they told each other about SL, and some members of the group began meeting occasionally in SL going sightseeing together or finding places to sit together and read. Their SL activities were similar to their *Skype* activities – except that in SL they were able to see each other sitting in comfortable chairs… or on a beach or in a garden, and indeed they used animations so that their avatars could lie on cushions reading their books (see Fig. 8.1). Many of the ELIP members could not access SL at all. Either their internet connections were not good enough, or the computers and graphics cards were not sufficiently powerful. But even so a growing number wanted to find a place in SL especially for the ELIP group. However, owning land in SL was not free like using *Skype*. So, *OpenSim*, the free open source version of SL was investigated and in May 2010 Homewood, the E~H world was created together with a website where ELIP members could register and create their own accounts in order to log into their own virtual world. Those who were familiar with SL knew what they wanted: beautiful places to 'hang out' together; a beach, a scripted dance floor, a 'British pub' (see Fig. 8.2). They also wanted lessons in the VW as well as in *Skype*.

As suggestions were made and ideas described and discussed, the islands or regions in the E~H virtual world were created and built to accommodate everyone's ideas. Unlike SL, an *OpenSim* world is elastic. If someone has a new idea

Fig. 8.1 Bassima reading in SL (With permission from Maryam Alansary). Snapshot from Maryam Alansary, who is called 'Bassima' in E~H (with permission)

Fig. 8.2 A beach, a pub and lessons in a virtual world. Snapshot from the 'Virtlantis' region in SL created by Kip Boahn in SL 'Kip Yellowjacket' (with permission)

and wants some space for it, it is the work of a moment to create an extra island or two to order. Students who had seen things in SL that they wanted, or thought would be good for language learning, described their ideas and helped put them into practice. One of the students, a computing undergraduate at Moscow State University, helped to set up the world and test it before it was opened to the rest of the group. Others with SL experience and skills have designed and created the

Fig. 8.3 Sharing screens in *Skype* to see the virtual world

avatar shapes and skins, and the clothes that are available for students to 'buy' in order to personalise their avatars when they first arrive. The 'Grammar Dungeon', shops of various kinds, a region-sized sandbox, areas for students to build houses, beaches, a 'British Pub', a lighthouse, are among those already built. The most recent request, scenarios for role-playing the dialogues used in the lessons is under way although a rather ambitious request for an island to role-play the BBC radio series 'The Archers' is still under consideration (BBC 2012a).

Whilst many members of the original ELIP *Skype* group have never actually visited the E~H VW, they have heard all about it and seen snapshots from inside the world. Using the 'share screens' option in a *Skype* call, those with inadequate computers or internet connections have been able to see fellow students' screens showing their avatars flying around in the VW (see Fig. 8.3) Even those who have never been there take great interest in Homewood's development and promise themselves that as soon as they get a better computer, graphics card or internet connection, they will be in there too.

The online language learners using the Homewood virtual world and the ELIP *Skype* groups are aware that these have been created in order to study their language learning and they have agreed to take part in the project. By observing, interviewing and questioning them, the intention is to find out why they are learning English, why they choose to do so online and how they do so, what other English learning activities they are engaged in and what they feel they gain from these online activities. Some of the group have created blogs on which they discuss their language learning and recommend resources and activities to others and in general they are very willing to discuss their views and experience of language learning and to suggest resources and activities that might be created. The experience of these students in E~H can be compared to that available to language learners in physical world classrooms or available from other online resources and the knowledge gained will help in the design of language learning resources in virtual worlds.

8.2 Affordances of a VW and of a Physical World (PW) Classroom

Table 8.1 shows the list of physical affordances that are generally used for teaching languages; that are used for the essential requirements of the P-P-P (Presentation, Practice and Production) of Situational Language Learning (Richards and Rodgers 2001); and for the essentials of Willis's Framework, the provision of Exposure, Use, Motivation and Instruction for Communicative Language Teaching (Willis 1996; Richards and Rodgers 2001). The diagram compares four different situations: the ordinary physical world classroom, a VW, a *Skype* group, and solo independent study on the net or a VLE. For the purposes of this discussion, we will assume that this PW classroom is exceedingly well equipped with an interactive whiteboard (IWB) and also assume that its computer is networked, that there is a VLE and the internet is available. For VWs here we consider only SL and the *OpenSim* private world of Elip~Homewood (E~H). We will mainly be interested in comparing the physical world classroom with the virtual one; the others are there partly for reference, but also because they can actually be easily combined. The physical world classroom can use elements of individual study on the web either in class or for homework, and *Skype* can be combined with a VW. This is in fact frequently done in E~H in order to include those members of the group who can access *Skype* but not the Homewood VW.

8.2.1 Pre-prepared Text for Use in Lessons

We can see that in all four situations both students and teachers can prepare text in advance. In particular the teacher can hand out or share text with each of the students, in a classroom by handing out printed worksheets and in a VW by distributing notecards. In the VW this can be done either by placing them in an object for avatars to click, by automatically offering them to avatars as they approach or enter the area where the class is taking place or by dragging them one by one from

Table 8.1 Comparison of affordances of physical world and virtual classrooms

Comparison of the physical world and virtual classes with Skype and the Internet				
Physical affordances for teaching languages	Physical classroom	Solo on the Internet or VLE	Virtual Worlds	Skype
Prepared text teacher + student	Yes but ...	Yes	Yes +++	Yes
Spontaneous public text	Teacher (s)	Twitter	T + S	T + S
Private notes	Restricted	Yes	Yes	Yes
Automatic logging of text	On IWB (T)	No	Standard T + S	Standard T + S
Text editing and correction	Yes T	No	No	Yes T + S
Prepared images, drawings and diagrams	Yes	Yes	Yes	Yes
Spontaneous images from the web	Yes T	Yes	Yes T + S	Yes T + S
Spontaneous drawings and diagrams	Yes	Not relevant	Can be organised	Yes
Spontaneous mime/action	Yes	Not relevant	Limited	Yes
Prepared mime/action	Yes	Yes	Yes	Yes
Prepared speech, dialogue, sound files	Yes	Yes	Yes	Yes
Spontaneous speech	Yes	No	Yes	Yes
Recording of speech	Can be organised	Yes	Yes	Easy
Display of film, music, etc	Yes T	Yes	Yes	Easy
Observation of mouth, lips, for pronunciation	Easy	No	No	With small groups
Role play	Yes	No	Yes+++	In voice only
Visiting places, excursions, trips	Difficult	Not relevant	Easy	No
Authentic use of language to perform real tasks with other students	Can be organised	No	Easy	Can be organised
Authentic use of language to perform real tasks with native speaking strangers	No	No	Easy	No
Automatic translation tools	No	Yes	Yes	Yes
Dictionaries	Yes but slow	Yes	Yes	Yes

T = teacher, S = all students, (s) = single students, yellow indicates advantages, orange strong advantages, grey disadvantage, green indicates the necessity for special equipment which is found only in the best equipped classrooms

inventory onto each avatar. This last is most similar to the PW scenario where worksheets would be handed out individually to each student in the classroom. In the VW, any of the students can equally easily distribute notecards they have written, but in the PW, the equivalent distribution of text written by students is less likely, as photocopying would have to be arranged in advance. There are far more

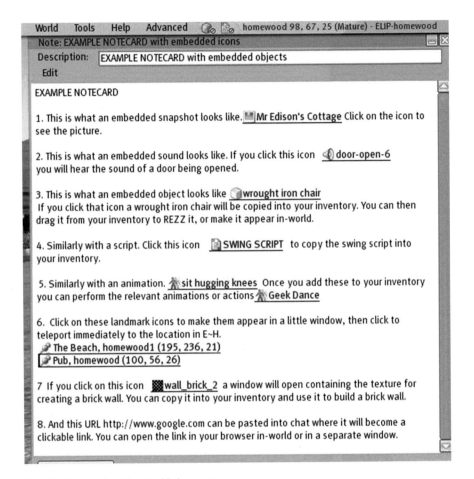

Fig. 8.4 Notecards with embedded resources

possibilities in the VW for the sharing of text items for private viewing. Of course in both situations pre-prepared text can be displayed on a screen for all to see. And in a PW class with an IWB, both students and teachers can interact with the board. This can actually also be done inworld; an IWB can be scripted and operated on a screen inworld (Design Digitally 2009). Although it is possible, this has not been tried yet in E~H. Virtual notecards do have some significant advantages over paper. Apart from the obvious environmental and financial advantages and the significantly easier-than-PW operations of copying and distribution described above, a virtual notecard can have embedded images, sounds, and URLs, landmarks enabling the avatar to teleport instantly to another location and even objects that can be copied then 'rezzed' or made to appear; all operable by a simple mouse-click. So VW notecards (Fig. 8.4) are considerably more versatile and powerful than photocopied worksheets in a PW classroom.

8.2.2   Text and Voice Chat; Logging and Recording

Although we learn to listen, and speak our first languages (L1) long before we learn to write them, this is generally not the case with second languages (L2) learnt after we can write in our L1. Some teachers consciously use methods, like the Direct Method and the Oral Approach, which avoid writing and follow the L1 order of listening and speaking first (Richards and Rodgers 2001), but teachers and students in language classrooms generally tend to read and write quite as much as they listen and speak. This is actually even more the case with distance or online language learning, since text is more faithfully and clearly transmitted than sound. To achieve clarity, we often spell things out on the telephone and often in *Skype* or VWs say, even in our own language, "I didn't quite hear that, can you write it?" Teaching a language, when students have a strong accent and the teacher has no idea what they are saying, the easiest solution is to ask them to write it out.

In SL and *OpenSim* (and *Skype*) text communication is automatically logged. Preferences can be edited to choose exactly what is logged, how and where; and it is all saved locally on the user's hard drive. So after a lesson or conversation the student or teacher can look at the text in a word processor and either make notes or notice and correct language constructions and errors. Both of these activities reinforce what has been learnt earlier in the lesson but this facility of a VW facilitates formative feedback and helps mitigate the effects of transcription errors introduced by a student copying notes off the board in the PW classroom.

Skype has the additional, unique facility of enabling a person to edit and correct text messages up to 20 min after they have been sent, and indeed the creator of a chat room can edit and censor messages up to 24 h later. This facility can be utilised in language teaching; after a student has sent a message containing an error the teacher or another student can draw their attention to it, and they can edit their message and correct it. Swain (1995), Hall (1995), and Long (1985) attest to the value of Corrective Interaction between more and less expert speakers, and Swain's Output Hypothesis in particular stresses the need for feedback on output in second language acquisition (Sheen 2004). It is also very useful for correcting typographical errors. It can be quite galling for teachers to correct a student's English, and then notice a typo in their own message. The ability to correct typos is most useful.

The text messaging in a VW chat is much clumsier, and any correction to a message containing a typo (or any other mistake) must be made in a new message. This is one of the reasons why, even as a greater proportion of the ELIP group (or even all of them) gain access to the VW, and inclusiveness becomes less of an issue, the E~H group will continue to use *Skype* in conjunction with presence inworld. An alternative scenario is of course that text chat with *Skype*-like correction tools might become available in *OpenSim*. Given the open source nature of the software this is a real possibility. During the installation of an *OpenSim* grid, there is choice in the modules implemented and, for example, some worlds use Vivox for voice, rather than Freeswitch. The development of a new messaging module for *OpenSim* affording a *Skype*-like correction facility in text messages would greatly enhance its potential for second and foreign language teaching and learning.

In a physical world classroom there is less text communication or at least less writing and such text is less easily shared, particularly when written by students. Even those notes seen by the whole class written on an un-digital black or white board would be lost unless students copied them into notebooks. And while it might be said that the exercise of writing those notes might reinforce the language learning, miscopying also occurs; so the possible benefit has to be weighed against that risk. With IWBs the notes made on the board during the lesson can be preserved and subsequent access by students can be arranged using a VLE.

Online, the students' ability to make audio recordings of themselves and each other is not automatically available but can very easily be arranged. There are several pieces of software that will automatically switch on and start recording the moment a call is made in *Skype* and voice in VW can also be recorded quite easily. Some students (with or without asking permission) regularly record the voice lessons, discussions and conversations in which they are involved. Using mobile phones and similar tiny devices, the same is true of PW classrooms, and open and even surreptitious recording can take place and indeed cell-phones can be utilised for teaching and learning in PW classrooms (Thornton and Houser 2005; Kiernan and Kazumi 2004; Devadoss 2011).

Pre-recorded voice is equally available in all settings whether this is the traditional tape recorder played in a language classroom or a sound file made available inworld or played through someone's microphone so that it can be heard inworld. Also sound and video clips from websites such as YouTube are equally available to VW users sitting at computers either streamed inworld or watched in browsers, and to the students in the PW classroom with an IWB connected to a computer and the internet. In the PW classroom this tool is generally available only to the teacher; inworld (or on *Skype*) teacher and students can find and play sound files and videos to the class and in fact in ELIP small groups of students frequently discuss music they like, each finding YouTube videos of the music they like and either playing it to the others through their microphones if they are together inworld or in a voice conference, or sending each other the URLs in text chat so that they can each play it independently and talk about it. This is a pleasant activity, involving real meaningful conversation in the target language. One cannot imagine a similar scenario in a language classroom, unless perhaps students used their mobile phones with incorporated MP3 players to play each other snatches of their favourite music, but such leisure activities are unlikely to be encouraged in a PW language classroom.

8.2.3 Spontaneous Images, Mime, Film and Inworld Animation

In a Modern Foreign Languages (MFL) classroom, the students generally all have the same first language and though the teacher may choose to teach primarily in the target language the common L1 *is available* for difficult explanations of grammar etc. Even if the teacher refuses to use it, the students can use their common L1 to confer and help each other. In an 'English as a Second Language' (ESL) classroom, the students have different L1s. Usually they are foreigners or immigrants learning L2 from a native speaker in a country where L2 is the normal means of communication. Although in the classroom there is no common L1 that can be used for instruction, ESL students usually have the advantage of immersion. They are in an English speaking country and, unless they live in exclusive immigrant communities, can practise their L2 every day outside the classroom in normal everyday activities.

The ELIP group come from all over the world. The only common language they have is English. So although the ELIP students are learning a language which, where they are living, is a foreign language, their classes must be conducted in English. The group has more in common with English as a Second Language (ESL) classes except without the advantage of immersion. E~H students do not live in an English speaking country they merely visit one in their VW. Outside the VW they are no longer in that country; after the lesson they return to their own countries and L1. So, while they may have more opportunities inworld for L2 leisure activities than students in a PW MFL class; outside their VW they do not have the same opportunities for immersive experience as most PW ESL students who are living in an L2 country.

In PW ESL classrooms the teacher cannot use the students' various L1s to explain something, and must use any means to hand including pointing to objects, spontaneous mime and gesture, drawing, whatever is available to elicit or explain vocabulary and to achieve understanding. In a VW, spontaneous actions are restricted; gestures and movements are confined to a portfolio of animations which have been created in advance. The PW classroom teacher's ability to sketch pictures and diagrams quickly on the board or a piece of paper is not generally available in VWs, although with recently developed inworld IWBs in both SL and *OpenSim* this is now more readily available (Design Digitally 2009). E~H, however, is not quite at the cutting edge of *OpenSim* worlds and the simplest solution for these problems in E~H is to use Google-image and paste a suitable URL into text chat for everyone to see the same picture in their browser. This method can be used to show the meanings of new words quickly although as a last resort students can use online dictionaries and translators. The creation and scripting of IWBs is on the Homewood to-do list.

8.2.4 Prepared Dialogues and Role-Play, Excursions, Extended Role-Play

Role-play is often used in communicative language learning classrooms; a search for 'language learning' + 'role-play' in any relevant archive of academic literature will bring forth a rich variety of references; Google Scholar presents over a million. In a PW language classroom, role-play can be used for an extensive range of activities from simple exercises like rehearsing sentences or questions and answers in order to practise the use of newly learnt grammar or vocabulary; for the 'production' part of the typical P-P-P lesson, or at the other end of the scale for extensive scripted or unscripted playlets or dramas acted out in class.

Role-play activities are much easier in VWs than they are in the PW, through the use of a holodeck. A holodeck is a scripted object which when touched offers a choice of scenes which can be 'rezzed' or made to appear in the VW. This is often used in SL where space costs money as it enables the same space to be used for several different purposes (Derrington and Homewood 2008). Holodecks can therefore be used for the instant creation of a great variety of scenarios for role-play and students can very easily change the appearance of their avatar to suit a character they are role-playing. Indeed whole regions in SL are devoted to extended role-playing activities.

Visits and excursions are sometimes used in physical world language learning and can range from group outings for social purposes to trips abroad to countries where the target language is spoken. The use of the teleport facility in a VW is obviously much easier and more convenient than travel in the PW. Sitting at home in front of a computer, a student can not only join other students in a language class, but with that class can go sightseeing to places of interest within the virtual world. It is very easy for the teacher in a virtual world to teleport the whole class to an art gallery, a concert, or a place of interest within the virtual world which can supply interesting subject matter for conversation and language learning.

8.2.5   Authentic Use of Language and Problem Solving

Lessons comprise only a small fraction of students' use of E~H. Students spend most of their time in other activities using English since it is the only common language in the group. In Homewood they spend most of their time building, socialising and in other organisational activities. Two of the students have shops in which they 'sell' products they have made to other students. Some of them have taken skills learnt in Homewood into SL where they interact with communities of native speakers. Use of the Sandbox, the building lessons and designing and creating their own DIY homes are all opportunities for using English to solve real problems. It is difficult to provide such activities in a PW MFL classroom, but of course for PW ESL students, living in a country where the target language is spoken such opportunities abound outside the classroom. The efficacy of Task-Based Learning and immersion for language learning has been documented by Ellis (2003), Willis and Willis (1996) and Skehan (1998) and many others.

8.2.6   Translation Tools and Dictionaries

In an ESL classroom although some are loath to relinquish their electronic translation dictionaries, as students progress they are encouraged to use English dictionaries, understanding new vocabulary from its English definition rather than from a translation. Similarly in E~H, students are used to the readily available Google Translate and, depending on which VW viewer they use, they can click to switch on an automatic translation device. This translates between two chosen languages enabling users to type in their L1, and produce text inworld in L2. Similarly, any inworld text in L2 will be translated for them into their L1. This can rather lose the point of learning an L2 at all, or alternatively it can help beginners to take their first tentative steps in L2 by providing the 'comprehensible input' that is one of the prerequisites for Krashen's Input Hypothesis for Second Language Acquisition (Richards and Rodgers 2001). There are also many free online English dictionaries which, since students are already sitting at a computer, are readily available when they are chatting on line or inworld. Students are encouraged to place a shortcut on their desktop or toolbar and consult English dictionaries themselves and indeed swap URLs of definitions.

Some of the students are always trying out newly learnt vocabulary and have recently started doing what they call the 'Google Collocation Test' to test how appropriate their usage is. For example in a discussion about the weather and use of 'nippy', 'chilly', 'keen' and 'frosty', they did the test googling "nippy weather", "chilly weather" etc in inverted commas and found out for themselves from the numbers of hits that although these four words were shown as synonymous in a dictionary, "keen" was not actually used like the other three as an adjective for "weather".

Woolard (2000) suggests the study of collocations as ideally suited to independent learning and indeed particularly important in raising students from 'intermediate' level to 'advanced'. The students' different linguistic backgrounds mean that they have different ideas and the easy availability of such tools to check these ideas can make their group discussions quite fruitful. By this means the 'instruction' mooted as desirable for language learning by Willis (1996) is available from online tools without a teacher, and such learning from peer collaboration is in line with constructivist theories (Vygotsky 1978; Papert 1980; Wenger et al. 2002).

8.2.7 Anonymity, Shyness; Benefits of Avatars, Nicknames and Alter Egos

One radical difference between face to face classes and language learning in E~H or any other online method is the anonymity afforded by an online identity and even more so the alter ego afforded by an avatar. There are two beneficial aspects to this. One is that students suffer less from shyness and self consciousness, and are less afraid of making fools of themselves when no one knows who they are (Moschini 2010) and particularly in role-play situations in virtual worlds (Robertson and Oberlander 2002). Trying to pronounce sounds that do not exist in their L1, and trying to acquire a good L2 accent both require a certain amount of confidence, or at least a willingness to experiment, and the cloak of anonymity or the adoption of a new persona can help.

The other benefit is that of adoption of an identity that they can talk about in the first person without either lying or giving away too much personal information. Students' conversational practice of their L2 often involves them in asking and answering biographical questions; supplying personal information that they would not usually give to strangers. Being able to answer questions with respect to their avatar rather than their physical selves removes a problem. The middle-aged female student who is asked her age can give the age of her avatar without guilt, embarrassment or loss of privacy.

8.3   Resources and Activities in ELIP-Homewood

The affordances discussed above can be summarised and compared in a table. As can be seen from Table 8.1, the affordances of a VW are not significantly different from those of a digitally equipped PW classroom and the differences in some cases favour the VW. Table 8.2 shows how various theories of Second Language Acquisition are supported by the affordances of these different worlds, physical and virtual. It can be seen how various Methods and Approaches used in Second language Teaching and Learning are supported by the affordances of physical and virtual classrooms. Having compared the affordances of a VW with those of PW classrooms we will now look in detail at some of the specific resources and activities in Homewood and examine exactly how they are used for language learning by the E~H group.

8.3.1   Vocabulary

Learning lists of vocabulary is an activity associated with twentieth century and earlier classroom language learning and was very much a behaviourist activity. Lists were learnt for homework (for example in Latin and French) for tests in class, and failure was rewarded with detention. In many ways this was very effective; students can still recall much of these lists decades later. These behaviourist methods of language learning may be very effective but the problem with it is that students learn to *translate*; they continue to think of the object and then its name in their first language (L1), and to translate the L1 name into its name in the target language (L2). To acquire fluency the object or idea must become associated directly with its L2 name. This activity of breaking and remaking links has been recognised in theories of language acquisition (McLaughlin 1990; Anderson 1989; Schmidt 1992; Zilberman 1999) and also in methods devised for fluent language acquisition. Immersion in an environment where the target language is used exclusively can help to create the direct links necessary for acquiring fluency.

Wandering through the huge supermarket in Homewood (Fig. 8.5), students see goods of all descriptions packaged and labelled in English. Looking at stacked, cans

Table 8.2 Virtual world support for different theories of language acquisition

References	Learning theories and issues	Effect of Skype or virtual worlds
Krashen 1982 & 1985 in Krashen 1998	Comprehensible input.	Aided by visual objects and translation tools.
Long 1996; van Patten 2002; Ellis 1995	The role of input.	Same as the physical world or similar, but notecards in virtual worlds much more versatile
Swain 1985; Swain & Lapkin 1995	Performance.	Same as the physical world or similar.
Long 1996; Morton & Jack 2005	Interaction (psycholinguistic and sociolinguistic). Conversational episodes involving negotiation of meaning.	More communication in second language because of a lack of a common first language.
Gardner & Macintyre 1993; Moschini 2010; Robertson & Oberlander 2002	Language Anxiety and Willingness to Communicate. Readiness to communicate with specific people	The anonymity of avatars and nicknames reduces embarrassment and shyness.
Gardner & Macintyre 1993; Dörnyei 1998, Dörnyei & Csizer 1998	Motivation and achievement.	Making real friends and communicating with them in a second language.
Oxford and Crookall 1989	Language learning strategies.	Advice and tips exchanged in Skype and other learner groups.
Swain 1995	Output hypothesis needed for modified output.	Skype's text correction facility. Peer assistance in online language learning communities. Better than the physical world.
Hall 1995; Peterson 2005	Negative evidence, correction interaction between more and less expert speakers.	
Long 1985	Noticing.	
Ohta 2001	Scaffolding into learning new second language forms. Peer and teacher correction.	Same or similar, possibly more scope for scaffolding in rich environment of virtual worlds.
Hall 1995	Second language learning processes as apprenticeship into a range of discourse practices, interaction between more and less expert speakers.	Much more interaction between learners than in ordinary classrooms.
Skinner 1957, 1969 in Skinner 1974	Behaviourism	Same or similar to physical world
McLaughlin 1990; McLaughlin et al.1983	Controlled and automatic processing, connectionism.	
Anderson 1989; Zilberman 1999	ACT* model declarative and procedural knowledge.	
Ellis 2003; Willis 1996; Skehan 1998; Morton & Jack 2005; Peterson 2009	Task based learning (TBL) and immersion.	Much more scope for immersion and authentic TBL in a virtual world than in a physical classroom.

Fig. 8.5 The supermarket

labelled 'peaches' can help the English word to become associated with peaches rather than their L1 word, or at least enable its quicker recall. Opportunities to use the target language and to associate it with real situations are easily provided in a VW. Furthermore objects in a VW are all named and labelled. Right-clicking an object, an avatar can see its owner, creator and its *name*, a simple direct way to check vocabulary. Objects in a VW must be named, so that users can find them in their inventories. Indeed objects can be even be scripted so that when touched by an avatar their names are spoken aloud and appear in text. This has been done in areas of Virtlantis, a language learning region in SL (Fig. 8.6), but not, so far, in Homewood. Some students have suggested it, and the counter suggestion has been made that they themselves could create such resources, and indeed the creation process would itself be a vocabulary learning exercise.

8.3.2 Places to 'Hang Out'; Presence and Immersion

ELIP Students who had visited SL had plenty of ideas about places to 'hang out' that could be created in E~H and many of these have already been built. There is a beach, complete with rugs, umbrellas, sandcastles, buckets and spades and even a camp fire (see Fig. 8.7). Rolling waves break on the shore, a couple of rafts float in the water and there are sailing boats out on the sea. There are many rural areas; parks and gardens with trees, flowers, butterflies floating in the air, birds flying above, and even bees buzzing round a hive (see Fig. 8.8). Rugs, cushions and logs and even a swing are available for avatars to sit and chat. There is a 'British pub' with a bar, a dance floor and cream teas available in the pub garden. Avatars can

Fig. 8.6 Virtlantis (With permission from Kip Boahn)

Fig. 8.7 Beach with sandcastles

Fig. 8.8 Rugs cushions and a swing

Fig. 8.9 Random chat and conversation

sit round the bar or the cosy fireside in the pub, or outside round tables under
coloured umbrellas (see Fig. 8.9). These areas are generally used for meeting for
random (informal) chat and conversation. The language learning that is achieved
in such situations takes place in the informal conversation, usually a combination
of voice and text. Students speak, but resort to text and the use of other online

resources, sometimes also to pasting URLs in the text chat for the others to access in order to clarify what they say, negotiating meaning to achieve Long's 'comprehensible input' gained through 'interaction' and 'adjustment' (Foster and Ohta 2005). This can be either directed at the language being learnt, (e.g. pasting a URL for a definition in an online dictionary) exchanging resources (e.g. a URL for a website one of them has found particularly useful or interesting) or they can be concerned with the topic being discussed; one of them wants to share an interesting article, maybe they are reading it together. Maybe one has heard or read something on the news about the other's country and wants to ask about it, or is reminded of a favourite song and is suggesting that the others listen to it. Obviously such conversations could take place just as easily in *Skype* as in a VW. So what is the difference and why would they choose to 'hang out' in the VW rather than just use a *Skype* conference?

Sometimes clearly the setting does provide some impetus to the conversation; the students may actually talk about their surroundings in the VW either seriously or in a playful way. But often the surroundings in Homewood or SL are of little or no relevance. However these surrounding do give the students some illusion of presence together in a shared space. Morton and Jack (2005) suggests that students' experience of 'presence' in VW makes it more likely that language skills learnt will be carried over into real situations.

Perhaps because of the ambient sounds inworld, they are less conscious than they would be in a *Skype* conference of their different individual surroundings. In a *Skype* conference, no one is particularly surprised when a students' telephone or cell phone rings. It is irritating but not surprising when we can hear someone's TV, or street sounds because they have an open window or when they are interrupted or speak to someone in their household. But when students meet in a VW, such interruptions seem more surprising and even if they know that they themselves are sitting in front of a computer, they do tend to think of the other students as being really present in the class, because they can SEE them, sitting there on the beach, or wherever.

8.3.3 *The Grammar Dungeon*

The Grammar Dungeon (Fig. 8.10) uses holodeck software to provide a reference area for grammar; apart from being beneath a castle it is quite unlike a dungeon. It is a very large airy room with two transparent walls looking out on the sea and is lined with large posters showing, explaining and giving examples to illustrate grammatical rules. These posters are rezzed by the holodeck so can be changed at the touch of a button. The posters showing verbs, and illustrating the difference between the present simple tense and the present continuous tense can be made to disappear, and be replaced by a new set of posters illustrating say phrasal verbs and the different verbs get up, get in, get out of, get into, get away, get away with, get up to, etc; idiomatic phrases based on the verb to get.

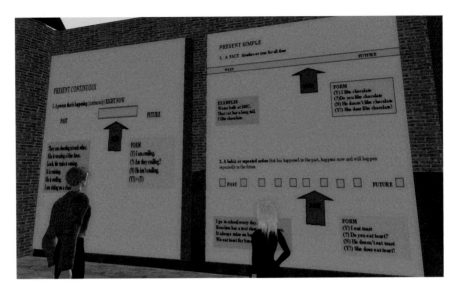

Fig. 8.10 The Grammar Dungeon

Such expositions of grammatical rules can be found in text books and on websites, so why display them on the walls in the 'Grammar Dungeon? Well partly in order to answer students' questions, partly to provide an innovative, fun way of accessing boring old grammar but mostly because by displaying them on these huge posters, it is easy for two or more students to see at the same time, to share and discuss and explain it to each other. It is a resource that turns private study into collaborative learning in line with Vygotskian constructivist principles. The same information could be provided privately on notecards, on a website or in a book but students seem to like these posters. It certainly seems quite dramatic, when the posters materialise above the holodeck prim and sweep into place on the walls of the room. In time the range of choices in the box can be increased, and indeed students themselves can be encouraged to devise new sets of posters to add to the rest.

8.3.4   The Sandbox; Building and Scripting 'Lessons in a Box'

Most areas of the VW are set to prevent students building and editing. This stops them accidentally damaging or destroying the resources, or untidily leaving abandoned creations lying around. The Sandbox (Fig. 8.11) is a whole region mostly covered by an isometric grid where the permissions are set for anyone to build, edit and script. On the perimeters of the sandbox are posters displaying the use of the building menus that are available on the recommended Hippo VW viewer. There is also a series of graduated 'Lessons in a Box' where students can

Fig. 8.11 Building lessons

learn right from the beginning to 'rez a prim' (create a 3D shape) and edit and script prims in order to create objects for use in the VW. Working through the series of lessons they create useful objects and learn skills and techniques which will help them to build their own unique creations. Each 'Lesson in a Box' has a small scaled model on the top showing the objects to be created by following the instructions inside and lessons start with the creation of basic cubes, spheres and cylinders ('prims') and include building a house, creating trees, flowers and plants and scripted objects like sparking fountains, shimmering ponds and streams with flowing water. There is also a DIY store near the supermarket where boxes of raw materials like scripts and textures can be obtained for further projects.

Some students have followed these lessons and have acquired considerable skill in building just by following the written and illustrated instructions provided. Some have needed occasional help. Not all language learners are interested, however, in acquiring building skills. They prefer to 'buy' objects from the shops in Homewood, or from fellow students and some persuade the more expert to build things for them. All of these activities, whether following instructions or persuading and negotiating with other students require authentic use of the target language. Students are also encouraged to attend building lessons in SL and some have done so. Requests have been made for building classes in E~H and although these are planned, so far only informal ad hoc help has been given with projects. Students are encouraged to help and instruct each other.

8.3.5   Students' DIY Homes

An entire island is divided into plots which are 'sold' to students so that they can build their own homes there. This is both to encourage them to build, learning and practising English while they learn and practise building skills, and also to give them spaces for meeting and practising conversation. One student has hosted reading parties in her home on the island rather than in the parks, gardens and other public spaces.

There are also shops where household furniture and other goods are for sale (for zero dollars; E~H does not have a currency) and whilst these were created primarily as places to explore, facilitating discussion and acquisition of vocabulary, they do also function as shops where objects can be obtained to adorn the students' inworld homes.

8.3.6   The Shops, Sightseeing Bus and Hot-Air Balloons

SL has special Orientation Islands where new arrivals, with avatars chosen during the account registration process, can learn the essential inworld skills immediately on arrival using specially prepared resources in an appropriate language. E~H, created with version 6.3 of *OpenSim*, is not quite so sophisticated. New students arrive with a default female avatar 'Ruth' dressed in a grey T-shirt and red leggings and especially if they are male the first thing students want to do is to get a more suitable avatar and clothing. Like everything else, this is an opportunity to learn and practise English, and resources are used to scaffold the process. Although registration takes place on a publically accessible website, so far at least no strangers have arrived by accident. New arrivals are generally helped by other students who shepherd them in, show them around and help them to get started. Since this process usually involves people with different mother tongues, the conversation is all in English; they use the target language in order to solve real problems.

Near to the default arrival area there are facilities for obtaining a new avatar and shops where the shape, skin and hair can be changed to personalise and improve the appearance of the avatar. There are also several shops and boutiques where clothes and shoes can be 'bought' to complete the process. These shops have been set in a village of small shops and boutiques selling everything from rugs and carpets, china, glasses and cutlery to washing machines, sofas, lamps, potted plants and vases of flowers. The rich variety of objects on view makes this a good place for students to window shop, just looking at things and chatting and of course acquiring new vocabulary and associating it directly with the objects in question rather than translations. This process of creating a direct L2 vocabulary link with the object rather than an object-L1, followed by translation L1-L2 helps develop fluency (Schmidt 1992; Zilberman 1999).

Fig. 8.12 Various ways to go sightseeing

There are also various methods of sightseeing. The most direct is to 'buy' the box of landmarks to be found at the base of several signposts dotted about the world. These landmarks are a collection of interesting places that they may have already heard about from other students in ELIP. Once bought, the landmarks appear in a folder in the students' inventories together with a collection of matching images. By clicking on the landmarks in their inventories, they can instantly teleport to the places in question. Using this collection of landmarks is a quick way of touring the VW (see Fig. 8.12).

There are other modes of sightseeing, vehicles or hot air balloons that can be scripted to follow a prearranged course delivering information and asking questions in text or sound. There is an open-topped Red London Bus all ready to go in the car-park outside the supermarket, and a couple of hot air balloons float above the sandbox on Homewood3. These have not yet been scripted. But once this is done they will provide further resources for language learning activities or for just having fun with other English learners, which is itself a language learning activity.

8.3.7   English Lessons in a Box

The E~H classes typically revolve around a series of scripted dialogues which chronicle the activities of a group of neighbours living in a street in a London suburb. They were inspired by the BBC's 'Flatmates' series, a weekly online soap opera for language learners. The characters in ELIP's version include Ann, a young science teacher and her husband Peter who is bored with his job in the civil service (BBC 2012b). There are also neighbours, David and Liz, who have three young daughters and an au pair from the Czech Republic and an elderly couple, Mr and Mrs O'Malley whose children and grandchildren have emigrated to Australia. The dialogues take place in many different locations; their various homes, at Ann's school, Peter's office, the local supermarket, Mrs O'Malley's hairdressers, the swimming baths, tube station etc. and involve other ancillary characters. The conversations are also arranged in a narrative, the story gradually unfolds of Peter's

DIY and gardening, Ann's application for promotion and her twin pregnancy, Jana's adventures with her young charges, her English course and her exams. The ongoing saga intrigues the students, they want to know what will happen next and discuss the possibilities. The variety of locations, the various activities and the informal nature of many of the conversations affords opportunities for the use of useful vocabulary and phrasal verbs and idiomatic expressions in use in normal conversational English. The conversations are all dialogues so students act them out in pairs concentrating on pronunciation, accent and on the 'tune' of the sentences. They are encouraged to continue the conversation beyond the script, to speculate on what may happen next and to discuss the pros and cons of the characters' actions. Using 'Focus on Form' (Long and Robinson 1998) grammar, idiomatic language and any queries about the content are dealt with as and when they arise. Independence is encouraged; the students use Google-image and the Cambridge online dictionary to look up new vocabulary. Idiomatic expressions and phrasal verbs are discussed and it is interesting to see how often these phrases occur in the online text chat in the days following the lessons. The same three or four dialogues are used for all (usually three) lessons each week, and new dialogues continuing the story are used each following week. Some students attend only one lesson but others like to attend two, repeating the same dialogues but more fluently at the second lesson. With or without permission, some students record the lessons and repeat them. Others reread and repeat the dialogues in groups at different times and more able students sometimes collect a little group to practise and read with at regular times to suit themselves – all in line with constructivist principles of social interaction and learning.

Some of the different settings for these dialogues are being built in Homewood. The supermarket is there, with Peter and Ann's trolley, full of the shopping detailed in the lesson dialogue. Ann's head of department at school, Mr Edison, is retiring to a little cottage on the south coast and Ann is applying for his job. Mr Edison's cottage can be found in Homewood, and his bicycle, together with Peter's and Ann's can be seen there leaning against the wall. Inside the cottage you can see the scrumptious tea that he prepared for them when they came to visit him and students can also walk down to the beach where the impetuous Peter took a dip in the sea. Peter and Ann's semi-detached house, next door to the gossiping O'Malleys' is in the process of construction. No doubt in time Ann's school and Peter's office will follow.

The scripts for the some of the series of prepared dialogues used in the ELIP lessons have been placed on notecards in E~H. There are 'English Lessons in a Box' on the sandbox next to the building lessons and also in the DIY store. Where the scenarios for these lessons have also been built, the relevant Lessons in a Box have been placed inworld. Appropriate lessons have been placed near the supermarket, and also near Mr Edison's cottage by the sea, and at the homes of the characters in the saga (see Fig. 8.13).

Students have asked for recordings of the dialogues to be included and these are in preparation. This will however change the character of these lessons. Currently the dialogues are acted out by pairs of students during lessons; they derive great amusement from dramatising the situations, and continuing the dialogue when the

Fig. 8.13 Lesson in a box near Mr Edison's retirement cottage

script ends. In class problems with accent, pronunciation, meaning and grammar are addressed if and as they arise in accordance with the ideas of Focus on Form (Long and Robinson 1998). There is a fear that using recordings, students will start merely listening and imitating the language spoken, problems will no longer be dealt with by Focus on Form but will have to be foreseen and appropriate notes provided. It will be a reversion to audiolingualism, which although it enjoyed some considerable popularity in the 1960s has been attacked on grounds of both language theory and learning theory and has long been discredited as a method of language acquisition (Richards and Rodgers 2001). So the current plan is to make just a few such recordings and see what happens. It could be that the recordings will be used just as a reference and activities will continue as before.

8.3.8   Task Based Learning (TBL)

There are many opportunities for TBL in E~H. Students spend the whole of their time in various activities which must be carried out in English. Observation shows that for most, possibly all, of the students engaging in the activities in the group their language has improved over time. There are particular members of the group who spend a great deal of time learning English both inside and outside ELIP and have made considerable gains in the accuracy and fluency of their English over the past 2 years but no systematic testing has been done. Indeed it would be difficult to plan any systematic, reliable testing given that there can be no knowledge or control over the activities of any of the members of the group outside their time online and activities inworld and in class. Indeed there can be no reliable check even of their identity.

Individual case studies might be used to throw some light on the process. Those individuals who became quite involved in the process of setting up Homewood are examples. The young Russian programmer who over a month or so while we initially set up and tested the *OpenSim* VW spent several hours each week talking and typing in English and having his English carefully corrected and mistakes explained at every step certainly made great strides, and I believe but cannot reliably know, shortly afterwards took and passed an IELTS exam. The young housewife from Saudi who has skilfully created the skins and shapes that are used for E~H's avatars and learnt English entirely on the internet in the past 3 years is another example. She has tried every way she can find to learn English for free on the internet and every week spends hours watching video clips on YouTube, reading books together with other students from ELIP; currently an abridged version of a Dickens novel and unabridged children's book. She is also a member of a group engaged in an extensive role-play (in English) on an island in SL (BBC 2012a). She follows *The Archers* and it is she who wants to set up Ambridge in Homewood and role-play the characters.

Studying such students and their learning of English can give some insight into whether and how E~H has helped them learn and how it compares with other online options. Most ELIP students use many different on-line resources in their language learning and some of them are also attending local face to face classes. Two ELIP members have actually arrived in the UK and are attending ESL classes in further education colleges as well as learning in E~H.

It may also be possible to test the efficacy of this VW for learning languages against other methods. Every year several thousand overseas students come to the UK to study. Many of these students come to the UK before the start of their course in order to improve their English and sit IELTS exams. By comparing three groups; one group coming to the UK for residential language courses, one group staying at home until the beginning of the course and using E~H to prepare and a third control group, the use of E~H could be compared to the much more expensive option of coming to the UK for English classes.

8.4   Language Learning in Virtual Worlds: Conclusion

The members of the E~H group receive free help with learning English and are told that the group is part of a research project studying online language learning. They generally express an eagerness to help and they often discuss their learning and their theories about the best ways in which to learn English. Some of the students are indeed language teachers and have studied linguistics and English as a Foreign Language in their own countries. They come from different cultures where different teaching methods are used and have views on whether or not they should learn grammar, whether listening to the radio is better than watching films, and how to get out of the habit of translating and improve fluency and so on. They tell each other about all the resources they use for learning outside the E~H group and they suggest new and additional resources and even help to create them.

The group has also evolved. Although many of the original members are still there some have disappeared to be replaced by a steady influx of new learners. Key members of the original group have grown considerably not just in their knowledge of English but also in confidence. The 'ladies only lessons' group, although it still exists, is hardly used as the original members have decided to join and take a full part in the mixed group. One of the regions in the VW, Lolland (Ladies-Only-Lessons-land, from the original ELIP~LOL) has been set aside for ladies only. It is far from the rest of the regions, very private, not overlooked, difficult to get to unless you know it is there, impossible to get to unless you are female and actually hardly used. In an elastic *OpenSim* grid there is no need for economy, so it can remain in case it ever is wanted or needed. It is not only the language learning in E~H that provides an interesting subject for research.

The use of *OpenSim*, open source software which can be edited and improved, also opens up other possibilities. The affordances of VWs for language learning could be greatly enhanced by the combination of the message editing and correcting facility available in *Skype* with a VW. The *OpenSim* VW software is a combination of different modules linked on the server, it only needs the messenger module to be rewritten so that it works like a *Skype* text chat. The search has begun for a programmer who can do this. Another proposed development in is the integration of a Moodle with E~H. SLOODLE and OSOODLE already exist (SLOODLE 2012) and provide the integration of a VLE into the teaching and learning in the VW so this is an obvious next step. The autonomous language learners of E~H can track their own progress using a Moodle VLE which will also provide the teacher/researcher with further insight into their learning. The current research will be extended by choosing individual learners for detailed case study.

The notes above have shown how VWs and in particular the E~H *OpenSim* VW can be and are being used for research into online language learning. The affordances of these virtual spaces have been compared to the affordances of a PW languages classroom; indeed of a very well resourced classroom complete with IWB, internet connected PC and a VLE allowing out of class access to the resources used in the class. It can be seen that in comparison, VWs are well designed for learning languages and indeed have some advantages over PW classrooms. The combination of *OpenSim* for a private, dedicated world in which a class can form a learning community, communicating, working and learning together and the public worlds like SL where communities of native speakers can be found works well. The experience can be compared with signing up to classes in a language school in Oxford Street in central London, learning with a teacher and practising with other students and then going out into Oxford Street and London and talking to the natives. A similar combination could be effected by buying several islands for a language school in SL but an *OpenSim* world is certainly more economical and it is also more adaptable since the space is expandable and the software is open source.

References

Anderson, J. R. (1989). Practice, working memory, and the ACT theory of skill acquisition: A comment on Carlson, Sullivan, and Schneider. *Journal of Experimental Psychology: Learning, Memory, and Cognition, 15*, 527–530.

BBC. (2012a). *The Archers*. http://www.bbc.co.uk/radio4/features/the-archers/

BBC. (2012b). *The Flatmates*. http://www.bbc.co.uk/worldservice/learningenglish/flatmates

Chen, H.-J., & Su, C.-C. (2011). Constructing a 3D world for foreign language learning based on open source software. In M. Chang et al. (Eds.), *Edutainment 2011* (LNCS 6872, pp. 46–53). Berlin/Heidelberg: Springer.

Derrington, M. de J. (2011). Setting up a virtual world for teaching language: Why OpenSim? In *Proceedings from the RELIVE11 conference* (pp. 43–52). Milton Keynes: Open University.

Derrington, M. de J., & Homewood, B. (2008). Get real – This isn't real it's second life: Teaching ESL in a virtual world. In *Proceedings from the RELIVE 08 conference* (pp. 106–120). Milton Keynes: Open University.

Design Digitally. (2009). *DDINC White Board for VWs*. http://www.youtube.com/watch?v=54UlMC3enkw

Devados, K. (2011). Utility of mobile phones in language classes. *Language in India, 11*. http://languageinindia.com/dec2011/devadossmobilefinal.pdf

Dörnyei, Z. (1998). Motivation in second and foreign language learning. *Language Teaching Research, 31*, 117–135.

Dörnyei, Z., & Csizer, K. (1998). Ten commandments for motivating language learners: Results of an empirical study. *Language Teaching Research, 3*, 203–229.

Ellis, R. (1995). Modified oral input and the acquisition of word meanings. *Applied Linguistics, 16*, 409–441.

Ellis, R. (2003). *Task-based language learning and teaching*. Oxford: Oxford University Press.

Foster, P., & Ohta, A. S. (2005). Negotiating for meaning and peer assistance in second language classrooms. *Applied Linguistics, 26*(3), 402–430. OUP.

Gardner, R., & MacIntyre, P. (1993). A student's contribution to second language learning. Part II: Affect variables. *Language Teaching, 26*, 1–9.

Hall, K. J. (1995). "Aw, man, where you goin'?": Classroom interaction and the development of L2 interactional competence. *Issues in Applied Linguistics, 6*(2), 37–62.

Kantalk. (2012). http://www.kantalk.com

Kiernan, P. J., & Kazumi, A. (2004). Cell phones in task based learning – Are cell phones useful language learning tools? *ReCALL, 16*(01), 71–84.

Krashen, S. (1998). Comprehensible output. *System, 26*, 175–182.

Livemocha. (2012). http://www.livemocha.com

Long, M. H. (1985). Input and second language acquisition theory. In S. Gass & C. Madden (Eds.), *Input and second language acquisition* (pp. 268–286). Rowley: Newbury House Publishers.

Long, M. (1996). The role of the linguistic environment in second language acquisition. In W. Ritchie & T. Bhatia (Eds.), *Handbook of second language acquisition* (pp. 413–468). San Diego: Academic Press.

Long, M., & Robinson, P. (1998). Focus on form: Theory, research and practice. In C. Doughty & J. Williams (Eds.), *Focus on form in classroom second language acquisition* (pp. 15–41). Cambridge: Cambridge University Press.

McLaughlin, B. (1990). Reconstructuring. *Applied Linguistics, 11*, 113–128.

McLaughlin, B., Rossman, T., & Mc Leod, B. (1983). Second language learning: An information – Processing perspective. *Language Learning, 33*, 135–157.

Molka-Danielsen, J., Richardson, D., Deutschmann, M., & Carter, B. (2007). Teaching languages in a virtual world. In *NOKOBIT proceedings* (pp. 97–107). Oslo: Tapir Akademisk Forlag.

Morton, H., & Jack, M. (2005). Scenario-based spoken interaction with virtual agents. *Computer Assisted Language Learning, 18*(3), 171–191.

Moschini, E. (2010). Chap 3: The second life researcher toolkit – An exploration of inworld tools, methods, and approaches for researching educational projects in second life. In A. Peachey, J. Gillen, D. Livingstone, & S. Smith-Robbins (Eds.), *Researching learning in virtual worlds*. London: Springer.

Ohta, A. S. (2001). *Second language acquisition processes in the classroom: Learning Japanese*. Oxford: Routledge.

Oxford, R. L., & Crookall, D. (1989). Research on language learning strategies: Methods, findings and instructional issues. *The Modern Language Journal, 73*(4), 404–419.

Papert, S. (1980). *Mindstorms children, computers, and powerful ideas*. Brighton: The Harvester Press.

Peterson, M. (2005, Summer). Learning interaction in an avatar-based virtual learning environment: A preliminary study. *PacCALL Journal, 1*, 29–40.

Peterson, M. (2009). Towards a research Agenda for the use of three-dimensional virtual worlds in language learning. *CALICO Journal, 29*, 67–80.

RezEd. (2010). *Language learning in virtual worlds*. Online at http://rezedhub.ning.com/group/languagelearninginvirtualworlds

Richards, J. C., & Rodgers, T. S. (2001). *Approaches and methods in language teaching*. Cambridge: Cambridge University Press.

Robertson, J., & Oberlander, J. (2002). Ghostwriter: Educational drama and presence in a virtual environment. *Journal of Computer Mediated Communication, 8*. http://jcmc.indiana.edu/vol8/issue1/robertson/robertson.html

Schmidt, R. (1992). *Psychological mechanisms underlying Second language Fluency*. Cambridge: Cambridge University Press.

Sheen, Y.H. (2004). Corrective feedback and learner uptake in communicative classrooms across instructional settings. *Language Teaching Research, 8*(3), 263–300.

Skehan, P. (1998). *A cognitive approach to language learning*. Oxford: Oxford University Press.

Skinner, B. F. (1974). *About behaviourism*. New York: Vintage Books Edition.

SLOODLE. (2012). http://www.sloodle.org/moodle/

Swain, M. (1985). Communicative competence: Some roles of comprehensible input and comprehensible output in development. In S. Gass & C. Madden (Eds.), *Input in second language acquisition*. New York: Harper Collins.

Swain, M. (1995). Three functions of output in second language acquisition. In G. Cook & B. Seidhofer (Eds.), *Principle and practice in Applied Linguistics: Studies in honour of HG Widdowson* (pp. 125–144). Oxford: Oxford University Press.

Swain, M., & Lapkin, S. (1995). Problems in output and the cognitive processes they generate: A step towards second language learning. *Applied Linguistics, 16*, 371–391.

Team Engage. (2009). *8D taps language learners, bots, microtransactions*. http://www.engage-digital.com/blog/2009/05/29/out-of-stealth-8d-taps-language-learners-bots-microtransactions/

Thornton, P., & Houser, C. (2005). Using mobile phones in English learning in Japan. *Journal of Computer Assisted Learning, 21*(3), 212–228.

VanPatten, B. (2002). Processing instruction: An update. *Language Learning, 52*, 755–803.

Vygotsky, L. S. (1978). Chapter 6: Interaction between learning and development. In *Mind in society: The development of higher psychological processes* (pp. 79–91). Cambridge, MA: Harvard University Press.

Wenger, E., McDermott, R. A., & Snyder, W. (2002). *Cultivating communities of practice*. Boston: Harvard Business School.

Willis, J. (1996). *A framework for task based learning*. Harlow: Longman.

Willis, J., & Willis, D. (1996). *Challenge and change in language teaching*. Oxford: Macmillan Education.

Woolard, G. (2000). Collocation-encouraging learner independence. In M. Lewis (Ed.), *Teaching collocation: Further developments in the lexical approach*. Boston: Thomson Heinle Language Teaching Publications.

Zilberman, A. (1999). *Language bridge: Acquiring language the natural way*. Grey Lynn: Future Marketing Group.

Chapter 9
Do Virtual Worlds Support Engaging Social Conferencing?

Andreas Schmeil, Béatrice Hasler, Anna Peachey, Sara de Freitas, and Claus Nehmzow

Abstract This chapter presents The Virtual World Conference, an online event that brought together top international researchers and pioneers in the fields of virtual worlds, from academia, education, and industry. The authors outline the challenges, successes, and problems of adopting the approach of structuring the global conference into three equidistant major time zones – East, Central, and West – resulting in a 24-h worldwide event. The chapter presents analyses of questionnaires that were completed by attendees, in an attempt to test the central hypothesis that virtual worlds can support engaging and effective social conferencing. We present innovations to be applied for further editions of the conference and close the chapter with suggestions and novel ideas for future virtual world events.

9.1   Introduction

As a result of globalisation, distributed work teams and groups of researchers undertake more international project travel than ever before, attending conferences on all continents. But financial cost, time spent and the impact on the environment

A. Schmeil (✉)
The University of Lugano (USI), Lugano, Switzerland
e-mail: andreas.schmeil@usi.ch

B. Hasler
Advanced Virtuality Laboratory of the Interdisciplinary Center Herzliya, Herzliya, Israel

A. Peachey
International Development Office, The Open University, Milton Keynes, UK
e-mail: a.peachey@open.ac.uk

S. de Freitas
Serious Games Institute, Coventry University, UK

C. Nehmzow
3D Avatar School, Hong Kong, Hong Kong

M. Childs and A. Peachey (eds.), *Understanding Learning in Virtual Worlds*,
Human–Computer Interaction Series, DOI 10.1007/978-1-4471-5370-2_9,
© Springer-Verlag London 2013

that international travel causes are all high, and many companies, organisations and institutions are looking for alternative methods for bringing people together in engaging and immersive ways that support social interactions and foster communities.

Over the last few years, virtual world platforms have proliferated. A range of platforms, such as *ActiveWorlds*, *Second Life*, *OpenSim* and *Olive*, allowing for large numbers of people to experience co-presence in virtual environments, are being used widely in many diverse fields. Conferencing in virtual worlds is becoming an increasingly popular solution for its cost savings and immersive interfaces. Virtual Worlds have the immersion to make participants feel engaged and part of the group (Schroeder 2006), and has the ease of access and low costs that enable participants to take part from their offices or homes or even on the move, without missing out on the socialising aspects of the conference. However, one of the major issues with using virtual worlds to support synchronous meetings lies in the imposed limits of physical world time zones; while users within a continent can relatively easily overcome the time zone barriers, when working between several continents, 6–8 h differences can be difficult to reconcile.

The common focus of the research team from different disciplinary backgrounds including computer science, psychology, educational research and collaborative work and organisational behaviour has been on how social collaboration can be best designed and supported in virtual and hybrid spaces. Social collaboration in virtual spaces has been investigated in psychological studies (e.g. Hasler 2012), in education research fields (e.g. Peachey and Childs 2011; Peachey et al. 2010; de Freitas et al. 2010; de Freitas 2006), from computer science, Human-Computer Interaction (HCI; e.g. Schmeil et al. 2012), and Computer-Supported Cooperative Work standpoints (CSCW; e.g. Schmeil et al. 2009).

The initial purpose of the conference was to bring together aspects of two physical conferences (the Serious Virtual Worlds and ReLIVE conferences, both based in the UK) into one virtual world conference that provided a platform for wider international dissemination, collaboration and networking. The virtual event was particularly appropriate in a period where budgets to attend physical conferences are reducing. For example with speakers and delegates from around the globe, the benefits of holding our conference in a virtual environment were considerable in terms of cost savings in travel alone. Rough calculations, allowing two-thirds of delegates to be one-third of the planet away from the conference home in Milton Keynes, suggest that 500,000 miles were travelled virtually to attend the conference. This reduces the environmental footprint of the conference, and saves on the time and cost of being out of the office for days either side of the main event, along with the conference fees needed to fund physical facilities.

In order to be truly global the idea was to organise an event spanning 24 h, divided into three equidistant conference time zones of 8 h each: East (Asia, Oceania), Central (Europe, Africa), and West (the Americas). With this unique perspective, we felt the need to implement a design science research (DSR; Hevner et al. 2004) approach.

The chapter first gives a background of virtual world conferences and other events, describes the case of TVWC, presents the evaluation of its first edition and discusses resulting implications for its second edition, closing with suggestions and novel ideas for future conferences in virtual worlds.

9.2   Conferences in Virtual Worlds

Many inworld conferences took place before the Virtual World Conference, for example a Second Life event for surgeons was very successful (Leong et al. 2008). However while there had been other attempts at conferences engaging audiences across time zones (most notably VWBPE: Virtual Worlds – Best Practices in Education), the Virtual World Conference was, as far as we know, the first to have adopted a 24 h approach that worked with the natural day of the speakers and audience.

In previous conferences held by the Serious Games Institute in the UK a hybrid model of combining physical conference space and lectures with remote participation (through inworld avatars) had been developed; the first Serious Virtual Worlds, was held in September 2007 with the launch of the Serious Games Institute (SGI). The event was well attended, both inworld and in the physical world. The virtual event however merely projected the actual event back into the *Second Life* auditorium (via video stream), and the link back to the physical conference was not established. For the next year Serious Virtual Worlds established a two-way communication system, and now inworld participants could ask questions and even present from *Second Life* lending a more international flavour to the event, and testing the video streaming technology. From 2007, the Second Wednesday monthly events were also piloted using the same technique, but held every month. These events brought four to five speakers a month into the virtual and physical hybrid event spaces, and remote participation with the events is still significant now.

The IEEE Virtual Worlds and Serious Games conference (VS-GAMES) in 2009 also adopted the hybrid model of virtual and physical presence. The main observation from the experience of hosting events in both settings is about the wider reach that has been established and the community that has been formed and supported through the 3 years, but also the connection of the community to industry gives the collaboration a focus upon physical world application of theory, and a strong connection with practices in education, health and the environment. Collaboration is the watchword of this type of community building, and supporting communities over long periods can be difficult but also rewarding. Intellectually, it has led to many new synergies being created; in particular innovation is well supported through this approach, due to the cross-disciplinary backgrounds of participants. Communities of interest as well as practice (Wenger 1998) emerge over time and people between sectors seem to become much more cohesive after several meetings.

9.3   The Virtual World Conference Approach

The organisation team of TVWC 2010 comprised four conference chairs (two in the UK, one in Hong Kong and one in California), two technical helpers in the UK, and a student volunteer in Turkey.

9.3.1   Scope

We titled the conference unambiguously *the Virtual World Conference* for its aim to cover applications of virtual worlds in the most diverse application areas, research done in and on virtual worlds, and current and future developments, also including combinations with real and other digitally-augmented environments.

9.3.2   Timing Structure

The event was organised as a 24-h around the world event, moderated by one chair for 8 h each (two co-chairs in the Central time zone). All presentations in all time zones were open to be attended for registered delegates, although it was expected that most delegates would spend the core of time in their own time zones. Table 9.1 shows the conference schedule to illustrate the timing structure of the conference and the timings of the talks in the East (E), Central (C), and West (W) for the other time zones. Conference presentation slots are in bold font in their respective time zones, night times are greyed out. With this timing structure, we aimed for each attendee to be able to attend all presentations in the time zone closest to their location, plus an additional four to eight presentations of other time zones. Note that attendees were not located only in one of the three time zones, but rather dispersed in all time zones in between.

9.3.3   Conference Environment

The 2010 event was hosted entirely inworld on the UK Open University island in the virtual world *Second Life*, which was chosen as the most popular immersive environment at the time (Kirriemuir 2009). The spatial organisation was conventional: rows of seats for the audience, directed towards a speaker podium that was flanked by two big screens – a bespoke slide presenter displaying the current presenters' presentation slides, and a video screen that could play videos from elsewhere on the Internet. This convention was a deliberate action, reflecting that the key drivers for being in the virtual world were considerations of physical practicalities rather than innovation. Providing a familiar space, icons and artefacts meant that both speakers and delegates would be comfortable with their environment and free to concentrate on the content rather than the delivery of presentations.

Table 9.1 Schedule of the virtual world conference 2010

	West (UTC - 8)	Central (UTC +/-0)	East (UTC + 7)
E: Speaker 1	17:00	1:00	**8:00**
E: Speaker 2	18:00	2:00	**9:00**
E: Speaker 3	19:00	3:00	**10:00**
E: Speaker 4	20:00	4:00	**11:00**
E: Lunch	21:00	5:00	12:00
E: Speaker 5	22:00	6:00	**13:00**
E: Speaker 6	23:00	7:00	**14:00**
E: Speaker 7	0:00	8:00	**15:00**
C: Speaker 1	1:00	**9:00**	16:00
C: Speaker 2	2:00	**10:00**	17:00
C: Speaker 3	3:00	**11:00**	18:00
C: Speaker 4	4:00	**12:00**	19:00
C: Lunch	5:00	13:00	20:00
C: Speaker 5	6:00	**14:00**	21:00
C: Speaker 6	7:00	**15:00**	22:00
C: Speaker 7	8:00	**16:00**	23:00
W:Speaker 1	**9:00**	17:00	0:00
W:Speaker 2	**10:00**	18:00	1:00
W:Speaker 3	**11:00**	19:00	2:00
W:Speaker 4	**12:00**	20:00	3:00
W:Lunch	13:00	21:00	4:00
W:Speaker 5	**14:00**	22:00	5:00
W:Speaker 6	**15:00**	23:00	6:00
W:Speaker 7	**16:00**	0:00	7:00

The *Second Life* island environment has an externally imposed limit of 100 concurrent users, and conference registration was restricted to manage an expectation of no more than around 60 users at any time in order to reduce lag and manage an optimum experience for the participants.

Figure 9.1 shows the inworld setup for TVWC 2010. The speaker podium contained the controls for the video screen.

9.3.4   Selection of Speakers

Following the conference goal of addressing global challenges, we invited 21 expert speakers to consider how virtual worlds can change the way that we learn, work and socialise and invited them to select a focus from:

- Social interaction, societies and communities in virtual worlds,
- Business applications and strategies for using virtual worlds,
- Formal and informal teaching and learning in virtual worlds.

Fig. 9.1 The setup of *The Virtual World Conference 2010*

Most of the speakers were familiar with *Second Life* but a small minority needed additional support to get an avatar and become familiar with the interface. All the speakers were asked to submit their slides and video in advance of the event and were invited to meet their session chair and technical support inworld for logistical and technical checks in the week leading up to the conference.

9.3.5 Management and Administration

A low registration fee for all attendees covered web hosting expenses and other organisational costs, as well as providing some measure of assurance that registered delegates would take up their places in the restricted space.

9.4 Evaluation of the Virtual World Conference 2010

A link to an online survey was sent to all attendees and speakers 1 week after the event to evaluate various aspects of TVWC and collect opinions and ideas for improvement.

Table 9.2 Mean ratings and standard deviations of technical aspects of TVWC

Items	Rating		
	N	*M*	*SD*
Sound quality (could understand the speakers)	27	3.44	.70
Graphics (could see the environment/people)	27	3.48	.58
User experience (could communicate/navigate)	27	3.41	.69

9.4.1 Participants of the Survey

Twenty-seven participants of TVWC (six speakers, nineteen attendants, and two who did not specify the type of their participation) replied to the survey. Eighteen participants were from the Central, seven from the West, and two from the East time zone. Most of the participants (85 %) reported to be frequent virtual world users. Only two participants rated themselves as occasional users or newbies. Two participants did not provide information about their virtual world experience. *Second Life* was the most frequently used virtual world (25 mentions). Participants stated that the main interests pursued in virtual worlds were educational purposes (36 %), followed by research (28 %), business (16 %), collaborative work (16 %), and design/arts (4 %). Eighty-one percent of the survey participants had attended events in virtual worlds before; TVWC was the first inworld conference for only five of them.

9.4.2 Quantitative Evaluation

9.4.2.1 Technical Aspects

Participants were required to rate the quality of technical aspects of TVWC on a scale from 1 = very poor to 4 = very good. The results are summarised in Table 9.2. Technical aspects were overall rated as very positive.

9.4.3 Setting

The setting of TVWC was evaluated with several aspects that were rated on a scale ranging from 1 = very inappropriate to 4 = very appropriate. The results are summarised in Table 9.3. The results indicate that attendees were in principle satisfied with the setting (this result though might have been influenced by the choice of the word "appropriate", because free-form comments suggest major changes to the conventional design, see below).

Table 9.3 Mean ratings and standard deviations of the conference setting

| | Rating | | |
Items	N	M	SD
Arrangement of seats	27	3.37	.63
Arrangement of slides/video screens	27	3.37	.63
Speaker space	26	3.27	.60
Location of conference program	27	3.22	.70
Location of posters	27	3.15	.60
Timing of sessions (to address the whole planet)	27	3.41	.74

Table 9.4 Subjective pros of virtual world conferences

Category	Count
No travel (time and cost savings; ease of access)	18
Real-time feedback/discussion during presentations	10
Additional/different features (e.g., recording, sharing links)	9
Global networking	8
Flexibility (e.g., to move around physically, tune in/out)	6
Different interaction styles (e.g., relaxed, informal, intimate)	5
Comfort and convenience (e.g., home environment)	5
Ease (e.g., sharing information, information cataloging)	3
Greater variety (e.g., topics, speakers)	3
24 h schedule	1

9.4.4 Future Attendance

Participants were asked to indicate the likelihood of their attendance of a future edition of TVWC. Eighty-one percent of the participants were sure that they would attend a future TVWC event, and nineteen percent indicated that they would maybe attend. None of the participants indicated that they would not attend.

9.4.5 Qualitative Evaluation

Participants were asked to compare their experience at TVWC with that of a physical-world conference, and to indicate the "pros and cons" of virtual world conferences. In addition, they were asked to provide suggestions for improvement of TVWC for future editions. Participants' free-text responses were categorised, and the number of statements in each category was counted. The results are summarised in Tables 9.4, 9.5, and 9.6.

Table 9.5 Subjective cons of virtual world conferences

Category	Count
Lack of socialising/networking possibilities (e.g., no lunch)	10
Technical problems	7
Not enough dialogue/interaction between participants	4
24 h schedule (e.g., missing talks, losing attention)	4
Face-to-face aspects missing (e.g., no real names/faces)	4
Too close schedule/information overload	4
Inadequate presentation styles (slides/video)	3
Overloaded chat (too much info, not enough time to respond)	3
No visual feedback from audience (e.g., speakers felt isolated)	2
Issues with sharing materials	2
"Value for money" (e.g., no "freebies")	2

Table 9.6 Suggestions for improvement

Category	Count
Presentation style (e.g., slides could not be displayed, more interactivity, inworld presentation skills)	8
Foster mingling/networking (e.g., enable small group discussions)	5
Guidance for newbies (e.g., use of camera; etiquette)	5
24 h schedule (more time/stretching the timetable)	5
More information on participants (e.g., bio of attendees)	4
Setting (e.g., rows and lecturer; satellites instead of one room)	3
Scope (e.g., open call/not limited to invited speakers; more frequent meetings and focused on themes)	3
Technical (e.g., SL alternatives, other presentation tools)	3
Archive materials	3
Thematic sessions/division	2
Conference announcement (earlier, more/better marketing)	2
Make use of embodiment (avatars/3D space) (e.g., visualise when avatars have ideas/questions; include virtual field trips)	2
Value for money/no payment for virtual conferences	2

As anticipated, the biggest advantage of using virtual worlds was considered to be the fact that no travel is involved to attend a conference, allowing greater flexibility and convenience while attending the conference. Also the great variety of topics and speakers was valued. On the other hand, the lack of travel was at the same time seen as the biggest disadvantage, as it prohibits most possibilities for networking, (face-to-face) dialogues, and socialising. Another cause for the lack of social interaction was considered to be the schedule, which was rated to be very dense; it was suggested to stretch it out, in favour of more informal social interaction and breaks.

For the topic of supporting interaction it was further suggested to introduce ways to actively foster mingling and networking, using features that are unique to virtual worlds. The conventional setting of the conference – basically copied from physical world conference setups – was criticised. This aligns with comments on the presentation style, where the use of virtual world tools was missed, as well as the use of visual cues and a solution to the information overload in the *Second Life* chat window (caused by everyone chatting in the same window, often discussing multiple topics at the same time).

Last but not least, technical problems were mentioned (mostly due to the *Second Life* viewer and platform), and more help for newbies and technical support would be appreciated.

9.5 Implications for the Next Edition

The subsequent edition of the Virtual World Conference will introduce some innovations and alterations to the ways the conference was organised in the first run, which we have derived from the evaluation analysis and comments from the attendees and presenters. This section provides an overview, along with explanations to each innovation.

9.5.1 Schedule

The second edition of TVWC will introduce a less tight schedule. Instead of 21 speakers, each time zone has merely five presentations, resulting in a total of 15 conventional talks. The presentations are further limited to 30 min, leaving another 30 for discussions or activities, before the next slot.

9.5.2 Format

All talks are divided into two sessions for each time zone, while keeping the highly valued diversity of topics. Apart from the 15 invited talks, the conference will include networking periods and designated time for informal mingling, engaging activities and planned discussions. Also a focus group will be offered to capture the best of each zone's discussion and feedback.

9.5.3   Real Identities

The possibility of displaying real names above the avatar name will be provided, in a non-obtrusive way. During the talks, the presenters' pictures, short biographies, and links to personal and/or project websites will be displayed on a dedicated screen, so that attendees are more aware of who is presenting and have immediate access to further information.

9.5.4   Tool Use

Presenters will not be limited to only slide show and video player as tools to support their verbal narration, but will also have a voting/polling tool at their disposal, in order to better include the audience in the presentations and discussions.

9.5.5   Participation

Throughout the conference, many boards will offer the possibility for attendees to leave comments in form of objects that attach to the boards upon click. This is useful for adding questions to abstracts before presentations (so the presenters can tailor their talks to the interests of the audience), for adding comments to particular slides or posters, for leaving notes and contact information to others on whiteboards, and for writing on whiteboards in general. Other boards can be equipped with a movable arrow, to point to a certain spot on it, for example on the current slide.

9.5.6   Networking

At the beginning of each time zone 'chapter', networking games and activities will be offered, making use of the attendees' virtual embodiment (i.e., their avatars) and their ability to navigate in 3D space. Interactive tools and a responsive environment will be used to create memorable experiences and persistent impressions. For the hour-long lunch break, semi-formal discussion rounds will be organised, centred around topics taken from the preceding talks. At the end of each time zone chapter there will be more time to network and discuss.

9.5.7   Collaborative Innovation

The focus group aims at creating innovative virtual world collaboration patterns for future editions of TVWC. Moderated by one of the conference chairs, attendees and invited speakers work on ideating novel practices for conferences and other social events in virtual worlds. This way the Virtual World Conference is forced to remain in its iterative redesign cycle (cf. design science research).

9.5.8 Setting

Harnessing the virtual world features of the availability of abundant 3D space and the possibility of scripting responsive environments and interactive tools, the conventional conference setting (lecturer-audience, static presentation slide and video screens) can give way to a dynamic platform accommodating the presenter and the audience; it moves back and forth between a persistent row of presentation slides in a spiral set up. Instead of switching slides on a static screen, the entire conference session moves along a path of presentations, traversing different topics, so to speak. Our basic policy is that every object has a function, in comparison to other virtual world events that focus on architectural extravagance and/or detailed decorations.

9.5.9 'Freebies'

All attendees receive an electronic version of the proceedings of the Virtual World Conference, including presenter biographies, abstracts of their talks, presentation slides, and possibly an edited version of the chat log of their session. These 'proceedings' will not otherwise be published.

9.6 A Plausible Future of Online Conferences

In future editions of this conference – or other virtual world events, for that matter – the following ideas could be considered.

9.6.1 Automated Presentations

Talks could be pre-recorded (in better audio quality), possibly edited, cut into pieces and attached to single slides, or just paused and resumed with buttons. The real-time interaction should focus more on the discussion; the speakers themselves could so join the discussion in text chat during their own talks.

Main caveat: The talk (the audio recording of the presentation) might run the risk of getting pushed in the background and losing its central role.

9.6.2   Interaction

Instructions for speakers on how to prepare their talks could be offered and live support could be given. This could allow for more engaging and effective methods of involving the audience using avatars, the 3D space, interactive objects, and external tools.

Main caveat: The content of the presentation might run the risk of getting pushed in the background, with too much attention on the use of novel tools.

9.6.3   Metaverse

Virtual field trips within *Second Life* and in other virtual worlds could be organised, and informal gatherings could be held between the main conference events (e.g. virtual lunches).

Main caveat: Field trips often end in losing most of the group while teleporting. With the abundance of virtual world group meetings, an innovative format has to be implemented.

9.6.4   Cross-Media Format

A combination of the real-time event in the virtual world and social networking tools might be a successful format fostering networking among participants.

Main caveat: Using cross-media approaches for social events is prone to end up in splinter groups, with attendees drifting off to different platforms.

9.6.5   Interest Communication

Attendees could be given hats or other props in different colours that display their main interest in virtual worlds

Main caveat: Too many props could clutter the conference.

9.6.6   No Proprietary Software, No/Fewer Costs

A switch from *Second Life* to the *OSGrid* as a location for the Virtual World Conference – or another virtual world based on open software – seems appropriate, already for technical glitches and limitations imposed by Linden Lab. In line with this, sponsors could be found (e.g., a virtual world news media channel), in order to cancel out the need for a registration fee.

Main caveat: *Second Life* is – still – the most popular virtual world, and the platform people think about when they hear of the Virtual World Conference.

9.7 Summary and Conclusions

This chapter has presented the Virtual World Conference, describing its organisation, unique format, and the novel and innovative approach of redesigning it immensely each edition. Its first year attendees greatly valued this new conference format, and expressed excitement about the event in general and participating in a live 24-h event around the world in particular. We have presented the lessons learned from the first edition of TVWC and described how we are implementing them in the redesign of the event for its next run.

In summary, while we have replicated a physical conference in the first edition of TVWC, the second edition will try out more innovative scenarios concerning the organisation, format, setting, and use of tools, and will introduce more varied elements to the program. An evaluation after the next TVWC is expected to provide more insights on whether we move into the right directions, and inform the redesign of the event for its third edition.

References

de Freitas, S. (2006). *Learning in immersive worlds*. Bristol: Joint Information Systems Committee. See: http://www.jisc.ac.uk/media/documents/programmes/elearninginnovation/gamingreport_v3.pdf

de Freitas, S., Rebolledo-Mendez, G., Liarokapis, F., Magoulas, G., & Poulovassilis, A. (2010). Learning as immersive experiences: Using the four dimensional framework for designing and evaluating immersive learning experiences in a virtual world. *British Journal of Educational Technology, 41*(1), 69–85.

Hasler, B. (2012). Intercultural collaborative learning in virtual worlds. In R. Hinrichs & C. Wankel (Eds.), *Transforming virtual world learning* (Cutting-edge technologies in higher education, Vol. 4, pp. 271–310). Bingley: Emerald Publishing.

Hevner, A. R., March, S. T., Park, J., & Ram, S. (2004). Design science in information systems research. *MIS Quarterly, 28*(1), 75–105.

Kirriemuir, J. (2009). *The spring 2009 snapshot of virtual world use in UK higher and further education*. Bath: Eduserv Foundation.

Leong, J. J., Kinross, J., Taylor, D., & Purkayastha, S. (2008). International conferences – Surgeons have held conferences in second life. *British Medical Journal, 337*(7661), 68.

Peachey, A., & Childs, M. (Eds.). (2011). *Reinventing ourselves: Contemporary concepts of identity in virtual worlds*. London: Springer.

Peachey, A., Gillen, J., Livingstone, D., & Smith-Robbins, S. (Eds.). (2010). *Researching learning in virtual worlds*. London: Springer.

Schmeil, A., Eppler, M. J., & Gubler, M. (2009). An experimental comparison of 3D virtual environments and text chat as collaboration tools. *Electronic Journal of Knowledge Management, 7*(5), 637–646.

Schmeil, A., Eppler, M. J., & de Freitas, S. (2012). A framework for the design of Avatar-based collaboration. In R. Hinrichs & C. Wankel (Eds.), *Engaging the Avatar in global education.* Bingley: Emerald.

Schroeder, R. (2006). Being there together and the future of connected presence. *Presence, 15*, 438–454.

Wenger, E. (1998). *Communities of practice: Learning, meaning, and identity.* Cambridge: Cambridge University Press.

Printed in the United States
By Bookmasters